THE ULTIMATE DREAM

THE ULTIMATE DREAM
75 YEARS OF THE TOTE CHELTENHAM GOLD CUP

BOB HARMAN

MAINSTREAM
PUBLISHING

EDINBURGH AND LONDON

To my children, Julia and Andrew

I would like to thank everyone who has assisted me in producing this book, in particular Brian Edgeley, without whom my task would have been considerably more difficult.

Copyright © Bob Harman, 2000
All rights reserved
The moral right of the author has been asserted
All photographs © Bernard Parkin

First published in Great Britain in 2000 by
MAINSTREAM PUBLISHING COMPANY (EDINBURGH) LTD
7 Albany Street
Edinburgh EH1 3UG

ISBN 1 84018 149 4

A catalogue record for this book is available from the British Library

Typeset in Garamond
Printed and bound in Great Britain by Butler & Tanner Ltd, Frome and London

Contents

Foreword

When Bob Harman approached me to write a foreword for this book and to include my earliest Gold Cup memory, I realised that although my first visits to Cheltenham were in the early 1950s I was either at school or abroad with the army in March and, therefore, my first Gold Cup was in 1964, also the first year that the great Arkle won.

I have not yet had the fortune of owning the winner of the Gold Cup, which is every National Hunt owner's dream, but I still vividly remember the excitement of What A Buck, my first runner in 1976, and the thrill of my wife's horse Drumadowney leading down the hill at the third last fence and eventually finishing fourth in 1985.

Anyone who has ever experienced the special atmosphere of the Gold Cup will have their own particular favourite. For me it has to be the three Gold Cups in 1964, 1965 and 1966 won by Arkle and, of course, the magnificent Irish participation which is such an important part of the Festival. For me as Chairman of the Steeplechase Company, the thrill of escorting Her Majesty Queen Elizabeth, The Queen Mother to the presentation after Imperial Call won the Gold Cup for the Irish in 1996 is something I will never forget.

The welcome sponsorship from the Tote that the race has enjoyed since 1980 has coincided with a period of tremendous progress for Cheltenham Racecourse, with the Tote Cheltenham Gold Cup itself going from strength to strength. At Cheltenham we are not afraid to look back as well as forward. To honour and meet the hundreds of past and present Gold Cup participants at our 75 years celebration luncheon held at Cheltenham has been just one of the enjoyable aspects of my position as Chairman. With Gold Cup representation from every decade, back to the origins of the race in 1924, it makes one take stock and wonder at the rich history of the race and exactly what it means to so many people and I regard this book as the perfect extension of that celebration.

Lord Vestey
Chairman,
The Steeplechase Company
(Cheltenham) Ltd.

Introduction

It all started with a splash, a striking chestnut gelding called Red Splash. The forward-thinking Cheltenham team, led by a certain Frederick H. Cathcart, had the presence of mind to introduce the Gold Cup as a championship race in the fledgling years of the Cheltenham Festival. The ripples have been emanating ever since from that first toe-dip, ripples that have reached the present tidal-wave proportions of Gold Cup celebratory mayhem – albeit well-managed mayhem – especially after an Irish winner. How right Edward Gillespie is when he describes the race as having grown from 'a novelty to a world-renowned institution'.

The Gold Cup is, and always will be, the jewel of the Festival crown. The Cheltenham package has been defined and refined by the Gillespie team over the past two decades and its popularity remains at an all-time high. But what exactly is Cheltenham's appeal? For one thing, the crowd is multi-faceted, which adds so much to the colour of the event. It offers different people different things.

For some, hopefully a minority, Cheltenham could be anywhere – simply another window of opportunity in a lifetime of opportunities. Skittish horses, nervous jockeys, stressed-out trainers and expectant owners – all simply become faceless, numbered players on the vast green stage. For these punting Philistines, the end result is everything, the means of achieving it immaterial – their level of personal success determining for them the value of a Gold Cup or even Festival vintage. For many, to soak up the unique atmosphere is everything, with no need for financial involvement. Just the joy of seeing top-class racing, the result being of virtually no consequence. For others it can be a curious mixture of both. One thing is certain – that the contents of the Festival melting pot can usually be guaranteed to produce something special for its recipients, on or off course.

1999 was no exception to this, with the classy See More Business a worthy Gold Cup hero. In the new millennium, we might see his half-brother, the embryonic Yet More Business, or even his Irish-trained cousin SeeMoreFestivalsbyRyanAir, winging their way up the famous hill. Maybe in 2001 A Space Odyssey will win our hearts and rocket to victory, his film star owner dedicating his win to the memory of the late Stanley Kubrick. Such is the mystery of the great race!

The inaugural Gold Cup, way back in 1924, was worth a princely 200 sovereigns, with £685 in prize money to the winner. That race somehow set the trend, fought out in typical thrilling Cheltenham fashion, with a three-horse thrust up the hill to the line, the novice Red Splash getting the verdict by a head and a neck from two vastly more experienced rivals. In this weight-for-age race for five-year-olds and upwards, Red Splash carried eleven stone five pounds, the other two twelve stone. It could be argued that the nine-pound age concession made to Red Splash was too great and tipped the scales in his favour. However, this wasn't a major talking-point in 1924, unlike the furore that surrounded Dawn Run's five-pound mares' allowance sixty years later when she became the first horse to achieve the Champion Hurdle/Gold Cup double.

At last year's northern launch of the pre-Gold Cup celebrations near Wetherby, the depth of feeling among some Dickinson owners concerned that this allowance tipped the balance in favour of Dawn Run against one of the Harewood stars, Wayward Lad, who lost the 'unequal' battle up the hill in 1986, was still tangible.

This subject soon became the topic of conversation around our table. With that adopted northerner, the Cork-born Jonjo O'Neill, Dawn Run's partner on that golden day, sitting within earshot, it promised to make good copy. But the ever-genial Irishman just smiled in his inimitable way and wouldn't be drawn into any argument, for or against the allowance. Whether this was on grounds of diplomacy, self-preservation or due simply to not wanting to dilute the memories of the mare's achievements was difficult to gauge. It could be that in his new life as a trainer, Jonjo has learnt to hone his diplomatic skills, especially where fickle owners are concerned!

Dawn Run's trainer Paddy Mullins told me last year that he had never known a mare that possessed so many masculine traits and the normally understated Mullins went so far as to describe her as a 'freak'. Would she have won without the mares' allowance? Nobody can say for sure, but it is both ironic and significant that if ever there was a mare built to carry the full complement of twelve stone with ease, it was Dawn Run. Despite Wayward Lad living up to his name up the Cheltenham hill, the North still had an enviable record in the race around this time, with six wins in a nine-year period.

Sadly, through no fault of the trainer, the Dawn Run saga often resembled a freak show and the anger and torment Mullins suffered, at the very moment his brave mare was making history at Cheltenham, tells you much about the frustrations he endured. He had little control: the mare's riding arrangements brought him untold and understandable paternal grief while the race targets led to a fateful journey to France that her trainer didn't want her to undertake.

Lows follow highs in racing as certain as night follows day and Dawn Run will definitely not be the last great horse to suffer such a tragic end. Owner's prerogative meant Mullins had no choice but to run Dawn Run in the French Champion Hurdle. Sadly, it ended in tears – doesn't it always seems to happen to the best ones?

✢ 1924 ✢

A bag of hot chestnuts and a clown called Koko

It is possible among the crowd bathed in sunshine, enjoying the very first Cheltenham Gold Cup were Sir Edward Elgar and the child prodigy Yehudi Menuhin. Based just down the road at Malvern, Elgar had invited the American violinist to join the local orchestra he was conducting. By all accounts, in a rush and having practised a piece straight through without a hint of a break, Elgar would often declare: 'That'll do – now we can go to the races.'

What inspiration they would have gained from the flowing movement of the horses' manes and the rhythmical pounding of their hooves on that glorious spring-like day. The young Menuhin probably wouldn't have known too much about racing, or that The Prince of Wales was there to support his steeplechasing mentor, the crack amateur rider Harry Brown, who was back from injury and hoping to perform a few tricks of his own on Conjurer II in the new race.

Harry Atherton Brown was a real character, a cavalier spirit who enjoyed life to the full. Riding in an era when amateurs were almost as abundant as professionals are now, he was without doubt the best in the post-war period and the most flamboyant. He began owning horses soon after leaving Eton and rode his first winner, at the age of eighteen, in 1907 and, within two years, he reached the top of the amateur tree. Incredibly, Brown was in such demand as an amateur after the war that, 80 years ago, as an amateur, he became national hunt champion jockey, a feat that will surely never be repeated.

Three years before the inaugural Gold Cup, Brown had further endeared himself to his adoring public by his actions in an eventful Grand National, riding the rather inappropriately named favourite, The Bore. After falling and breaking his collarbone at the second last, Brown remounted and, with his right arm hanging uselessly by his side, bravely finished second to Shaun Spadah, ridden by top professional Dick (F.B.) Rees.

It wasn't just his bravado in the saddle that helped mould the Brown legend. He was a prolific shot, an expert stalker and a fisherman. Typically, when he arrived early at Hereford races one day, he decided to put his unexpected free time to good use, catching a record 44-pound salmon on the Wye. Certainly, Brown will never be forgotten. He was caricatured as 'Charlie Peppercorn' in Siegfried Sassoon's *Memoirs of a Fox-Hunting Man*. Somehow, though, and through no fault of his own, he seemed always to just miss out on the big occasion.

This was never better illustrated than with his ride at Cheltenham on Conjurer II, who came an unlucky third in the 1923 Grand National. Owned by Mr Dewhurst, Conjurer II had been ridden by a very inexperienced amateur, the owner's son and an undergraduate at Oxford. It was felt that greater experience and strength was needed to get the best out of the horse and Brown was their man.

Eight runners went to post, with one of the top professional riders of the time, Jack Anthony, riding Forewarned. Although Forewarned started favourite, Alcazar had been expected to be market leader, until his unexpected withdrawal only hours before the race. Red Splash's participation had also been in serious doubt, due to a number of factors. First, although the gelding had already won four chases, including one at Cheltenham's November meeting, he had had an accident at home resulting in interrupted and hurried preparation. Secondly, his trainer, the popular Fred Withington, had been dubious about running his five-year-old chestnut against the likes of Alcazar in receipt of only nine pounds (after all, in a handicap he would have been far better off at the weights). Finally, he had wanted to engage Dick Rees, who had ridden Red Splash before and knew him well, but Rees was committed to the George Poole-trained Alcazar. How delighted Withington must have been on his arrival at Cheltenham that morning to find Rees without a ride. He snapped him up in an instant and declared Red Splash for the new race. Rees's renowned judgement of pace and superior course knowledge would prove to be a significant factor.

Rees took the bull by the horns right from the off and set out to make it a strongly run race. He soon had more than half of the field in trouble and continued to pile on the pressure from the front. With six furlongs to go, Red Splash began to drop back through the field, appearing to run out of steam and looking to be in trouble. However, Rees was just giving his partner a well-earned breather. Coming down the hill, Rees set him alight again on the run to the second last, by which time he was back in front, but only just in front of Conjurer II and Gerald L, who still appeared to be full of running. The three protaganists breasted the last in unison and set off up the notorious climb to the post. Harry Brown on Conjurer II mastered Gerald L in the final few yards of the race, but could never quite peg back the 5–1 outsider. Red Splash battled on in most determined fashion for his pilot, clinging on to his slender lead all the way from the final fence to win by a head and a neck. Rees had proved himself to be the master of his profession. He was also the supreme stylist of his day, with wonderful hands and a tactical brain to match his physical qualities.

Dick Rees and his brother Bilby (L.B.), sons of a Pembrokeshire vet who rode in point-to-points, began riding at a tender age for the Harrison stable at Althry, within sight of Bangor racecourse. Dick Rees turned professional in 1920 and became champion jockey at the end of that first professional season and again a further four times, up until 1927. Winning every major race in Britain and the Grand Steeplechase de Paris, Rees was to renew his Welsh links for two further Gold Cup wins in 1928 and 1929.

Red Splash's victory was deemed to be no flash in the pan – the two placed horses were classy performers and both had previously won the valuable National Hunt Handicap Steeplechase. Conjurer II's trainer, the Lancastrian Tom Coulthwaite, was one of the more eccentric of trainers and had never sat on a horse in his life! He started out as an athletics trainer and applied similar principles to horses with great success. He had already trained two prestigious Grand National winners before this race and another was to follow in 1931 with Grakle, a horse that figured prominently in several future Gold Cups.

With this in mind, this may not have been Withington's finest hour, but to win the new race with such a young horse (in effect not yet a five-year-old, as the gelding was a May foal) was, nevertheless, a superb feat of training. Withington had already carved himself a niche in racing, in particular Grand National history, by achieving the seemingly impossible back in 1908 when, in an incredible one-two, the American-bred Rubio beat his more-fancied stable-companion Mattie Macgregor by ten lengths.

Red Splash's victory was achieved at a time when Withington had cut down considerably on numbers, having returned to Oxfordshire after the war and selling Red Splash to one of his owners, Major (later Colonel) Wyndham. Unlike Withington, Wyndham was a noted horseman, a winner of two consecutive Grand Military Gold Cups, riding his own horse, Another Delight.

Withington remained at the top of his profession until his retirement in 1930 and thereafter served a term as a Steward, the first national hunt trainer to do so, acting at Cheltenham and many other courses. Both Wyndham and Withington went on to become members of the National Hunt Committee and Wyndham was even elected to the Jockey Club, despite never having a runner on the flat, such was the esteem in which Withington was held. He was also godfather to *Sporting Life* journalist Tom Nicholls. Withington died in 1951 and Cheltenham still run a race in his honour to this day.

The inaugural race had been a resounding success and the public instantly latched on to Red Splash, hoping he would reach his full potential. The young chestnut was heralded as a potential champion – an extremely good-looking racehorse, almost anything seemed possible for him. At only five years of age, he didn't need to go to Aintree yet – if at all. In fact, most people firmly believed him to be too good to risk amidst the Grand National mayhem that prevailed year in, year out. Many considered him too much of a proper racehorse to be asked such a question, in spite of the massive crock of gold that invariably landed in the lap of fortunate winning connections.

Sadly, these concerns would never turn out to be a factor in Red Splash's career. Rumours about Red Splash being unsound gathered pace through the year and he didn't see a racecourse until mid-January, and then only a small chase at Leicester. He had blossomed into a superb physical specimen, but his looks were deceiving. He faded well before the finish and, after the race, Withington declared that Red Splash would now miss both the Gold Cup and the National and aim instead for the Champion Chase at Liverpool.

Unfortunately, Red Splash never got to contest that race, or run in another Gold Cup. Oddly enough, 75 years on from this disappointment, champion trainer Martin Pipe has a horse similar to Red Splash in the shape of the precocious Cyfor Malta. A typically tough French-bred six-year-old, the gelding has carried all before him over the past two seasons, winning a Cathcart Chase at the 1998 Festival as a five-year-old before injury stopped him in his Gold Cup tracks. He had beaten the best – including the subsequent Gold Cup winner and runner-up – in the Cheltenham trials leading up to the 1999 Festival. Whether he will ever return to his best form remains to be seen, but he's young enough and certainly in good hands. For whatever reason, the list of Gold Cup possibles that never fulfil their potential is endless.

A two-horse race at Sligo in Ireland that ended in a dead-heat wouldn't normally deserve much of a mention, not even in *The Sligo Weekly*. However, this particular result was to have a more far-reaching significance. The two horses in question, Ballinode and Koko, would both play starring roles in the next two Gold Cups.

I wonder how aware form students were of that race? If only Phil Bull had got his *Timeform* act together a bit sooner, punters could have been singing the Halifax sage's praises even then! He might well have given Koko, ever the clown, a squiggle, or even the dreaded double one for allowing Ballinode to reach him in the shadow of the post. Could this be what Bull was referring to when he described racing as 'that great triviality'?

RED SPLASH (1924)

ch.g. 1919 (Copper Ore – La Manche)
Owned by Major E.H. Wyndham, trained by F.E. Withington and ridden by F.B. Rees

✢ 1925 ✢

The Sligo Mare, Guinness and all that

> Some of the most distinguished Irish steeplechasers and winners of the
> Grand National have been reared and schooled under conditions that an
> English stableman might describe as 'not 'arf rough', though the 'hovels'
> that we sometimes read of in the old books and magazines are a trifle highly
> coloured. The Irish farmer who had 'a good harse' – and those fellows
> always knew – saw that he was as well 'done' as the members of his own
> family. As a foundation he had the magnificent limestone pastures, and
> there was plenty of corn and oats grown on these same pastures. If a little
> rain came through the stable roof, well it helped to make the horse hardy
> – 'He'll have t' run in the rain sometimes, won't he!' – and if there was more
> litter about the yard than the discipline of a good stable allows: 'Clane that
> up, Boy . . . when y' have toime.' If the Boy seldom had hygienic time, it
> did not matter a great deal.
>
> Captain T.H. Bird, *The Horseman's Year 1947–48*

Surely, in one succinct paragraph, Captain Bird has captured the essential qualities
of the Irish steeplechaser – a formidable opponent, particularly around such an
unforgiving course as Cheltenham.

Trainers in Ireland often doubled as farmers at that time. There was no danger
of over-pampering here, no hint of encouraging 'soft' performers and, it must be
said, all the earliest Irish challengers for Gold Cup glory fell neatly into the 'good
harse' category.

They were, almost without exception, extremely hardy individuals. Golden
Miller's arduous journey to join Basil Briscoe's stable is just one good illustration
of the ability of the Irish chaser to cope with just about anything – a characteristic
that would later be seen to greatest effect in that chaser's incredible run of victories
in the early '30s. It would have been interesting to have been able to compare
Frank Morgan's training base at the Curragh with his 'stop-over' for his regular
British raids. Perhaps the Morgan team, both human and equine, trained on
Guinness in the same way Alf Tupper, comic-book hero and athlete extraordinaire,
trained on fish and chips *en route* to his meetings! Joking apart, whatever the
conditions Ballinode and the others endured during their frequent stays, Morgan
rarely went home empty-handed (if he ever went home at all) and the 1925 Gold
Cup was no exception – it set the trend for the perennial Anglo-Irish battle at
Cheltenham.

Born in County Waterford, Morgan had been a top-class flat jockey in Ireland,
winning the 1904 Irish Derby on Royal Arch before combining riding and
training over the jumps at the Curragh. From a large family of accomplished

horsemen, Morgan's four sons were all successful jockeys, as well as his nephews Tommy and Danny (DJ). Danny appeared on the Gold Cup roll-call, both in a riding and training capacity in future years. Frank Morgan would have been a Gold Cup-winning jockey too, if he had not been taken ill on the eve of the race and forced to miss the ride on Ballinode.

Morgan's challenger was a chestnut mare and such was her popularity that she became affectionately known as 'The Sligo Mare'. Very talented and a fast jumper, she was inclined to take the odd chance with her fences. However, the 1925 Gold Cup lacked both quality and quantity, and didn't take that much winning. With only three opponents, Ballinode, ridden by Ted Leader, was second favourite at 3–1 behind the 8–13 favourite Alcazar, trained by George Poole. Generally regarded to be the best three-miler in Britain, Alcazar had the invaluable assistance of Dick Rees. The other two runners were old Conjurer II, by now a light of former years, and Patsey V, former winner of the valuable four mile National Hunt Chase and ridden by his owner, Mr B.B. Lemon.

Ballinode's form had been impressive over the past two seasons, having finished second in the 1924 National Hunt Handicap Chase over the Gold Cup distance. The Sligo Mare had won on her two previous visits to England, including at Nottingham in February, and was primed to do herself justice. On a fine day, with the going described as good, the four runners jumped away to contest the increased prize money of eight hundred and eighty pounds. It was soon effectively a two-horse race, Conjurer II breaking down after making a bad mistake and Patsey V never getting a blow in at any stage. Alcazar bowled along in front, with Rees trying to repeat his winning tactics of last season. They were being tracked by Leader on Ballinode, that partnership going particularly well. It was only a matter of time before the mare was sent to the front, which she duly did at the second last to win in a hack canter by five lengths.

Although Ted Leader kept the ride on the mare for the majority of her career, like Red Splash before her, Ballinode didn't bear much more fruit. Later that month, Aintree was a bit of a disaster, the Gold Cup winner falling when well fancied for the Grand National. As for Ted Leader, he would soon become champion jockey, keeping up great family traditions. During his riding career, which lasted until 1934, he won just about every major race, including the Grand National on Sprig in 1927 and Dorothy Paget's famous Champion Hurdle/Gold Cup double in 1932, the opening gambit of Golden Miller's remarkable record at Cheltenham.

BALLINODE (1925)

ch.m. 1916 (Machakos – Celia)
Owned by Mr J.C. Bentley, trained by F. Morgan and ridden by E. Leader

✢ 1926 ✢

No longer the clown

With the out-of-form Ballinode not even entered for this season's Gold Cup, it was left to another Frank to follow in Morgan's footsteps. This was Frank Barbour, a wealthy linen manufacturer who had trained privately at a magnificently equipped stable at Trimblestown in County Meath. In similar fashion to Morgan, Barbour would invade the mainland, basing his string of horses at a pub in Tarporley, Cheshire. Although Barbour masterminded the operation, his horses were, at least officially, trained by his capable head lad, Alfred Bickley.

Barbour was a bit of an eccentric to say the least, as his behaviour at a Westmeath point-to-point illustrates. After falling off his own horse in the Members' race, he picked himself off the ground, headed straight out of the course, hitched a lift on a pony and trap, caught a train to Dublin and sailed off to New York for a holiday – still in his hunting clothes and without any luggage!

Despite such moments, Barbour was an astute horse dealer during his time at Trimblestown and the steeplechase course he built there provided a wonderful grounding for not one but two Gold Cup winners.

First there was Koko and then came the horse that did more to popularise the Gold Cup in its infancy than any other, Easter Hero. Back home in Ireland, Barbour taught his young charges to jump replica Aintree fences, no easy task with tearaways like Koko and Easter Hero. It transpired that this novel experience was wasted on the latter, certainly in the light of his first taste of Aintree's delights when he managed to get himself straddled across the open ditch at the Canal Turn, causing untold havoc in the process. Some two years older than Easter Hero, Koko made his first appearance in the Gold Cup at the age of eight. An imposing bay gelding, he was deemed to be about as impulsive as his owner, but when things went the right way for him in a race, and he was allowed to dictate, he was a very difficult horse to peg back. And so it was when he was teamed up with Tim Hamey, a local Bishops Cleeve-based jockey, who was to make this, his only Gold Cup ride, a winning one.

The first local to make an impact in the Gold Cup, Hamey, originally from Essex, had moved to the Cheltenham area and was riding for Arthur Saxby. Aged 21, it must have been quite a daunting task for the young jockey to take on the front-running role in a race that was already beginning to capture the imagination. After all, the prize money on offer was not inconsiderable – and not far behind some of the better established races. Hamey knew that he had a horse with a tremendous engine.

Koko had not impressed on his previous outing at Sandown, making numerous jumping errors. Now at Cheltenham, he appreciated being given his head right from the start, allowed to make his own pace in front. As an unfancied 10–1 shot in the betting, Koko proceeded to demolish a field generally made up of much slower Grand National types, including Old Tay Bridge and Ruddyglow, with Ruddyglow ending up a hot favourite on the day.

Koko, the Greta Garbo of the chasing world, was undoubtedly at his best ridden in this fashion. This win was the real launching pad for Hamey's career and he began to pick up the level of rides that befitted his undoubted talents. He teamed up with Koko again in the 1926 Grand National, but only got as far as Becher's Brook first time round. Hamey enjoyed a remarkable 12 successive rides in the National, winning in 1932 on Forbra for trainer Tom Rimell. He eventually took up training alongside the racecourse at Prestbury and in 1958, when Cheltenham were looking to expand the course, his farm was bought in what was, for all intents and purposes, a compulsory purchase order. Hamey retired from training in the mid-'70s and, in his latter years, was the oldest surviving winner of the Gold Cup. He died in April 1990. Koko, ever the character, would return to Cheltenham twice more in search of further glory. Without Tim Hamey, though, he would disappoint Barbour. Realising that the writing was on the wall for his enigmatic performer, Barbour sold him after his disappointing effort in the 1928 Gold Cup. It was an astute move that he would never have cause to regret.

KOKO (1926)

b.g. 1918 (Santoi – Persister)
Owned by Mr F. Barbour, trained by A. Bickley and ridden by J. Hamey

✣ 1927 ✣

A hot chestnut, Thrown In for good measure

The 1927 Gold Cup signalled the beginning of a period of domination by the Anthony brothers, Jack, Ivor and Owen – without doubt the most outstanding national hunt racing family of the period between the wars. Apart from all three being top-class jockeys, Jack and Ivor were both champion jockeys as amateurs and professionals. Remarkably, all three would train at least two Gold Cup winners each, amassing an incredible seven wins between them in a golden 14-year period. Owen Anthony's main claim to fame as a jockey had been a distant second in the 1913 Grand National riding Irish Mail. Eight years later and after becoming too heavy to ride, he started training at Lord Stalbridge's Pounds Farm stables at Eastbury, Berkshire, where he enjoyed virtually instant success, winning the 1922 Grand National with Music Hall.

The whole Cheltenham meeting was run in glorious weather and the Gold Cup, worth seven hundred and eighty pounds, attracted a field of eight. Silvo, a handsome dark bay and a prolific winner throughout his career, went off a well-backed 13–8 favourite. Trained by Percy Whitaker, who, then at the ripe old age of 53 rode him to win the 1923 Champion Chase, Silvo won the Grand Steeplechase de Paris in 1925 and finished a creditable third in the 1924 Grand National. His owner, W.H. Midwood, had already splashed out an incredible ten thousand pounds to buy him outright, having owned him in partnership with Sir E. Edgar. With these wins behind him, Silvo was fully expected to make short work of a sub-standard field which included the rookie amateur the Hon. Hugh Grosvenor, son of Lord Stalbridge, on one of the outsiders, Thrown In.

Two years earlier, Lord Stalbridge had bought the chestnut while he was still an entire horse. Thrown In was subsequently gelded and proceeded to double his tally of seven wins prior to the Gold Cup itself. However, nobody really took Grosvenor very seriously as he had ridden in only eight steeplechases and was facing possibly the stiffest fences outside Aintree. Indeed, the fences had been made much stiffer for this Gold Cup than for previous races and good jockeyship was now accepted as a prerequisite for success in the race. One of the joint-second favourites, Amberwave, came down at the first open ditch and the other, the five-year-old gelding Grakle, a headstrong individual making the first of four appearances in the race, proved to be a very difficult ride for his young Irish jockey, Jack Moloney.

Silvo had cried enough at the second last and it was left to Grakle, trained by Tom Coulthwaite, and Thrown In to fight out the finish. There was only one winner up the hill, Thrown In pulling clear of his only serious rival, Grakle (who had spoilt his chances running down the last) to win by a comfortable two lengths. Grakle's day would come, not at Cheltenham, but four years later in the Grand National.

The canny Coulthwaite was destined never to win a Gold Cup and his quirky Grakle re-opposed Thrown In at Aintree. Both fell – Thrown In only got as far as the first fence. Sadly, Hugh Grosvenor would never be seen in the saddle again. He took up a military appointment in Australia shortly after the National and was killed in an air crash 12 months later. Lord Stalbridge sold Thrown In, who disappeared without trace, having been exported to race in Denmark.

THROWN IN (1927)

ch.g. 1916 (Beau Bill – Va Largo)
Owned by Lord Stalbridge, trained by O. Anthony and ridden by Hon. H.R. Grosvenor

✛ 1928, 1929, 1930 ✛

A Welsh saint, and a hero in the making!

Not too many Cleopatras around at this time, but quite a number of Anthonys! Jack Anthony, the youngest of the three popular Carmarthenshire brothers, was the only one to ride in a Gold Cup, finishing down the field on Forewarned in the inaugural race and similarly out with the washing on Hackdene three years later. But these were simply minor blips on Jack Anthony's otherwise brilliant riding career, which included an incredible three Grand National wins, as well as being crowned champion jockey, both as an amateur and as a professional.

Like his brother Owen, it didn't take long for the Anthony magic to work in Jack's new guise as a trainer. Turning his back on riding in 1927, he set up at Letcombe Regis on the Berkshire Downs, where the newly ensconced Anthony quickly received the biggest boost anyone in his position could wish for – an equine star that would instantly elevate his standing in the training ranks.

Beautiful to behold, sleek, streamlined, powerful yet supremely elegant – not the soundtrack to a car advertising campaign but a set of adjectives aptly applied to a lean machine – a horse without the bulk of his predecessors, destined to change the face of national hunt racing some seventy years ago. Here was a hero in the making – Easter Hero.

He was bred within shouting distance of Greenogue, County Dublin, where in future years Tom Dreaper would train the greatest Gold Cup hero of all. Easter Hero's breeder, Larry King, a local farmer who trained and rode the majority of his horses, decided to sell the chestnut son of My Prince and Easter Week after his initial flop at Baldoyle. Mr Bartholomew, an English trainer, bought the cast-off cheaply and campaigned his new acquisition here, there, and everywhere, both in England and Ireland, culminating in an unplaced run in the 1925 Irish Grand National at Fairyhouse. At this early stage of his career, Easter Hero's jumping was distinctly unimpressive, although the five-year-old did manage to get his head in front on one occasion over the minimum trip at Manchester. It was only when Frank Barbour managed to buy him from Bartholomew for a paltry five hundred pounds that Easter Hero began to show his true potential on the racecourse.

Danny Morgan, nephew of Frank Morgan, did the majority of Barbour's work-riding around this time and would carve his own niche in racing history by eventually becoming the first to both ride and train a Cheltenham Gold Cup winner. There would be nobody better qualified to assess the relative merits of the free-spirited Easter Hero and Danny Morgan wrote about these early experiences in *The Horse In Ireland*, published over thirty years ago.

> Easter Hero was more like a hurdler than a chaser. He stood about 16.1 hh, was light-framed and lacking in bone, but he was electrifying to ride against

or watch! I rode him in a gallop once and he confirmed all I'd seen and felt racing behind him. No jockey could ever hold him: the only thing to do was try to give him a 'breather' halfway through a race, then he was off again. I never saw a horse get within ten lengths of him on a Park course, except Gib who tried to take him on in the Cheltenham Gold Cup and paid the penalty when he fell close home. Yet Gib had won his previous six races off the reel, the last with twelve stone nine pounds in the saddle. To show his versatility, Easter Hero went on to win a good class hurdle at Newbury by ten lengths!

Racing scribes at the time didn't quite know what to make of the glamorous chestnut with the broad white blaze, so obviously full of character. In many quarters, he was dismissed as a 'speedster', one who couldn't possibly stay extreme distances. Very soon, Easter Hero made them all eat their words, just before the 1928 renewal. By winning the Coventry Chase at Kempton, a recognised Gold Cup trial over three and a half miles, he proved himself to be eminently adaptable. Carrying the mammoth burden of twelve stone seven pounds and giving upwards of two stone and more to creditable opposition, Easter Hero was a real eye-opener.

All of a sudden, Barbour was spoilt for choice in terms of targets for his new star. Would he decide to go for the Gold Cup, or the valuable National Hunt Handicap Chase followed by a cut at the pot of gold that the National represented? As it turned out, Barbour decided to bypass the Gold Cup and concentrate on the latter options. However, on the eve of Cheltenham, Barbour typically shocked the racing world by announcing that Easter Hero had been sold and would go straight to Aintree. He was always a man ready to listen to offers for any of his horses, irrespective of their talent. In this case, no details of the deal or of the purchaser were revealed for some considerable time.

Despite fears that snow and frost would lead to the 1928 Gold Cup being abandoned, the race went ahead thanks to a fortuitous break in the bad weather – but sadly without the much-heralded chestnut to spice up matters. However, Barbour still had Koko in the field and, as a ten-year-old, Koko was generally regarded at being at the peak of his powers and a more than able substitute for Easter Hero. Sent off at a shade of odds-on, Koko looked to be in control as he was sent to the front a mile from home. But the artful Dick Rees had Patron Saint, a young five-year-old bay gelding, in Koko's slipstream and, nipping around the inside on the home turn, Patron Saint jumped the last in front, albeit under severe pressure. Breathing down Patron Saint's neck, it looked for all the world as if Koko's superior pace would be the telling factor up the hill. Amazingly, though, Koko stopped dead in his tracks and was even passed by the unconsidered Vive for second place. Later, it transpired that Koko had broken a blood vessel, which had undoubtedly cost him his chance of a glorious double.

Patron Saint, trained in sight of Bangor racecourse by Stanley Harrison, next ran third in a two-mile flat race, ridden by Noel Murless, a young amateur who would go on to make an indelible mark in that sphere as a trainer. Expected to challenge Easter Hero the following year, the wretched Patron Saint was continually beset by training problems – the only subsequent win he ever achieved was in the quaintly named Plodders' Chase at Nottingham in 1930. He was basically a one hit wonder. Thanks to the brilliance of Dick Rees, he had enjoyed his fifteen minutes of fame in one of the slowest and probably one of the worst Gold Cups on record.

Meanwhile, ending much speculation, which had seemed only to intensify public interest in Easter Hero still further, his mystery buyer turned out to be almost as much of a shock as the amount of money involved in the sale. Captain Alfred Lowenstein, a wealthy Belgian financier who hunted in Leicestershire, was the man in question and the deal was a staggering seven thousand pounds, with a contingency of three thousand pounds if the horse won the National. The Captain's new purchase certainly would make an impression at Aintree – unfortunately not the one he and others had hoped for.

Easter Hero faced 41 opponents and set off like a scalded cat, jumping in magnificent fashion to end up several lengths clear at Becher's. The Canal Turn was an open ditch in those days and Easter Hero completely misjudged the fence on take-off, hit the top of it and ended up straddled across it, causing mayhem behind him and taking out around three-quarters of the field in the process.

Ironically, but not entirely surprisingly, Koko, not to be outdone by his stable-companion, managed to fall in spectacular fashion and was dragged unceremoniously out of the ditch in which he had got himself wedged, only seconds before the five remaining runners bore down on him. Only one horse finished the race unscathed, the tubed and parrot-mouthed Tipperary Tim. The 100–1 outsider was ridden to victory by Billy Dutton, a young amateur jockey who will feature much later in the Gold Cup annals as the trainer of Limber Hill, the first northern-based winner of the Gold Cup.

The Easter Hero saga took a further twist a few months after his Aintree débâcle when his owner vanished while flying to Brussels over the North Sea. Whether he fell out of his private aeroplane or actually committed suicide, nobody will ever know as his body was never found. Six months later, Lowenstein's executors put his horses up for sale and in stepped John Hay Whitney, a dashing American multi-millionaire sportsman who bought Easter Hero and another of the Captain's good horses, the Grand Steeplechase de Paris winner Maguelonne, for eleven thousand pounds. Surprisingly, it was believed that Maguelonne was the more expensive of the two purchases. Whitney promptly sent them both to be trained by Jack Anthony.

Looking back, it almost beggars belief that the outcome of the next seven Gold Cups would rest between Whitney and his cousin, the wealthy young heiress the Hon. Dorothy Paget, the daughter of Lord Queensborough. The impact their star performers had on raising the profile of national hunt racing in the eyes of the general public should not be under-estimated. Indeed, it became very fashionable for a number of rich American and British businessmen to try and emulate Whitney's involvement in the winter game. In contrast, nobody could begin to – and probably lacked the desire to – mirror the inimitable Miss Paget's bizarre behaviour, which at the time became almost as much a topic in racing circles as the exploits of all her numerous top-class horses put together.

Meanwhile, Easter Hero had a Gold Cup appointment to take up this year and an old friend to bump into on the way to the start – Koko.

Koko's new connections were hoping he would enjoy better luck than last year. His pilot was the lanky Tommy Morgan, a nephew of Frank Morgan. He had followed in the footsteps of his father, one of seven jockey brothers and as a 13-year-old apprentice on the flat had won the 1920 Great Metropolitan Handicap at Epsom before increased weight forced him to switch codes. However, it would be Tommy's brother, Danny, who would uphold the Morgan traditions in years to come, both as a jockey and a trainer. Koko, not for the first time, would prove to be an unwilling partner.

No longer carrying the famous Barbour colours of steel and vermilion and making what would turn out to be his final appearance in the race, Koko reverted to his old habits. Resenting being held up, he dragged his feet literally through every fence before he eventually parted company with Morgan at the water first time round. It was sad but somehow almost inevitable that Koko's links with the great race would end in this fashion. Having looked a dual winner before 'bursting' in last season's renewal, Koko was now a spent force. He had simply taken one liberty too many over the years and ended his racing career doing the rounds in soldiers' races at places such as Aldershot and Windmill Hill – a far cry from his glory day at Cheltenham.

As for Morgan, he went on to train from Ivy Lodge, Letcombe Bassett, more recently the late Captain Forster's former base. At the 75 year celebrations at Cheltenham, Tommy Morgan, 92 years old, enjoyed the distinction of being the oldest representative from the heady days of Easter Hero.

On paper at least, the fit and fancied 7–4 favourite Easter Hero faced a tough task in the 1929 Gold Cup against so many capable and experienced rivals. The weather leading up to the meeting had been appalling, with frost and snow having caused a complete cessation of racing right back to early February. The race was postponed for a week and Easter Hero's meticulous pre-race preparation included a number of exercise canters on the sands at Tenby.

Rees took the bull by the horns and drove Easter Hero straight into the lead from the off and never saw another horse. More than 30 lengths clear passing the stands on the first circuit, Rees gave him a breather down the far side before piling on the pressure again coming down the hill for the final time. Bright's Boy fell at the third last in vain pursuit and Grakle, ridden by Keith Piggott, Lester's father, couldn't make his presence felt in the last half mile and was caught for second by another seven-year-old, the outsider Lloydie. Rees was on fire, following up in the Champion Hurdle on Royal Falcon to become the first jockey to complete the Gold Cup/Champion Hurdle double.

Easter Hero's connections decided to try again in the Grand National, for which the chestnut had been allotted twelve stone seven pounds and went off a heavily backed 9–2 favourite. Once again, Easter Hero's luck ran out, twisting a plate at Valentine's and, despite this obvious handicap, running a remarkable race to finish second in the hands of Jack Moloney, only failing by six lengths to give more than a stone to Gregalach, one of Newmarket-based Ted Leader's five entries.

Easter Hero was given a well-deserved rest after such a gruelling contest and made his re-appearance a winning one, hacking up in a minor chase over three miles at Wolverhampton. He would be ridden this year by Tommy Cullinan, an Irish ex-amateur who had turned professional in 1928. The new combination proved to be successful. Showing his versatility, Easter Hero reverted to the minimum trip for his next outing at Leicester, where he picked up the princely sum of £88 for 'Jock' Whitney after winning with his head in his chest. So Cheltenham beckoned once again for the 10-year-old, with another attempt at Aintree to follow, assuming all went to plan in the 1930 Gold Cup.

Cullinan, in a bid to win his first and Easter Hero's second Gold Cup, faced a serious challenge in the shape of Gib, a young seven-year-old chaser trained by the vastly experienced Percy Woodland at Cholderton in Wiltshire. Gib had been bred and owned in Ireland by Lord Killeen, who had horses with Woodland. Gib was sold in 1930 to Mr B.D. Davis, who kept the horse in training at Cholderton – not that the horse spent much time in the stable. He was unbeaten in seven starts that season prior to Cheltenham, admittedly all handicaps, and had the advantage of the incomparable Dick Rees in the saddle.

Gib was being aimed specifically at the Gold Cup and had not even been entered for the National, which was a serious worry to Jack Anthony. Would the champion be able to fend off the young upstart? In all truth, Easter Hero's preparation this season had been almost negligible and Anthony knew it.

However, come Gold Cup day, with the Tote operating for the very first time, the disappointing field of only four runners failed to dampen the enthusiasm of the record crowd who were enjoying the fine weather and eagerly anticipating the clash of two exciting front-runners.

The 50–1 outsider Donzelon was clearly out of his depth and had fallen after one circuit. Grakle, a poor second in last year's race, not surprisingly couldn't live with the strong pace set by Easter Hero, a solid 8–11 favourite. Gib enjoyed plenty of support in the ring at 13–8, his proximity to Easter Hero due mainly to the Rees factor.

The favourite set off like a scalded cat and proceeded to take the first fence by the roots. He repeated the dose at the second fence, just managing to get away with hitting the deck. After these initial shocks to the system, the flamboyant chestnut began to settle and after the first circuit a repeat win certainly looked to be on the cards. Cullinan managed to get a Rees-style breather into him, which allowed the great man himself aboard Gib to make some ground on the leader. Despite a couple of errors in the latter half of the race, Gib was upsides with two to go, but under pressure when he ploughed through that fence, giving Rees very little chance of staying in the saddle. Easter Hero was left well clear and sauntered home twenty lengths clear of Grakle, who was a similar distance behind last season.

Grakle's finest moment would come in the Grand National in 1931. Now owned by a local Liverpool businessman, he vindicated Tom Coulthwaite's belief that he would one day make a name for himself at Aintree.

Undoubtedly, Easter Hero's style of running and zest for racing from the front had elevated considerably the status of the Gold Cup, and indeed Cheltenham in general. Already as popular as the Sandown Military meeting, the National Hunt Meeting still had a long way to go to match the thrills and spills of Aintree, although the cavalry charge mentality and the standard of some of the National entries left a lot to be desired. Tipperary Tim's win had lent a certain farcical, almost comic aspect to the historic race and every Tom, Dick and Harry who owned a chaser of any ability whatsoever was more than willing to stump up the £100 entrance fee. This helped to swell the National first prize to a mammoth thirteen thousand pounds, hence the previous season's record field of sixty-six, but only ten finishers!

Returning to a hero's reception, Easter Hero was immediately installed as 5–1 clear favourite for the National, despite being made to shoulder twelve stone seven pounds once more. However, dreams of Aintree glory swiftly became academic, following the discovery that the first dual Gold Cup winner had gone lame during the Gold Cup race. The National bid would have to wait another year. Additionally, Easter Hero was found to have strained a tendon in one of his forelegs, putting an end to his whole season there and then.

Tommy Cullinan had created history on Gold Cup day, going on to land the Champion Hurdle for Jack Anthony riding Brown Tony – the first trainer and jockey combination to do the big race double. Any hopes of a unique treble culminating with the National seemed to be dashed. Yet talk about the luck of the Irish! Cullinan picked up a spare ride on the fancied Shaun Goilin, trained by Frank Hartigan at Weyhill, and beat none other than Sir Lindsay, Jock Whitney's substitute for Easter Hero, into third place in a thrilling finish.

Strangely, in the years following his exploits with the likes of Easter Hero, Tommy Cullinan found rides increasingly difficult to come by and retired from the saddle in 1935. He trained without much success, briefly as a permit holder and even more briefly as a licensed jumps trainer, based at Didcot, in the late '30s. At the start of the Second World War, a private in an English anti-aircraft unit, he suffered severe depression and sadly, in a fit of depression, took his own life.

There was no Gold Cup in 1931, in fact no National Hunt Meeting at all due to the terrible weather. Only the National Hunt Chase, still the most valuable race at the meeting, though not the most prestigious, re-opened and was run in April. This decision raised a number of eyebrows in racing circles and prevented the champion from bidding for his hat trick.

Easter Hero, now an eleven-year-old, headed for Aintree instead but seemed a shadow of his former self when beaten at long odds-on at Lingfield shortly before the National – his first defeat on a Park course. Things didn't improve much in the big race itself. Carrying his usual welter burden and starting the 5–1 favourite, he was brought down at Becher's second time round. Amazingly, Easter Hero was pulled out to run again the very next day in the Champion Chase, only managing to scrape a dead-heat at level weights with an unknown and unconsidered French raider, Coup de Château.

Fittingly, with Dick Rees back in the saddle, the Champion Chase was to be Easter Hero's last race as both Whitney and Anthony sensibly decided that enough was enough – they had been to the well often enough with Easter Hero to know when to make that decision. There are more than enough examples in racing history of former top-class horses shuffling round gaff tracks in their old age. Fortunately, this was never going to be the case with Easter Hero. It made sense to go out on a winning note, even if the performance itself was not up to Easter Hero's usual standard (albeit against specialist two-milers and the day after an exhausting run in the National).

Jack Anthony declared that this was the best horse he had ever known and one of the best never to win a Grand National. In all probability, he would have won three consecutive Gold Cups had he been allowed to take his chance back in 1928. He missed a great opportunity to put his poor National record straight when injured at the peak of his powers following his second Gold Cup win.

Jock Whitney shipped him out to Virginia, where he enjoyed a well-deserved retirement at his owner's stud, living to the ripe old age of 28. Easter Hero left a lasting impression with his flamboyant, cavalier style of racing and proved to be exactly the boost that national hunt racing – and the Gold Cup in particular – was crying out for.

Nobody in their wildest dreams could have hoped for a successor to the Gold Cup crown, let alone one even better equipped than Easter Hero to carry on the good work. Did such an animal exist? Surely not. The racing hacks at the time had waxed lyrically about their champion, and rightly so. Yet within two years, there would be a Gold Cup winner that would eclipse even The Hero's achievements. It was to be a period of overwhelming dominance that only Arkle would ever threaten to match. Chaucer detailed the exploits of a certain hell-raising miller in his *Canterbury Tales* – another Miller, a Golden one, proceeded to raise hell amongst his peers too.

PATRON SAINT (1928)

b.g. 1923 (St Girons – V.M.C.)
Owned by Mr F. W. Keen, trained by H. Harrison and ridden by F. Rees

EASTER HERO (1929 AND 1930)

ch.g. 1920 (My Prince – Easter Week)
Owned by Mr J.H. Whitney, trained by J. Anthony and ridden by F. Rees (1929) and T. Cullinan (1930)

✢ 1932 ✢

It's Miller time

> The prospect of having a good story to tell of the race for the Cheltenham
> Gold Cup was dashed when the three most interesting horses in the small
> field of half a dozen came to grief in circumstances that were most
> deplorable, at any rate, in the case of the favourite, Grakle (10–11), who,
> as the world knows, is favourite for the Grand National . . . all the bottom
> seemed to go out of what should have been an interesting and instructive
> affair.

Hindsight is a wonderful thing, but how Hotspur of the *Daily Telegraph* must have
looked back in anger at his report on the 1932 Gold Cup and wished he had been
a little less downbeat and given the shock winner, Golden Miller, a tad more credit
for his victory. After all, it is not beyond the realms of possibility, given his
Cheltenham record thereafter, that 'The Miller' might have beaten all the fancied
horses if they had all played a part in the eventual finish.

So what if Grakle, the odds-on favourite, had been brought down by another
fancied horse? Fair enough, he had won the Grand National the previous season,
but his actual form in the Gold Cup didn't exactly inspire overwhelming
confidence – he had failed three times already and to make him such a short price
on what he had actually achieved at Cheltenham was ridiculous. The up-and-
coming young Miller had already proven himself to be an above-average
five-year-old by winning three of his four chases. His young trainer, Basil Briscoe,
was perfectly entitled to expect great things from the promising novice.

Hotspur's throwaway line that as the world knows, Grakle is favourite for the
Grand National, typified the perception of public interest in the Aintree
spectacle at that time, which, for all its possible accuracy, should in fact have
had very little bearing on the market for a top-class race on a park course. If
ever there was a '30s 'Bismarck', Grakle fitted the bill perfectly and he
proceeded to sink on the day. While one light was extinguished, however,
another burned brightly and would light up the whole of Cheltenham for many
a year, providing good copy for the likes of old Hotspur – even if he didn't
realise it back in 1932!

The press were usually more than ably assisted off-track by The Miller's
extremely newsworthy connections, who were quite often embroiled in tempes-
tuous disagreement over some particular aspect of their shared interest. This shared
interest eventually led to disaster for the headstrong Briscoe, the trainer in
question, whose fall from grace was almost as dramatic as his climb to the top,
which he enjoyed courtesy of The Miller and others on behalf of the Hon.
Dorothy Paget. Keeping this particular lady happy was no easy task, and the

owner/trainer relationship was doomed eventually to break down – but, for a time, what glorious success they enjoyed together!

In her defence, Paget always had the interest of her horses uppermost in her thoughts, but she was a control freak and an obsessive one at that. She had an army of female secretaries buzzing around her like mini satellites, informing her of anything and everything that appeared to hold the slightest significance for her quest to gamble. As a wealthy heiress, she could afford to bet telephone number sums and invariably did, usually on her own horses and often for astronomical sums. This would test the nerve of any self-respecting trainer. Over the years, some coped better than others, but nobody got better results for her than Basil Briscoe. He certainly didn't deserve the bullying he endured from Paget, which would take place even in front of his own staff, but for the most part he accepted it as part of the package deal. He knew that if he didn't turn the other cheek, the horses would soon be moved elsewhere.

Briscoe certainly bucked the trend when it came to his involvement in racing. Only the Leader family had successfully produced top-class national hunt horses while training at Newmarket, the headquarters of flat racing, and the Briscoe story is not the usual one of generations of the same family involved in the sport. Quite the opposite, in fact. Briscoe's family completely disapproved of his compulsion for matters equine. Willy Briscoe, head of a prosperous hardware empire, was determined that his son, educated at Eton and Clare College, Cambridge, would study estate management. But Briscoe had caught the racing bug with illicit trips to Windsor racecourse and later to Newmarket.

Although he acquiesced to his father's demands and spent two years in an estate office, it was plain for all to see that young Briscoe had made up his mind to train racehorses, whatever career his father had planned for him. The biggest mistake his father made was to set him up as a pupil under Lord Ellesmere's agent at Stetchworth, almost within sight of the July Course.

Briscoe spent more and more time on the gallops and even became an owner, staking considerable amounts based on inside information gained from his involvement with his friend and trainer, Joe Orbell. It was at Orbell's stable near Bury St Edmunds that Briscoe met his future head lad and former jockey, Stan Tidey, who would play a considerable part in Golden Miller's development.

In 1926, Briscoe took the opportunity to work as pupil assistant to Harvey Leader, uncle of that great jockey Ted Leader. Leader trained at Beechwood House, Exning, where Briscoe would eventually take over. But, for now, Briscoe was in his element, receiving the best grounding available in both codes and it proved to be a year that both men would remember. Leader won the Grand National with the ex-hunter Jack Horner, as well as taking many valuable prizes on the level. Briscoe, for his part, took part-control with Leader of the Cambridgeshire Harriers, kennelled at Bottisham, and brought over May Crescent, Golden Miller's older half-brother, from Ireland as a hunter and rode him to win a race at the long-established Pytchley point-to-point meeting in early 1928.

When Joe Orbell decided to retire, Stan Tidey joined Briscoe, who had rented stables at Madingley in order to start his own training career with his own horses, which now included his useful Pytchley winner. Although initially listed as Leader horses, Briscoe's string soon assumed the mantle of being 'privately' trained. May Crescent, ridden by the owner/trainer himself, made the first breakthrough under rules in February 1929, punted significantly, as usual, by Briscoe. Twelve months on, Briscoe returned, with an apparent seal of approval from his father, to the family mansion of Longstowe Hall near Royston, where his father had set aside some land for his youngest son. It didn't take long for Briscoe, now listed as a professional trainer for a number of owners, to break the ice under rules – a feat achieved by the appropriately named Longstowe.

While the racing world became Briscoe's oyster, opportunity certainly wasn't knocking for millions unemployed in the depression, and the Wall Street crash in October did nothing to help matters either. However, many rich Americans still wanted to indulge in their favourite leisure pursuit, so the likes of Briscoe were generally not touched by the financial problems that beset the majority of the nation. Cocooned in Longstowe, the young man with the Henry Cecil mannerisms started to attract wealthy owners and better quality horses. In March 1930, around the time that Easter Hero was about to consolidate his position as the best chaser in the land, Briscoe arrived home from racing to receive a telegram from a friend Captain Farmer, a Leicestershire horse dealer. He was offering May Crescent's younger half-brother for £500, an offer which Briscoe gratefully accepted. Farmer had been to County Tipperary to check out the latest bunch of horses that the legendary farmer/horse dealer Paddy Quinn had assembled down in Fethard ready to sell on and had picked one that he knew would interest Briscoe.

Within a week, the unseen purchase made the arduous journey from Ireland. A bedraggled and miserable-looking animal turned up at the railway halt at nearby Old North Road Station to be collected by one of the staff at Longstowe. Briscoe got the shock of his life when checking over his new arrival, wondering whether Captain Farmer was beginning to lose his touch. He described the incident in his book *The Life Of Golden Miller*, which he wrote during the war.

> My goodness, I had a shock. He stood there, head low to the ground, his wet bear-like coat sticking up in places like a porcupine and plastered in mud from head to tail; he turned his head slowly round to greet me and with the most downcast look in his eyes seemed to say to me, 'Well, I've arrived; I'm a disgrace to the stable, but be kind to me just the same.'

Although one gets the impression that Briscoe may have ever-so-slightly over-loaded on sentimentality here, it is doubtful that any horse enduring the train-ship-train passage that the three-year-old had suffered would be bounding with health in the aftermath of such an arduous journey. In fact, unbeknown to Briscoe at that time, it was probably the horse's superb temperament that had seen him through on the economy-class trip he had encountered. This was no ordinary horse – nothing seemed to phase him, with the possible exception of hunting, as his trainer would soon find out.

After getting over the initial shock and threatening to return 'the carthorse' to Quinn, Briscoe set about the task of schooling the raw recruit, who seemed to do what was required of him, but certainly no more. Tidey famously remarked shortly after Briscoe had registered the gelding: 'What a good name for a bad horse!' His first outing in August, in a well-contested but poor hurdle at Southwell, did nothing to change that opinion, although Briscoe believed that 'Golden Miller had been tremendously admired by the experts'.

Sure enough, he had grown significantly and his coat was beginning to take on that rich hue that would stay with him almost throughout his lengthy career. But, for now, the hullabaloo that he encountered at Southwell was a world apart from the tranquillity of Longstowe and he trailed in well behind, finishing in the pack. Briscoe decided that a spell hunting would benefit his latest Irish import. This wasn't the best of the impetuous Briscoe's brainwaves. Together they crashed through fences and rails and, in his words, 'The horse seemed so slow that I couldn't even keep up with the hounds, he had no interest in foxhunting at all and went through the roots of every fence we jumped.'

Never had truer words been spoken, but The Miller had shown something that the demanding Briscoe hadn't thought to give him any credit for – the ability to stay upright, despite blundering through every obstacle in his way. Not unexpectedly, The Miller had sustained a sprained tendon for his troubles, but this didn't stop Philip Carr, one of Briscoe's owners, showing surprising faith in the gelding, paying Briscoe a reputed one thousand pounds for him. Carr took the view that The Miller had something to offer and it didn't take long for this to be confirmed. A sudden transformation seemed to come over The Miller. Miraculously, the tendon sprain responded to treatment almost immediately and he began to display some of the awesome power he would become famed for, starting at Newbury in November and finishing a very creditable third in a handicap hurdle over two miles, the rain-sodden ground bringing his undoubted stamina into play.

His next outing came at Leicester in January, interestingly on the same card as Easter Hero who was making his first appearance since winning the 1930 Gold Cup. The Miller managed to emulate the great horse's impressive display on the day, both winning as they liked. Naturally, all the plaudits were for Easter Hero, but the raking stride of the passive bay was there for all to see, even over hurdles, and would become an even more familiar sight over the bigger obstacles.

Less than a week later, Golden Miller followed up in bizarre fashion at Nottingham. He got caught up in the starting tape and lost a tooth in the process! It seemed nothing could stop him. In the hands of Briscoe's old friend Ted Leader, he made up all the lost ground after the problems at the start and cruised past his 23 rivals to win by an effortless five lengths.

Briscoe decided the time was right to blood his pride and joy over fences at Newbury, despite being thrown in at the deep end against more experienced rivals. The Miller performed with immense credit, only going down by a short-head in a bobbing finish, with Gerry Wilson in the saddle. Wilson made sure that the new recruit didn't have too hard a race, much to the annoyance of Philip Carr, who had backed him to win a considerable sum.

The 1931 Cheltenham Festival was cancelled due to frost. Briscoe couldn't resist trying The Miller on the level and ran him in a handicap at Warwick in April, swiftly followed by a stakes race over a mile and a half at Newmarket. Even The Miller couldn't bridge this particular gap, finishing down the field in both races. Carr, whose health had been deteriorating for some time, decided to sell The Miller along with the rest of his horses. At around this time, Dorothy Paget was moving away from racing uncompetitive Bentleys at tracks like Brooklands, her team never even having won a race. She began to concentrate her efforts on buying top-class horses that would fuel the competitive Paget instincts. The desire to better her cousin Jock Whitney's impressive record of owning a host of useful animals, including, of course, the dual Gold Cup winner Easter Hero was an overriding factor, as was the enjoyment Miss Paget derived from gambling on her own horses. She rang Briscoe to enquire if he had any horses she might be interested in. Briscoe's reply was typical of the man. 'I have the best chaser in the world, Golden Miller, and the best hurdler in England, Insurance.'

Within a year, nobody could disagree with him, least of all his new owner, who, according to Briscoe himself, happily paid some twelve thousand pounds for the two geldings. This was an astonishing amount of money considering the paltry prize money on offer at a time when the country faced deep financial crisis. Everybody was expected to be frugal and play their part in facing up to the deflationary measures that the emergency budget had introduced – except the likes of Dorothy Paget. Money had long since ceased to have any real meaning for her, so much had she inherited. This hardly changed throughout her life, despite gambling losses of up to fifty thousand pounds in one year alone. Paget's gambling was one aspect that, in years to come, would cause her trainers much anguish, though not Briscoe.

In many ways, Briscoe was as impetuous as his new owner and took on the bookmakers regularly, in much the same way as young Vincent O'Brien would in a decade's time. One significant difference set the two men apart: in contrast to Briscoe, O'Brien was the ultimate shrewd operator and had to gamble to survive and succeed. For a while, Briscoe and Paget were an irresistible combination, though dealing with 'D.P.', as she became generally known, was like holding a grenade with the pin gradually slipping out, as Briscoe would soon find out. It was one thing coping with comparatively difficult owners, quite another dealing with D.P.

The Miller achieved instant success for his new owner, winning four times over fences in the run-up to the 1932 Gold Cup, although he was disqualified from the strangely named Moderate Chase at Newbury because Briscoe had misinterpreted the race conditions and The Miller carried insufficient weight.

Although The Miller was impressive in his races, it was asking a lot of the inexperienced five-year-old to take on the older brigade at Cheltenham. However, with no horses of the calibre of Easter Hero to worry about, Paget and Briscoe were confident that The Miller wouldn't let them down. Yet the ground was rock hard on the opening day of the meeting and Briscoe was loath to risk his stable star on the prevailing ground. Stabled overnight, The Miller was taken by Ted Leader for a tune-up on the morning of the race. Leader felt that The Miller wasn't letting himself down and was moving very gingerly indeed. Trainer and jockey reluctantly agreed that he was unfit to run. D.P., though, having already punted, would hear none of it, insisting, 'He's here, the money is down and I want him to run.'

The day started off well for the Briscoe/Leader/Paget combination, with the Champion Hurdle falling to the impressive Insurance who enjoyed a scintillating 12-length win over his expected main rival, Song Of Essex. The scene was set for a unique Champion Hurdle/Gold Cup double in the next race. Grakle, the Grand National hero, was in great form, unbeaten in his last three runs carrying huge weights and making his fourth and final attempt on the winner's purse of six hundred and seventy pounds, and backed as if defeat was out of the question. Starting at a shade of odds-on at 10–11, he had been expected to revel in the ground conditions and the stiff fences – so stiff that the course inspector was unhappy with them and ordered that six inches be lopped off them. This meant there was no 'soft top' to the fences and no margin for error, which could have had a considerable effect on the eventual outcome of the race.

Other challengers included second favourite Kingsford, a renowned hard-pulling chestnut trained by George Poole. Brilliant on his day, the nine-year-old Kingsford had blotted his copybook at Gatwick with a fall in his final warm-up race. Also in the race was Lady Lindsay's useful six-year-old brown gelding Inverse, a Becher Chase winner and a similar proposition to Kingsford. Gib was back to try and lay to rest the ghost of two seasons ago, though he was now a light of former years.

During the race itself, Gib proved his unreliability by departing at the second fence. The running was made by the complete outsider Aruntius from The Miller. The Miller's early fencing left much to be desired, but he warmed to the task as the race progressed. Grakle looked to be on good terms with himself, coasting along at the back of the field, when disaster struck. Heading out on the far side for the second time, Aruntius jumped sideways and almost fell, causing Kingsford, on the heels of the leader, to clatter the fence and fire Billy Stott into the ground. Grakle was also caught up in the mayhem, jinking in mid-air to avoid the fallen Kingsford and catapulting the amateur Jack Fawcus out of the saddle, ending his chance of finally grabbing Cheltenham gold. As they reached the top of the hill, The Miller had been given time by Leader to recover from a blunder on the far side and so the two principals were left to fight it out virtually on their own as Aruntius was now a spent force. Bob Lyall on Inverse was the first to go for his stick but his efforts were in vain. The Miller was now in overdrive and put the issue beyond any doubt at the second last, pulling clear of Inverse. Clearing the last in effortless style, the era of The Miller had well and truly begun – the first steps on a Gold Cup odyssey that would stretch for a further six years.

Briscoe couldn't contain his excitement any longer, exclaiming, 'He's won it, he's won it!' – much to the disapproval of the surrounding connections of the vanquished. Ted Leader then provided probably the rarest moment in Gold Cup post-race history. Ever the horseman and typical of his character, he had the presence of mind to grab hold of Grakle's reins as he ran loose and rode his second Gold Cup winner and the reigning Grand National champion into the unsaddling enclosure, to a chorus of cheers. Tom Coulthwaite was there to meet them and gratefully took control of his charge, before Grakle could do himself any more harm. To show his eternal gratitude, Coulthwaite subsequently presented Leader with a silver cigarette case with the inscription 'Actions speak louder than words'.

Briscoe now knew he had something special to go to war with, even if the racing scribes were more preoccupied with the well-being of the nation's (and National) favourite, Grakle. They had given The Miller some credit for his rugged performance and for this Briscoe was grateful. It had been a slowly run race, taking well over half a minute longer than Easter Hero's record. Nevertheless, to his credit, The Miller was inexperienced, still only five years old (which excluded him from any thoughts of a follow-up in the Grand National), yet he certainly had more to offer than the other Gold Cup-winning novices. This was an animal that kept something in reserve, doing just enough to keep one step ahead of the opposition. His economical jumping coupled with his raking stride would stand him in good stead for the countless battles that lay ahead.

As for Briscoe, he was the original leopard who couldn't change and, as we will see, his temper finally got the better of him. When it came to coping with the inevitable disappointments that racing throws in the direction of its players from time to time, Briscoe was found wanting. This was a great pity because he obviously had the talent, if not the temperament.

GOLDEN MILLER (1932)

b.g. 1927 (Goldcourt – Miller's Pride)
Owned by Hon. D. Paget, trained by B. Briscoe and ridden by T. Leader

✛ 1933 ✛

Briscoe plays Newmarket. What a card he is!

By the time The Miller returned to Cheltenham to defend his Gold Cup crown, Briscoe's burgeoning operation had moved to Exning, Newmarket. D.P. had rented Beechwood House from Harvey Leader (who had decided to move to a stable in Newmarket itself) believing that this was the logical move for Briscoe. He duly took up her offer to move to larger premises.

Although only some thirty miles down the road from Longstowe, Exning was a far cry from the Briscoe family home in terms of training 'behind closed doors'. Not that Briscoe had anything to hide; it simply meant Briscoe's training methods, and, more importantly, those used on The Miller would be there for all the racing world to see and comment on. In time, as events conspired against Briscoe, this would prove to be a significant factor in his eventual downfall. Had he stayed at Longstowe, things might have been very different. Yet this was Basil Briscoe: youthful, impetuous, confident, cocking a snook at establishment and more than happy to show the wagging tongues at headquarters just what he was capable of.

You couldn't really blame Briscoe for wanting to rid himself of the logistical problems that he was increasingly facing at Longstowe. It must have seemed to be the right thing to do at the time as he shot up the ladder of success. The new yard had a rustic charm about it, which would have appealed to Briscoe. With roses climbing up between the doors of the boxes, it seems Briscoe shared not only the Cecil mannerisms but also Cecil's love of roses. The Miller had spent the summer grazing in a paddock at the adjoining Brickfield Stud and had learnt to cope well with the wide open spaces of Newmarket Heath and the introduction of a new jockey, the latter something that the champion would have to get used to throughout his career. D.P. had fallen out with the forthright Ted Leader and had employed five-times champion jockey Billy Stott in his place. A diminutive rubber ball of a man, the powerful former flat-race jockey had already enjoyed success on The Miller when he partnered him to his first win over fences.

Having been trained with the National in mind, The Miller remained unbeaten in four outings prior to Cheltenham. One particular example of his titanic strength, even as a six-year-old, stands out above all the others. His final prep race for Cheltenham had been Lingfield's valuable Troytown Chase, which he took in his stride despite having to shoulder a mammoth twelve stone ten pounds. Even in those days, Lingfield in midwinter could turn into a real bog. It made no difference to The Miller who brushed aside all challengers up the straight before delivering the killer blow over the last to a young horse of immense talent, Buck Willow in receipt of thirty-one pounds, to win comfortably by a length.

The Miller had improved race by race throughout the season and the Gold Cup seemed to be there for the taking. On the day, it was very much a case of *déjà vu*. The

Champion Hurdle once again went to The Miller's stablemate Insurance, who showed his liking for the prevailing soft ground. Stott steered the champion hurdler to a fluent win over last year's runner-up Song Of Essex, who had done his best to bite through Stott's arm as they were milling around at the start before the tapes went up!

D.P. was wearing a new long, tweed coat, bought specifically for the big day, as she led her dual-champion hurdler. This coat would become a very familiar sight over the years – she wore it day in, day out. That she wouldn't go racing without wearing it, for purely superstitious reasons, is questionable. It certainly didn't always do the trick, even with The Miller! Nobody in her hand-picked entourage would ever dare to question her choice of attire, but fashion icon she clearly wasn't – the only thing that mattered to her was winning races, thereby waging war against her bookmaker.

The Festival continued to go D.P.'s way, but not before Stott returned to the weighing room to have his wound dressed.

According to the market at least, this Gold Cup appeared to be a formality. The Miller was on offer at 4–7, which reflected the high regard in which he was now held by both his connections and the public. Second favourite at 11–4 on the day was Thomond II, a remarkably tough, almost pony-sized chestnut gelding who was a year older than The Miller and whom Jack Anthony and owner Jock Whitney thought could go some way towards emulating the great Easter Hero.

Thomond II, who was unfashionably bred in Ireland, had been earmarked as a Gold Cup hopeful after his success in a handicap chase at the Festival the previous year on his very first outing in Whitney's colours. This season he had been partnered to four impressive wins by Stott's great pal Billy Speck, including a dynamic performance to gain the day, despite a slipping saddle in Aintree's Becher Chase. Although at all times a formidable terrier-like opponent, Thomond II was an infinitely better horse when the ground was riding lightning fast. The conditions for this Gold Cup were certainly stacked in The Miller's favour, which wouldn't always be the case in future Gold Cups.

Other principal contenders included the promising Kellsboro' Jack, another nine-year-old who was at his best on firm ground and who turned out to be a top-notch performer for his owner Florence Ambrose-Clark. There was also the useful Delaneige, cleverly named by J.B. Snow, his American owner, who had changed the gelding's name from Sanstrome to the French equivalent of his own surname.

A massive crowd had gathered to enjoy the spectacle and they weren't disappointed. Delaneige made the running, with The Miller and the others grouped up behind for the first circuit. Stott made the decision to bide his time on the favourite and as he moved out into the country on the far side for the final time, Speck took up the running on Thomond II and tried to steal a march on the field, suddenly injecting some real pace into the race. The Miller went about his work like the true professional he was. Tracking the leader with three to go, Stott set The Miller alight, knowing that his partner had stamina and speed in abundance. Gutsy though he was, Thomond II simply couldn't live with The Miller. Stott was almost toying with his great friend Speck, who was working overtime on the tiring chestnut. Despite making a hash of the second last, The Miller was kept up to his work on the run-in to win by an impressive ten lengths, with the gutsy Thomond II managing to hold on for second place from Delaneige.

There could be no doubters now, no jibbing of The Miller's destruction of a quality field. He hacked up and the cheering that met the conquering hero as he was led in by his proud owner and trainer spoke volumes for The Miller's increasing popularity. By the end of next season, his actions would make him truly public property, a scenario that Briscoe would find increasingly difficult to cope with.

For now, however, the Grand National beckoned for The Miller, who was immediately made favourite for the race. The Gold Cup/Grand National double had eluded even Easter Hero, The Miller too for now. As an acknowledged master around Aintree, Ted Leader was called on to replace Billy Stott, who apparently didn't feel he that had the physique to be able to overcome the more daunting fences and do The Miller justice in the race.

Despite the ground being on the firm side of good, The Miller still went off a well-backed 9–1 favourite on the day. Unfortunately for connections, who had punted sizeable amounts on their charge, things certainly didn't work out for the reunited Leader. After a number of clumsy leaps that would have downed a lesser horse and jockey, The Miller finally parted company with Leader at the Canal Turn fence, firing Leader into the ground.

The race was won in record time by Kellsboro' Jack. His American owner vowed after the race that she would never again allow her pride and joy to face the daunting prospect of taking on the Aintree obstacles. According to Danny Morgan, who rode Kellsboro' Jack to finish in the frame in the next three Gold Cups, she actually went much further than this. 'Although he was not so spectacular as The Miller, Kellsboro' Jack was my favourite. He was a good horse – especially when you think that after winning the 1933 Grand National his owner said that he was never to be trained seriously again – and I know he wasn't, as I rode him from 1934 to his retirement in 1938' (*The Horse in Ireland*). The same could certainly not be said of The Miller. His owner and trainer were both equally determined to push on with their plans for 'Miller immortality' and the Aintree hiccup had been brushed aside within days of the race.

Ted Leader's mutterings that The Miller would never make an Aintree horse were totally dismissed by both Briscoe and Paget. Leader was no longer available to ride due to starting up as a trainer, which meant that a new jockey would be needed next season. Billy Stott was unavailable to take his place, having been badly injured in a car crash just days after the Grand National. In stepped Gerry Wilson, champion jockey-elect, to renew his partnership with The Miller. Wilson, who even at this stage of his career was generally regarded as the ultimate professional, had ridden The Miller in his first chase and knew the horse well, having schooled him at Longstowe prior to that Newbury race. It would be the end of November before The Miller was back on the racecourse proper, by which time he had, almost unbelievably, strengthened up yet again. Briscoe had spent the summer formulating a new plan of action for his great champion, working the seemingly indestructible Miller day in day out to get him as fit as possible.

The Miller's extravagant labours on the Newmarket gallops would soon bear the fruits that his efforts deserved and ensure his place in racing history – the only horse in the twentieth century to achieve the Gold Cup/Grand National double in the same season.

GOLDEN MILLER (1933)

b.g. 1927 (Goldcourt – Miller's Pride)
Owned by Hon. D. Paget, trained by B. Briscoe and ridden by W. Stott

✢ 1934 ✢

The Miller grinds his way into history

If ever a horse was fed up with suffering the all-too familiar sight of The Miller's powerful hind quarters disappearing into the distance, it must have been poor Thomond II. Thomond II was victim to The Miller yet again on his re-appearance at Lingfield; it didn't make a scrap of difference that his shrewd handler Jack Anthony had honed the bonny chestnut to race fitness. Thomond II, two facile wins behind him, was put firmly in his place once more, on this occasion by six lengths, when The Miller won on a tight rein. The Miller's performance, in the light of Briscoe's remarks that his horse was 'only one quarter fit', must have sent shudders down the spines of a few trainers.

Nevertheless, even The Miller's greatest season was not without its setbacks and his next two appearances, both defeats at odds-on, must have given hope to many rivals and led to some concern within the Briscoe camp, despite the usual public show of confidence. First, and for a change, Thomond II was able to exact at least some revenge when Wilson was unable to reel in the runaway winner on fast ground and over the shorter trip of two and a half miles at Kempton's Christmas meeting. Second, The Miller had failed to give upwards of two and a half stone to the useful Southern Hero and Persian Sun at Hurst Park.

Yet Briscoe made sure come Cheltenham that The Miller would be 100 per cent on the day, leaving no stone unturned in his champion's preparation. He brought in Harry Beasley, the top-flight flat-race jockey, to complete The Miller's workouts at Newmarket. Come Gold Cup day, the quantum leap made in the champion's conditioning since the Hurst Park defeat would prove to be a significant factor – it needed to be! The small but select field of seven for the 1934 Gold Cup presented a rare cocktail of talent and experience. Some of the experienced horses, such as the precocious Avenger, were beyond their tender years.

The Black Gauntlet gelding bred by Lord Derby, still only a five-year-old, had already clocked up eight chase wins, of which six had been gained as a four-year-old! To add to this, in his last race at Manchester Black Gauntlet had given weight and a beating to competent performers such as Inverse. Inverse was in opposition again here and not fancied to reverse places, being considerably worse off at the weights. Another challenger reckoned to have a touch of class was the Percy Woodland-trained French import, El Hadjar, a whippet-like gelding who had caused a considerable stir by winning his initial outing in Britain only a week before the Festival over three and a half miles at Kempton. In that same race, Jock Whitney's Royal Ransom had fallen while in close contention at the second last. Royal Ransom was to represent the owner here in preference to Thomond II, who was being specifically aimed at the National. Old adversaries Kellsboro' Jack and Delaneige completed the line-up.

Conditions on the day of the race were, to say the least, difficult. The prolonged drought followed by the recent rains had made the track very slippery, placing the accent on sure-footedness and quality jumping. This combination of factors meant there was plenty of opinion on the outcome of the race and no shortage of opposition in the ring to The Miller. Despite this, he went off a short-priced favourite, with El Hadjar, Avenger and Delaneige all vying for second favourite just before the off.

In an eventful race, such as was only to be expected given the tricky conditions, Inverse was the first to fall, sadly breaking a leg in the process, in full view of the packed stands. Delaneige had made the running, with Wilson tucking Golden Miller in behind the leader and travelling on the bridle throughout the first circuit. With over a mile to go, Wilson decided to make use of The Miller's superior stamina and immediately kicked him clear at the water jump. Billy Parvin, riding El Hadjar, tried to respond but had cried enough when tiredness took over and he crashed at the fourth last fence. There is an old saying in racing: disaster only ever strikes with good horses, many a rogue lives to a ripe old age. This was undoubtedly the case with El Hadjar, who was to fall fatally in his next race, the Champion Chase at Liverpool.

It was now Kellsboro' Jack's turn to take on The Miller running towards the third last. As quickly as the challenge materialised, Wilson asked Golden Miller to respond. In a couple of strides Kellsboro' Jack was a spent force. The final threat to The Miller's supremacy came from Avenger, with Bob Lyall doing his utmost to take advantage of Avenger's useful nine-pound allowance and closing in on the favourite coming to the last. But nobody was going to spoil the party and The Miller breasted the last and drew away to pass the post six lengths clear of Avenger.

It had been a remarkably easy win and, with his ears pricked to listen to the rapturous applause around him, he strode into the unsaddling enclosure to a memorable reception, a champion among champions. He had beaten Easter Hero's record of two Gold Cups and had achieved it with the minimum of fuss.

Sixteen days later, The Miller's already increased popularity rocketed into orbit when he beat Delaneige and Thomond II by five and six lengths respectively to win the Grand National in record time. Hotspur of the *Daily Telegraph* changed his tune in no uncertain terms. 'Coming to the second fence from home there were actually two in it, Delaneige and Golden Miller. Which would win? I looked for the proved fine speed of Golden Miller now to determine the issue, having got so far. Delaneige put up a game response to the limits of his endurance, but Golden Miller came galloping home like the champion that he is.'

Incredibly, just twelve months later, things were to turn extremely sour for the infamous Miller team. No trainer in the world, let alone the unfortunate Briscoe, could persuade the reluctant Miller to reach the expected high notes at Aintree again. The Exning maestro found himself washed up like a shipwreck cruelly stripped of its assets and laid bare on the beach for all to observe and pass comment on. Briscoe's pride would come after a fall that would ultimately change his life, though not before Golden Miller returned to Cheltenham to fill his lungs to capacity yet again in search of further Cheltenham glory.

GOLDEN MILLER (1934)

b.g. 1927 (Goldcourt – Miller's Pride)
Owned by Hon. D. Paget, trained by B. Briscoe and ridden by G. Wilson

✛ 1935 ✛

'The greatest race of my life'

The options for the phenomenal Miller, who had now reached the zenith of his career, were endless. His connections could have tried to muscle in on the legendary Brown Jack's territory, the Queen Alexandra Stakes at Royal Ascot. The Grand Steeplechase de Paris, a race which Grand National winner Troytown had won as a six-year-old, was mooted as another alternative. While these were all possibilities, the one problem was the timing of these events as high summer usually meant hard going, which was definitely unsuitable for the champion. For once, D.P. displayed remarkable restraint and, much to Briscoe's relief, took the easier options.

The Miller had been given the summer off on the way to targeting both Cheltenham and Aintree again and this time round it was very much a softly, softly campaign in true Briscoe style. By the time March came, The Miller was unbeaten in four runs, all at restrictive odds but for the final run at Sandown. In fact, the £670 on offer at Cheltenham would more than double the season's earnings for The Miller – but his team were glory hunting and prize money really didn't enter the equation. Quite correctly, Briscoe firmly believed that a fourth Gold Cup was there for the taking, albeit a mere trifle in his greater scheme of things, and who could blame him? Surely nothing could stand in the champion's way after last year's rout and well before Cheltenham? The Miller was already as low as 2–1 to wear the Aintree crown once more.

However, Jack Anthony and Jock Whitney had other ideas – their 'ham sandwich'. The narrow Thomond II entered unexpectedly the Gold Cup calculations and threw a monkey wrench in the Gold Cup works. With fast ground on the cards for the National Hunt Meeting, it made total sense for Anthony to advise his owner to take on the champion, not only at Aintree but also at Cheltenham.

There had been other bad news for The Miller team in the week leading up to Cheltenham. Wilson had suffered a fall, tearing shoulder muscles. However, he declared himself fit after riding in three minor hurdle races at Shirley in Warwickshire. Wilson kicked off the meeting on the Tuesday, winning the Champion Hurdle on the aptly named Lion Courage, a difficult ride at the best of times. His brilliance as a horseman saw him through the arduous task of guiding the local Frank Brown-trained gelding home with a truly masterful ride, without having to resort to the whip and so exacerbate his shoulder problems. The champion jockey sensibly gave up all his rides on the Wednesday and, after extensive physiotherapy, he declared himself ready to do The Miller justice on the Thursday.

Meanwhile Briscoe was busy trying to persuade Whitney not to run his Thomond II in the Gold Cup. He argued that it would be a disastrous move for both sets of connections, bearing in mind the effect an unnecessarily hard race would have on their respective chances in the forthcoming Grand National. Whitney subsequently denied this approach from Briscoe, although in hindsight he did think that it probably had been a mistake to run Thomond II, despite everything looking to be in his favour.

So, Thursday, 14 March 1935 turned out to be a red-letter day for the Cheltenham executive as the crowds flocked to the course on a beautiful spring day to witness a Gold Cup to savour. The quintet of top-class chasers, all in their prime and ready to do battle in the heat of the Prestbury cauldron, was made up by Kellsboro' Jack, Southern Hero and Avenger. The market wholly reflected The Miller's achievements. He was well supported down to 2–1 on, with his great rival Thomond II second best in the exchanges at 5–2. The pained expression etched across Wilson's gaunt face as he was led out of the parade ring was there for all to see. The question on everyone's lips was what effect would his injury have on the outcome of the struggle that lay ahead?

Scottish National winner Southern Hero set off to try and make all, with the four remaining runners closely packed up behind, all waiting to pounce. The pace set by Southern Hero was a generous one but he dropped back after the third last, leaving the two principals to slug it out for supremacy over the final two fences and up that famous hill.

Wilson acknowledged after the race that they had been up against a formidable opponent. He reflected post-race:

> We fought it out neck and neck and there was never an inch between us as we headed for the last fence. We took off together and the two horses didn't jump it as you and I know jumping. They flew over it and flew the distance of the run-in too. It's a short run-in from the last to the winning post at Cheltenham, no more than 240 yards – but it is a tiring uphill climb and any horse the least bit short of stamina falls back beaten as so many do year after year. Both Golden Miller and Thomond were thorough stayers and Specky as well as myself could ride a strong finish. But my horse found rather the better speed and we won all-out by three-quarters of a length – the greatest race of my life.

A sad irony from the epic battle was the remark made by the diminutive Billy Speck to his friend Gerry Wilson as they sipped champagne in Sir John Grey's box after the race. 'It was a grand race, mate. Well, here's one thing, when we are old and grey sitting back and enjoying a drink, we can tell them how we did ride at least one great horse race, one day in our lives.' Tragically, that would never happen. A few weeks later, Speck was dead. He broke his back when he was unseated from the unreliable Gwelo, trained locally by Len Lefebve, in the first race at the Cheltenham spring meeting. The fearless Speck had taken on one rogue too many and died six days after the fall at the tender age of thirty-one. The racing world mourned his death and turned out in droves to attend his funeral. Hundreds of people followed the cortège as it came past Prestbury Park, where the flag flew at halfmast, *en route* to the churchyard at Bishops Cleeve, the village that was home to both 'Billys', Stott and Speck. The famous Speck name lived on in national hunt racing through Billy's son Vic, a jump jockey who became a dual-purpose trainer at Melton Mowbray.

By winning his fourth successive Gold Cup in record time, The Miller confirmed his status as the greatest steeplechaser of the twentieth century. Briscoe and D.P. proudly confirmed to the assembled press their intention to head for Liverpool in search of the double again – a move that would ultimately prove to be the undoing of their unlikely partnership.

Briscoe went about the champion's defence of his Aintree crown in typical fashion. Three and a half mile gallops across Newmarket were the order of the day. Interval training this certainly wasn't! But Golden Miller seemed to thrive on it, although a number of good paddock judges reckoned he looked to be 'running up a shade light'. This was a view that D.P. herself subscribed to, having been fed copious amounts of damning information by her Newmarket spies concerning the nature of the training schedule that Briscoe was supposedly subjecting The Miller to on a regular basis. For his part, Briscoe became almost paranoid about the dangers of someone nobbling The Miller prior to the race; even Gerry Wilson came under suspicion from the trainer, following warnings from Briscoe's friends in the betting industry. Concerns were voiced that the sheer volume of money riding on The Miller in the National meant that Briscoe could well face a serious attempt to prevent his champion from even making the race. Not surprisingly, in the days leading up to the race, Briscoe played safe and security, at D.P.'s expense, was considerably stepped up, especially at Liverpool. The Miller would eventually go off a ludicrously short-priced favourite, as low as 2–1 on the off, despite the firming up of the ground which considerably lessened the chances of a repeat of the heroics of the previous year.

Everything appeared to be going to plan for most of the first circuit as The Miller warmed to his task. Wilson kept him covered up in behind the leaders over the first few fences before urging him along to close into second place as the field approached Becher's. On the heels of the front-running Castle Irwell soon after Valentine's, The Miller safely negotiated the next fence before disaster struck at the open ditch. The seemingly invincible champion seemed to falter close to the obstacle, appearing to try and refuse altogether. Wilson struggled to change his partner's mind and almost succeeded but the laws of gravity took over and all his efforts counted for nothing. The usually ultra-reliable Miller tilted sideways in mid-air and over-pitched on landing, giving his rider no chance whatsoever of staying in the saddle. Wilson was catapulted through the air, landing in a heap on the unforgiving ground. As so often happens in such incidents, which occur in the blink of an eye, the majority of the expectant crowd were initially unaware of exactly what had taken place. Not so Briscoe – he had his binoculars trained on his beloved Miller. By the time Briscoe had scampered to the bottom of the stands, head bowed and pushing past row upon row of soon-to-be disgruntled punters, his world was already crumbling. It took a while for the penny to drop among the thousands in the stands but, when it did, as the field headed back into view with no sign of The Miller, they were stunned into a disbelieving silence. Within minutes, every possible scenario had been reenacted by the countless Miller fans, some blaming Wilson, some blaming Briscoe. Watching the remainder of the race unfold in an eerie silence must have been almost as surreal an experience as witnessing Esha Ness 'win' the void National some sixty years later. Just for good measure, Reynoldstown came back and repeated the dose again in 1936.

The Miller was to have a second chance at glory. The decision was taken to run him the very next day in the Champion Chase. However, the famous partnership got no further this time. Internal recriminations, held back from the previous day in the vain hope of an improved performance, were now vented in full by Golden

Miller's connections. It was the final straw for the excitable Briscoe, who had already been taken to task by D.P. for overworking her champion, insisting that he was unfit to do himself justice as a trainer. When two worlds collide in this manner, there has to be a loser and that loser was Briscoe. Shooting his career well and truly in the foot, he told D.P. in no uncertain terms to remove her horses from Exning. In a matter of days, The Miller and all her other horses were taken to her cousin-in-law Donald Snow's yard at Eastbury in Berkshire until Owen Anthony took over as trainer. Briscoe recalled that dismal day in *The Life of Golden Miller*. 'He was seen out of the gate by his faithful friend Grouse, my huge Great Dane. When The Miller left the stable gate Grouse sadly trotted back, and lay in the straw in the empty box.' Perhaps if Briscoe had stood up to D.P. in the early days of their relationship things might have been very different. Certainly, Owen Anthony was, in many people's eyes, bravely accepting a poisoned chalice in taking on D.P.'s jumping string. However, this move was on Anthony's own terms and unlike Briscoe he did not mince his words with the redoubtable D.P. Interestingly, this seemed to do the trick for Anthony. Irrespective of The Miller's future performances – some of which were undoubtedly in and out – no blame was ever apportioned by D.P. to her new trainer. Perhaps she had met her match in Anthony.

As for the unfortunate Briscoe, things went from bad to worse. Gambles went repeatedly astray and despite making a sensible move in late 1935 to accept an offer to train from Roy Pope's stable in Royston, he never recovered from the blow of losing The Miller. Briscoe's famed generosity continued, despite his ailing financial situation. Tragically, his young wife died after falling ill with tuberculosis, only months after Briscoe had been declared officially bankrupt and forced to leave his stable. He contracted the same illness as his wife, while working as a driver for the Royal Army Service Corps in Egypt, and returned home to treatment at Papworth Hospital in Cambridge. In August 1951, Briscoe died, aged 48, after seriously injuring himself in a fall at the Crown Inn at Swaffham Prior, where he had been living and working as a lorry driver, collecting manure from Newmarket stables. He was buried next to his wife in the churchyard at Longstowe.

I felt compelled last summer to visit Longstowe, a sleepy rural village nestling off the main road near Bassingbourn in Hertfordshire. Paying my respects to Briscoe was tinged with sadness and exasperation as I struggled even to find the grave of the man responsible for moulding one of the greatest chasers ever seen. I remember thinking that surely the folk of Longstowe hadn't forgotten Briscoe. After all, the pub in the village bears the name of Golden Miller. I honestly don't know what I thought I would find. I wasn't prepared, however, for the weather-worn, moss-covered headstone with the barely legible inscription with seemingly no mention of his achievements with The Miller. Somehow, that cold, granite stone seemed to encapsulate everything that went wrong for Briscoe. Not someone usually prone to great sentimentality, I admit to shedding a few tears that afternoon, standing in that leafy old churchyard. Somehow Briscoe the character, the entertainer, deserved better in his latter years.

GOLDEN MILLER (1935)

b.g. 1927 (Goldcourt – Miller's Pride)
Owned by Hon. D. Paget, trained by B. Briscoe and ridden by G. Wilson

✣ 1936 ✣

Sitting with a nap hand, then
mugged by the elements

With Golden Miller now stabled within throwing distance of Thomond II, it must have been tempting for his stable staff, ahead of a new season, to bait their counterparts at Jack Anthony's yard with stories of their new arrival's legendary prowess. It wouldn't have mattered if they had.

In October 1935, Thomond II had run extremely disappointingly, beaten in a minor two-horse race after an equally deplorable attempt at the Grand Steeplechase de Paris on his previous outing. Not surprisingly, the famous Gold Cup war with The Miller had 'bottomed' the brave chestnut and, despite being only a nine-year-old, Thomand had effectively already been round the clock twice and was sensibly retired after the Wincanton match defeat.

In contrast to this, nothing had been expected of The Miller early season and he was given time to settle in to his new surroundings. Anthony simply popped him over a few hurdles prior to a pipe opener in a national hunt flat race at Sandown. His lack of conditioning showed in the latter stages of the contest and his amateur jockey sensibly eased him home in third place. With Gerry Wilson back in the saddle for his next outing in December, the champion restored public confidence in him by taking an ordinary Newbury chase over an inadequate two miles. Next time out, in February back at Newbury, The Miller disgraced himself, for no apparent reason, running out at the fifth fence from home and dumping Gerry Wilson unceremoniously on the ground. Wilson, perhaps wisely, decided to announce the severance of his partnership with The Miller.

Arguably, D.P. would have made the decision to jettison Wilson anyway. Wilson's timing was usually right, however, and this was no exception. Anthony didn't have to look far for Wilson's replacement. Evan Williams, a willowy 23-year-old Welshman who had been attached to the Anthony stable as an amateur, was given the dubious pleasure of taking over on The Miller from the champion jockey for the forthcoming Gold Cup. Williams had already proved himself capable in the saddle, having turned professional a couple of years earlier. He was currently riding for Owen's brother Ivor for whom he rode the youngster Royal Mail.

The going come Gold Cup day was more or less ideal for The Miller, with plenty of give underfoot. This suited him better than it did his old rivals, Southern Hero and Kellsboro' Jack. Royal Mail, ridden in this race by Fulke Walwyn, would provide the stiffest challenge to the would-be nap hander.

The Miller was back at his favourite stamping ground and facing only five opponents. His jumping, although slightly unorthodox, was at least effective. His capable young jockey enjoyed an armchair ride throughout the race, keeping the champion under restraint until the turn on the far side, when he suddenly injected a burst of pace that soon had the others in trouble. The race was over in an instant. He scooted clear over the last, putting twelve lengths between himself and Royal Mail with a further two back to Kellsboro' Jack.

Not surprisingly, there had been some opposition to The Miller in the market. But, considering his fantastic record at Cheltenham, his starting price of 21–20 was remarkably generous. Breaking with her usual tradition, D.P. didn't lead The Miller in but instead waited to greet him in the winners' enclosure. With his reputation restored, the plan was now to capture the English and Welsh Nationals, in the space of 18 days. But there would be no recapturing of former glories at Aintree.

The Miller was market leader overnight until a flood of money came on the day for the dashing Avenger, pushing The Miller out in the betting. Sadly, The Miller, through no fault of his own this time, got no further than the first as Oeil de Boeuf, the French outsider, fell directly in his path giving him no chance of staying on his feet. While The Miller lived to fight another day, Avenger, Gold Cup runner-up in 1934 owned by Violet Mundy, wasn't so fortunate. The talented seven-year-old, ridden by Fred Rimell, was challenging for the lead when he fell heavily at the 17th fence, breaking his neck. Year in, year out even the most innocuous of the Aintree fences can prove most unforgiving.

Sensibly, the option to run The Miller in the Champion Chase the following day was declined and he ran, as planned, in Cardiff carrying a mammoth twelve stone seven pounds, yet still going off as the 4–6 favourite. The Miller could never get on terms throughout the contest with the winner, the well-handicapped Sorley Boy, trained by Ivor. Although beaten only four lengths into third place, it was, nevertheless, a disappointing effort. Anthony took the decision to put The Miller away for the rest of the season. In November, The Miller would once again face his personal nightmare – a return to Aintree, this time with a view to establishing whether it would be worth attempting the Grand National later in the season. He didn't disappoint his Aintree detractors, with Royal Mail reversing the Gold Cup form in no uncertain terms. After this latest defeat, it seemed that nothing would go right for The Miller. Suffering a conclusive defeat at the hands of Royal Mail in the Becher Chase was bad enough in the eyes of his demanding owner, but his performance at Gatwick two months later must have had even Owen Anthony scratching his head. Evan Williams was riding him for the final time and The Miller put in a below-par performance, managing only a last-gasp dead heat with the Ivor Anthony-trained Drinmore Lad.

Drinmore Lad, having won a number of steeplechases in America, including the Deep Run Hunt Cup twice, was shipped to race in England and became the first in a long line of Paul Mellon standard-bearers. Mellon, who was fabulously wealthy, had studied at Clare College, Cambridge and his famous black and gold cross colours would, in time, be immortalised by the exploits of Mill Reef. He sent Drinmore Lad to Kingsclere. Until the American philanthropist's death in February 1999, that same yard, still occupied by Mill Reef's trainer Ian Balding, enjoyed Mellon's loyal patronage for 63 years. His father, Andrew W. Mellon, once said, 'Every man wants to connect his life with something he thinks eternal'; his son certainly achieved this through his love of horse-racing, and the memory of the generous-spirited Mellon will live on through his many charitable trusts and foundations.

Although Mellon himself never had a Gold Cup runner, the Mellon name does appear in the Gold Cup records through his cousin Dick (R.K.), whose wife owned the Tom Dreaper-trained Leap Frog, a creditable second to dual winner L'Escargot in the 1971 Gold Cup. Later that year, Leap Frog's success in the Massey Ferguson ensured that Dreaper's last runner at Cheltenham completed his remarkable record there which was started by the mighty Prince Regent in the 1946 Gold Cup – the next horse to capture the public's imagination after The Miller himself.

With less than a month to go before returning to Cheltenham to attempt an incredible sixth consecutive Gold Cup, it wasn't all doom and gloom in The Miller camp. After all, this was The Miller's favourite course and despite the renowned burst of speed having been seemingly blunted, the indomitable fighting spirit appeared to be still there in abundance. Also, with no serious challenger coming through the ranks it was highly likely that another Gold Cup was well within his capabilities. In his final prep race, The Miller was ridden for the first time by Herbert 'Frenchie' Nicholson. In years to come, Nicholson would prove to have a considerable influence on horseracing, jockeyship in particular. But for now, the young gun was concerned with coaxing the champion to do the business at Birmingham with the minimum fuss and the maximum impact. D.P.'s pride and joy obliged in impressive fashion, unchallenged by 15 lengths, and the stage was set for his return to Cheltenham.

But it wasn't to be. The National Hunt Meeting, set to take place in the first week of March, was initially put back for a week due to some truly appalling weather. When it did eventually get under way on the following Tuesday, the first day of the meeting just about survived, with Free Fare, trained by Ted Gwilt, winning the Champion Hurdle. However, snow covered the course on Gold Cup morning. Although a rapid thaw ensued soon after midday, it was too late. The stewards had made their decision to abandon an hour earlier and The Miller's chance of Gold Cup immortality had gone for another year. It was a crying shame for everyone concerned, for had racing taken place, the hock-deep conditions would have been eminently suitable for the champion. So it was back yet again to Aintree in the vain hope that he could recapture his best form there once more.

With Danny Morgan taking over in the saddle, The Miller started market leader for the National again, but without the weight of money that was seen for him two years ago when he was the hottest favourite on record. All seemed to be going well until The Miller refused once more at the fence after Valentine's. Meeting the obstacle side on, The Miller was in and out of the ditch in a flash. For a change, it was Royal Mail's turn to grab the limelight. The previous year's Gold Cup runner-up went one better at Aintree in the hands of Evan Williams, the almost black gelding emulating the heroics of Reynoldstown, his dual-Grand National-winning half-brother. Never again would The Miller be subjected to the terrors of Aintree. Enough was enough. He was now to be campaigned solely with that elusive sixth Gold Cup in mind.

GOLDEN MILLER (1936)

b.g. 1927 (Goldcourt – Miller's Pride)
Owned by Hon. D. Paget, trained by O. Anthony and ridden by E. Williams

☩ 1938 ☩

So near, yet so far

Now rising eleven, The Miller wouldn't be seen again in public until mid-December, having enjoyed a nine-month break in order to freshen up for another assault on the Gold Cup. Following a pipe opener at Sandown, where he finished down the field – patently unfit but running to Anthony's expectations – The Miller managed to win three of his next four starts, albeit in fairly weak company. His only reverse had been at Hurst Park in February, where he was beaten at level weights by Macauley, a useful young horse bred by Lord Rosebery and trained by Peter Thrale.

Regular partner Frenchie Nicholson had been in the plate for the best of those wins – the valuable Prince's Chase at Sandown. This long-distance chase, still one of the Esher course's main attractions, is now known as the Mildmay/Cazalet. The Prince's Chase had been renamed the Mildmay Memorial following the death (presumed by drowning) of the late, lamented Lord Mildmay in 1950. The last of the true Corinthian riders, Lord Mildmay had actually won the Prince's Chase riding his beloved Cromwell only months before his disappearance. (Cromwell went on to record a poignant victory in the 1952 renewal.) It had, however, been a hard-fought victory for The Miller and Anthony was under no illusion about the difficulty of the Gold Cup task that would face the ageing champion in two months' time.

Nearly twenty thousand spectators, more than four times the number that had witnessed his first win back in 1932, enjoyed what would turn out to be The Miller's Gold Cup swansong. With the ground riding on the fast side of good, The Miller went off a drifting 7–4 favourite. Things looked ominous for the champion until the popular front-running Airgead Sios, third favourite behind Macauley, failed to make the running as expected. The hard puller did eventually claw his way to the front, but he had used too much of his energy in the first half of the race to make a serious impact here. The ensuing crawl was always going to make life difficult for The Miller, especially if it came down to a sprint up the hill.

The Miller, who was fencing indifferently, had been tracked for the majority of the race by Danny Morgan on Morse Code, a strangely wishy-washy-coloured nine-year-old liver-chestnut trained by Ivor Anthony. Morse Code, despite his unappealing colour, was a fine, athletic-looking beast of the highest quality. He had proved his ability when he finished a close third to Airgead Sios and Macauley in his final prep Gold Cup race. He had won the Grand Annual two years earlier and, like The Miller, had been trained specifically for this Gold Cup race.

As the leaders approached the second last, there were still four in with a chance. Suddenly, four became two as Airgead Sios crashed through the fence, miraculously staying on his feet, but losing all chance and badly interfering with

Macauley in the process. With only Morse Code to beat, the crowd began to roar The Miller home over the last, knowing that he had never been beaten up the hill – until now. The Miller had already given everything and it soon became obvious that the younger Morse Code was full of running and unlikely to relinquish his lead, even to the greatest of all chasers. Silence reigned as Morse Code passed the line two lengths clear of The Miller – a temporary silence, broken by muted applause for Morse Code, the party pooper that few, it seemed, could forgive. Instinctively, the crowd then began to cheer for the brave, yet vanquished, Miller, almost as if he had won. He had given his all but it simply wasn't enough against an opponent on top of his form.

It was the end of the road for The Miller, who would make only one more racecourse appearance, eleven months down the line at Newbury. This almost half-hearted attempt at a prep race for the 1939 Gold Cup led to a performance from a portly Miller that secured the decision to retire him. This prep race might have been a superfluous gesture but, given the unconventional nature of the owner, it probably wasn't a surprise to most observers.

Comparing the Gold Cup merits of The Miller and his predecessor Easter Hero, both equally dominant in their own era, is no easy task. Without wishing to diminish or dilute Easter Hero's tremendous achievements, there is no doubt that his consecutive 20-length wins were a slightly false reflection of his superiority over his peers. His main challengers made his task that much easier by exiting stage right at crucial times in both races, although it goes without saying that such was his brilliance that he could and would have pulled out much more if the need had arisen. The Miller never seemed to have that luxury afforded him, but his sheer consistency at the very highest level, especially at Cheltenham, tips the scales slightly in his favour. He kept coming back for more, year after year, at times on totally unsuitable ground. Briscoe could never dissuade D.P. from running any of her charges – not that he needed much encouragement to run his champion. It actually makes one wonder how many times The Miller ran, particularly during the Briscoe years, when it would have been more prudent for him to have stayed in Exning. Only Briscoe could have known the true answer to this, but such was his growing belief in his champion's ability that that question became irrelevant. One indisputable fact that sets The Miller apart, not just from Easter Hero but from every other horse that has ever attempted to repeat it, is that Gold Cup/Grand National double achieved in the same season. Only one horse has truly come within a whisker of repeating it – Garrison Savannah in 1991. His trainer, the recently-retired Jenny Pitman, would be the first to tell you how special he was and, considering the odds that were stacked heavily against him on account of all his physical problems, you cannot argue with her assessment. Yet the fact remains that where others have so far failed – including Easter Hero before him – Golden Miller succeeded.

MORSE CODE (1938)

b. or ch.g. 1929 (Pilot – Heliograph)
Owned and bred by Lt.-Col. D.C. Part, trained by I. Anthony and ridden by D.J. Morgan

✛ 1939 ✛

Morse Code to dot up? By George no!

With Golden Miller now in retirement at D.P.'s Elsenham Stud in Essex, the burden of expectation fell on Ivor Anthony to win consecutive Gold Cups with Morse Code. However, despite a significant increase in prize money to top the magical one thousand pounds mark for the first time, no opposition of any quality seemed to be coming through to challenge the current champion. In a very sub-standard year, there seemed to be absolutely no reason why the favourite shouldn't follow up with ease.

With only four opponents on the day, Morse Code's starting price of 4–7 utterly reflected his chance. However, as so often happens with expected formalities, the rout didn't happen, despite the paucity of runners. Gerry Wilson, by then six-times champion jockey, had the ride on Bel et Bon, the second favourite at 11–4, and the nine-year-old Brendan's Cottage was next in the betting at 8–1, the only other in the field deemed to have any chance at all. One of the outsiders, L'Estaque, was ridden by the useful amateur Mr Harry Llewellyn (later Sir Harry), better known for winning a showjumping gold medal riding Foxhunter at the Olympic Games at Helsinki in 1952.

Morse Code's preparation, in similar vein to last season, had been geared all season towards Cheltenham and the meticulous Anthony arranged a final racecourse workout at Kempton only a week before the big race. The race itself was run at a crawl, with nobody wishing to commit too early in the race. Alarmingly, even at this early stage of the race, Morse Code wasn't moving all that well. Travelling down the far side for the final time, Brendan's Cottage and Morse Code took over in the lead, but the writing was on the wall for supporters of the favourite as they turned for home. George Owen, the rider of Brendan's Cottage, was sitting motionless, unlike Danny Morgan, who was bustling up Morse Code to try and keep him in contention. It was all to no avail as Owen confidently swept past the beaten favourite over the last and pulled away up the hill to win by a comfortable three lengths.

Just what happened to Morse Code was a mystery. Connections could offer up no excuses. The going was admittedly heavy, but nothing that the reigning champion hadn't coped with in the past. For his part, Brendan's Cottage had proved himself to be a most versatile performer, having won on the flat as a two-year-old. Cottage, the bay's sire, would create history when another of his sons, Workman, went on to win the Grand National in the same year, a feat repeated nine years later with Cottage Rake and Sheila's Cottage. The winning trainer, George Beeby, had recently moved to Hamilton House, Compton, having trained since 1924 at Melton Mowbray. He became associated with Lord Bicester around this time, although he trained Brendan's Cottage for Mrs Arthur Smith-Bingham, the daughter of a keen American owner, Charles Garland. Owen became the first northern-based jockey to win a Gold Cup. After his riding career was over, he went on to train from a base at Malpas in Cheshire and will probably be best remembered for his ability to produce top-class jump jockeys, Dick Francis and Stan Mellor being just two of his pupils.

This turned out to be Brendan's Cottage's only appearance in the Gold Cup. He suffered a serious leg injury and died the following year.

BRENDAN'S COTTAGE (1939)

b.g. 1930 (Cottage – Brendan's Glory)
Owned by Mrs A. Smith-Bingham, trained by G. Beeby and ridden by G. Owen

✤ 1940 ✤

D.P.'s hackles are raised by an ugly Latin brute

Following the outbreak of war, a considerable number of owners declined to run their horses because they were of the opinion that horseracing was detrimental to the war effort. Not everybody saw it that way, including D.P. Her horses continued to dominate what racing there was and the 1940 National Hunt Meeting was no exception. Accused of being unpatriotic, she explained her obsession away by claiming that racing is essential for preserving the morale of the country.

It was generally felt that because of the boycott, the top races at the National Hunt Meeting would take less winning than usual. Due to the ploughing up of the National Hunt Chase course, the Gold Cup course was shortened by two furlongs and the start moved, with the horses starting with their backs to the second fence.

Not surprisingly, D.P. enjoyed her usual strong Cheltenham entry and on the opening day of the curtailed two-day meeting she took the Champion Hurdle with the Owen Anthony-trained Solford, who redeemed himself after falling when he looked set to win the previous year. Roman Hackle, her Gold Cup hope, had won the Broadway Novices Chase the previous year as a six-year-old and was well fancied to follow up the following day. There would be a new name on the Gold Cup roll-call, along with the likes of Airgead Sios, Rightun, the quaintly named five-year-old Hobgoblin, as well as the Grand National favourite, Professor II.

Roman Hackle, a giant, raw-boned bay, was in desperate need of a run, having had only one race prior to Cheltenham. Anthony's prayers were answered as snow fell on the eve of the Gold Cup, causing it to be postponed for six days. This gave him time to get a run into his stable star in a minor race at Windsor. He sluiced up, despite having to give a considerable amount of weight away. Others who tried the same trick were not so lucky. Airgead Sios broke down at Wolverhampton, only two days before the Gold Cup, while the winner of that race, Professor II, was sensibly taken out to ensure that he would be able to take his place at Aintree.

That talented Welshman, Evan Williams, was by this time back in favour with D.P. He rode Roman Hackle, the even-money favourite, with supreme confidence, riding a waiting race as, one by one, he picked off the fancied horses ahead of him. Hobgoblin had fallen quite early in the race and would never fulfil the early promise. Gerry Wilson failed once more on the well-fancied Bel et Bon and it was left to Fred Rimell, riding 20–1 outsider Black Hawk, to chase home Roman Hackle, albeit at a discreet distance of ten lengths. Roman Hackle was immediately dubbed a 'super champion' by one or two experienced racing scribes, though on this occasion they were wrong. Twelve months later, he was to dispel any hopes that he might become the next Golden Miller. Like Morse Code 12 months earlier, Roman Hackle would prove to be a major disappointment.

ROMAN HACKLE (1940)

b.g. 1933 (Yutoi – Waraya)
Owned by Hon. D. Paget, trained by O. Anthony and ridden by E. Williams

It shouldn't happen to a vet

As leading owner once more in 1940–41 by virtue of having five times as many runners as anybody else, Dorothy Paget's name had already appeared on more equine invoices than that of anyone else in the history of the sport – a veritable Maktoum of her time. It has been mooted that her total outlay on horses exceeded five million pounds – a mere bagatelle to the daughter of Lord Queenborough. Ironically, the Gold Cup hero of 1941 cost only forty guineas. He had presumably been bought cheaply by his owner, Mr Sherbrooke, not only because the market was in such a dire state but also because the owner just happened to be a practising veterinary surgeon and the horse had a breathing problem.

With the loss of good chasers such as Airgead Sios at the start of the year, many observers felt that the way had been left clear for D.P.'s Roman Hackle to follow up. However, he had been fairly unconvincing for most of the season, although he had managed to put himself back in the picture, winning a small race at Plumpton on the previous Saturday. Giving weight and a beating to Sable Marten, though, by no means proved that he was back to his best. But at least he had shown himself to be in good shape and was allowed to take his place in a field of ten.

Others believed to be in with a chance, according to the betting, were the nine-year-old Savon, Lord Stalbridge's Red Rower and the bargain buy, Poet Prince. Savon was a difficult horse to keep sound and the two Wroughton runners were both expected to put up a good show. Lord Stalbridge had leased his home-bred to Lady Phipps for the day with Danny Morgan in the saddle. Poet Prince, the more fancied of the Wroughton pair, was due to be ridden by his owner, the amateur rider and vet David Sherbrooke. However, riding plans had to be changed at the eleventh hour as the owner had injured himself in a fall only the day before. Young Roger Burford, second jockey at Wroughton, came in for the ride on the second favourite and grasped his chance with both hands.

In an uninspiring race, it seemed that his winning effort at Plumpton had taken more out of the favourite than even Owen Anthony had expected, the bay son of Yutoi struggling to keep tabs on the principals and finishing well in arrears. Poet Prince, well handled by his last-minute deputy, took over from his more illustrious stable-companion coming over the last and pulled away up the hill to finish three lengths clear of Savon, who pipped Red Rower for second place near the line.

Burford had gone one better than his father, himself a Wroughton man through and through who had finished second on The Turk II in the 1920 Grand National, beaten by the useful Troytown. Burford kept the ride on Poet Prince the following year, but made no impression against stiffer opposition. Poet Prince did manage to win a total of nine races, but never attained the same level of performance as for this Gold Cup win. In fact, he ran twice more at Cheltenham, culminating in his last appearance, as a thirteen-year-old, with Fulke Walwyn, finishing well beaten.

POET PRINCE (1941)

ch.g. 1932 (Milton – Welsh Princess)
Owned by Mr D. Sherbrooke, trained by I. Anthony and ridden by R. Burford

✠ 1942 ✠
'Côtes de Rhonehurst, m'lord'

Pendley Farm, Peter Harris's ultra-modern, open-all-hours concept, is about as far removed in terms of customer care as you get from your average yard of sixty years ago. Reg Hobbs, like most trainers of that time, believed Sundays and owners simply didn't mix. He once famously referred to the prospect of a visit from one of his principal owners, Lord Bicester, as follows: 'I'm not having that old bugger coming here on a Sunday – I won't see people on Sundays.'

In his early twenties Hobbs worked in the States for Ambrose-Clark, a wealthy American owner and grandson of the founder of Singer Manufacturing. He returned to England in 1922, specifically to look after Ambrose-Clark's hunters at Melton Mowbray, which he did until 1931 when he took out a trainer's licence at Lambourn, where he remained until the mid-1950s. Rhonehurst, Hobbs's base in the tiny hamlet of Upper Lambourn has been a racing stable for over a century and is currently occupied by Oliver Sherwood. It took Hobbs a short time to find his feet in his new venture, but by 1938 he had become a household name, winning the Grand National with the pony-sized entire Battleship, ridden by his 17-year-old son Bruce, the youngest rider ever to win the National. Battleship was owned by one of a number of Hobbs's wealthy American owners, Mrs Marion du Pont Scott, wife of the film star Randolph Scott. In fact, Battleship went on to win six races for Hobbs before returning to become champion sire back in the States. Hobbs had tasted success and, although he might not have enjoyed the attention that went with it, his talents were such that things weren't likely to change. He went on to become champion trainer for two consecutive seasons from 1940 to 1942.

Hobbs's championships came at a time when, because of the war and its obvious implications, there was a distinct lack of quality horses around, never mind opportunities for them (in England at least). This didn't stop Hobbs continuing to enjoy high-profile success, this time with Lord Sefton's French-bred Medoc II. Medoc II was an eight-year-old bay full brother to Roi d'Egypte, winner of the Cathcart at the 1942 Festival and sire of Leney Princess, who would produce numerous winning foals, the first being Fort Leney, the 1968 Gold Cup winner.

This 1942 Festival took place on consecutive Saturdays, 14 and 21 March, with most of the fancied challengers for the Gold Cup turning out for the Grand Annual on the first Saturday – effectively a dress rehearsal for the real thing. The Hobbs-trained Savon, runner-up to Poet Prince the previous year, fell and had to be destroyed. Lord Stalbridge's Red Rower took the Grand Annual comfortably from Medoc II and, not surprisingly, was installed as clear favourite for the Gold Cup itself.

The sparse crowd that turned out to brave the elements on the following

Saturday were treated to a very fast-run race that was full of incident. A blanket of thick fog engulfed Cleeve Hill and lingered on the racecourse itself, a fact that was not mentioned by radio commentator Raymond Glendenning to avoid giving weather information to 'the enemy'. From the start, Solarium, one of the outsiders, had disputed the lead most of the way and came to the last open ditch with Broken Promise, bracketed on 10–1 with former winner Roman Hackle, breathing down his neck. The leader toppled over and took the unlucky Jimmy Rank-owned Broken Promise, who was looking all over the winner, down with him. To cap it all, Red Rower managed to get entangled with both the stricken horses, just as it looked as though he had the race at his mercy. Meanwhile, Nicholson and Medoc II escaped the mêlée and found themselves in front, with Danny Morgan – having performed miracles to keep Red Rower upright – setting off again in vain pursuit of the new leader. But his efforts were to no avail. Medoc II, second favourite at 9–2, ran on strongly to claim victory for Hobbs, which gave him some compensation for the sad loss of Savon. Lord Bicester's Asterabad claimed third place, with Schubert, trained by Cliff Beechener, back in fourth.

Lord Sefton, a wealthy and distinguished figure, looking resplendent in the uniform of the Royal Horse Guards, was there to greet his winner, who meant so much to him – the winning prize money of a mere five hundred pounds certainly didn't! His family had owned Aintree racecourse and associated land for over eight hundred years. A former Lord Mayor of Liverpool and a lifelong supporter of national hunt racing, he had been elected to the National Hunt Committee in 1936. During the war years, he became the senior steward of the Jockey Club and owned horses on the flat, as well as breeding them. His best subsequent chaser was Irish Lizard, trained by Frenchie Nicholson himself who, incidentally, received a hundred pounds from Lord Sefton for his sterling efforts on Medoc II that foggy day. Nicholson's delight in victory was understandable following his near miss in 1938. It was fairly late in Frenchie Nicholson's career when he become probably the greatest ever mentor of apprentice jockeys, both on the flat and over jumps. The list of his pupils is endless and includes his own son, David, Michael Dickinson, Paul Cook, Walter Swinburn and Pat Eddery. Nicholson's classic remark, 'They came on bicycles and left in Rolls-Royces' accurately summed up the long-term effect on the lucky recipients of his expert tuition.

Lord Sefton and other wealthy owners would soon be forced to run the likes of Medoc II in Ireland following the news that national hunt racing in Britain would be grinding, at least temporarily, to a halt. On 10 September, 1942, this notice appeared in the *Racing Calendar*: 'The Stewards of the National Hunt Committee have received notification from His Majesty's Government that they are unable to sanction National Hunt Racing during the season 1942–3.' Few words, but far-reaching in their consequence.

It would be two years and more before the sport got back on its feet, to recommence at Cheltenham in January 1945.

MEDOC II (1942)

b.g. 1934 (Van – Menthe Poivre)
Owned by Lord Sefton, trained by R. Hobbs and ridden by H. Nicholson

✢ 1945 ✢

Equine *Dad's Army* won by Jonesy? Never

6 January 1945 – a red-letter day for national hunt racing in Britain when it resumed, appropriately, at Cheltenham. Two months later the Gold Cup would be part of just a one-day meeting. A record number of runners were cheered on by a massive crowd, keen to show their support of jump racing again.

So who was left? A mixture of old and even older faces! Red Rower, now an eleven-year-old, had proved his fitness by sluicing up at Windsor in February and was made favourite. He had a new jockey in Davy Jones, a natural lightweight from the flat who would be forced to carry no less than three stones of dead weight. Jones, taking over from the brilliant Danny Morgan, rode his first winner on the level in 1925 and eventually became very successful when he reverted back to flat racing after the war. He must have been a bit of a character, as he had developed a very odd habit. Hanging well back from the tapes at the off, he would suddenly wail like a banshee, thrusting his way through the waiting pack. I understand it was done not to announce the impending death of members of his family but as a clever way of clearing a path for himself among his fellow jockeys as their horses panicked! I don't suppose Jones would have got away with this trick for long, even 50 years ago, but it was still wartime and men did strange things. He went on to ride extensively abroad, booting home his last winner in Kenya at the age of sixty-five, and was still schooling at his home near Cheltenham in his eighties!

Everything about Red Rower had Stalbridge stamped on it: he had bred him, was officially training him and had him back running in his own colours. He may not have been a great horse, but Red Rower was certainly good enough to cope with this field, which resembled, like any number of races around this time, an equine *Dad's Army*.

Sixteen starters lined up on a glorious day with perfect going. Trainer-ridden Schubert made the running from Paladin, a horse that had looked very promising three years ago but that had been unlucky with injuries. Red Rower's jumping was sketchy, but he was still well in contention just behind the leaders with three to go. Old Poet Prince, now with Fulke Walwyn, was running a blinder and looked the likely winner approaching the second last, until problems with his wind got the better of him and he went out like a candle. Schubert and Paladin were neck and neck coming down to the last and their connections must have thought they had the race to themselves. However, Jones knew better and jumping upsides at the last left them for dead up the hill to score by three lengths.

If Lord Sefton's prize money for Medoc II's victory back in 1942 was bad, then the £340 that Red Rower earned the good Lord for his efforts here was almost derisory. But at least there was racing at Cheltenham when the rich cousin, the

Grand National, was still out of commission. It must be said, though, that for Lord Stalbridge and his peers the winter game wasn't about money. It was all about taking on a challenge. The sporting landed gentry of the time enjoyed the prestige that went along with winning a Gold Cup.

With the wartime Gold Cup years coming to a close, it was time to look ahead to the beginning of a new era. It was time for the Irish bid to become rocket-powered, with a twin-turbo assault for glory by two masters of their craft, who, over the next twenty years, would amass a staggering nine Cheltenham Gold Cups between them! Exciting times certainly lay ahead and they began with something a little out of the ordinary – an Irish Prince, a Prince Regent.

RED ROWER (1945)

b.g. 1934 (Rameses II – Red Maru)
Owned by Lord Stalbridge, trained by the owner and ridden by D.J. Jones

✛ 1946 ✛
A princely exodus

Prince Regent's fame effectively began the mass exodus from the Emerald Isle to Cheltenham that we now take very much for granted each March. While postwar rationing continued in England through to 1950, and the likes of Tom Dreaper and Vincent O'Brien were concentrating on getting their powerful strings of horses over to compete, the invading army of punters brought over their own strings – of sausages! Always inventive, they brought along many other epicurean delights that would make up a full English breakfast and which could be used as virtual currency. This ingenuity supplemented their Festival pots and made a welcome change from Spam for the locals.

Thomas William Dreaper, born in 1898, was the most successful trainer in Gold Cup history. He trained horses from his farm at Greenogue, Killsallaghan, for more than 40 years, until finally handing over the reins to his son Tom in 1971. The unassuming Dreaper never had any great ambition to train a large string of horses, regarding himself first and foremost as a cattle and sheep farmer. Consequently, he trained no more than around 35 horses at his peak, which he felt was an ideal number. He had been a useful amateur jockey and partnered Prince Regent to his first win in 1940. His involvement with Jimmy Rank's Prince Regent came purely by chance after Bobby Power, who was to have broken the horse in, was killed in a road accident. To compound this, Gwyn Evans, who was due to train him at the owner's Druids Lodge in England, also died in tragic circumstances. The horse returned to Dreaper, who had broken him in, and the link-up between man and beast proved to be an irresistible one. Rank invited Dreaper to go over to England as his private trainer, but the offer was politely declined. Dreaper was a County Meath man through and through and that was where he wanted to stay. Rank solved the problem in an instant. 'Alright then, I will have my horses in Meath.'

James Voase Rank was the son of a prominent flour miller from Hull and elder brother of the film magnate J. Arthur Rank. He first became associated with the turf in 1920, but it was some ten years later that he really expanded his racing interests. Jimmy Rank, like Tom Dreaper, didn't want much out of life, but demanded from his trainers the very best for his horses and spent vast sums of money trying to achieve his sporting ambitions. We have already touched on the misfortune of Broken Promise, his Gold Cup runner in 1942. Rank had been dissuaded by a friend from buying Reynoldstown, dual winner of the Grand National in 1935 and 1936, on account of the horse being black! Early Mist did win the 1953 Grand National, though sadly not in Rank's famous quartered colours. Rank died in 1952 and at his dispersal sale Early Mist was bought by 'Mincemeat Joe' Griffin, who enjoyed brief notoriety as a lucky owner with

Vincent O'Brien before his business empire suddenly collapsed. Rank also owned Southern Hero, who had won three Scottish Nationals but who wasn't really good enough to make an impact at Cheltenham, running in three Gold Cups without ever troubling the judge.

It was to be another famous son of My Prince who changed Rank's luck. Purchased as a yearling at Goff's Sales, Prince Regent was subsequently resold as a two-year-old to Jimmy Rank through Harry Bonner, who was buying horses for him at the time. Prince Regent started his career running in three bumpers in 1940, winning on his third outing at Naas when he was ridden to victory by none other than Dreaper himself. Two years later, having blossomed into a clearly striking individual, he began to show the sort of promise over fences that had been expected of him. His initial tasks were to give lumps of weight away to inferior horses, but he did the job with the minimum of fuss. Four races went his way that year, including the Irish Grand National, carrying the welter burden of twelve stone seven pounds. The following year, he ran up against considerably more experienced types such as Medoc II, transferred over from a barren England to continue his chasing career, which never really got off the ground in Ireland. Prince Regent won the 1942 Irish Grand National, giving nearly a stone to Dorothy Paget's Golden Jack, then finished runner-up in the race twice, again giving up to three stone in weight away.

He had been ridden to victory at Fairyhouse by former showjumper Timmy Hyde, who rode the great horse twenty-eight times consecutively in five seasons, having been given his chance as a late replacement in November 1942 for the injured Jimmy Brogan. The partnership clicked on no less than 12 occasions, winning the Irish Grand National in 1942, a race that Hyde had won in 1938 on Clare County. Hyde was persuaded by Irish trainer J. Ruttle to turn professional. Ruttle knew that only Hyde was right for Workman. How right he was, with the partnership winning the 1939 Grand National in fine style.

Hyde was paralysed in a fall in 1951 and spent the rest of his life in a wheelchair. He trained a few horses at his home in Cashel, County Tipperary, assisted by his son Tim, himself a useful rider and now a world-famous bloodstock agent.

Prince Regent was forced to miss the 1945 Gold Cup due to a warble just behind his withers, which meant that putting a saddle on him was totally out of the question. In November, after nine months off the track, Prince Regent met Roman Hackle at Leopardstown and failed by only a head to give three stone to the old 1940 Gold Cup hero. It is no wonder that Prince Regent was held in such high esteem by his trainer and public alike. He had faced the cream of Irish talent throughout the war years and won 12 races. Now it was time to try and emulate Golden Miller's famous race double.

An intrigued crowd, for so long starved of racing, packed the stands to see the new Irish folk hero at the Bradford Chase at Wetherby (one of the first courses to resume after the war), his first port of call in England. All the pre-race hype was justified: he looked magnificent and won the race at odds of 1–10, hard-held by a cheeky half-length. His next sojourn would be more important – a March date with destiny in the shadow of Cleeve Hill. Only five acceptors took on the brilliant seventeen hands bay in front of a record thirty-five thousand crowd. Poor Flame, trained by Tom Rimell, and Lord Stalbridge's Red April were fully expected to present the Irish champion with his biggest test, although the former was little more than a unpredictable novice, despite winning all his races to date that season. Red April had been third in the Champion Hurdle last season and although a half-brother to Red Rower, he was never as good.

The other three runners were the extremely average French raider Jalgreya, the totally unfancied African Collection, and a fruitcake of a horse called Elsich, the complete outsider at 200–1 ridden by ex-squaddie Bill Balfe from Swindon. If they continued to issue medals for bravery after the war, Balfe would have been at the front of the queue. Needs must and, in late 1945, the bombardier, awaiting demobilisation, hitched a lift to Cheltenham from Larkhill Barracks in the hope of a spare ride. Balfe recalled: 'A staff car driven by a full-blown Colonel picked me up and dropped me right by the old weigh room where I met a trainer, Charlie Kelly. He told me that he had a spare for me – he didn't want his son Glen to get hurt! Naturally I grabbed at the chance, not knowing it had run the previous day and his jockey had jumped off between the second and third fences. I actually got him round for the first time in his life and the owner threw his hat in the air saying, "From now on he is your ride – if you can qualify him for the National, you can ride him in the Gold Cup as well."'

For his pains, Balfe, who had had only two rides the season before, got to know Elsich quite well over the next few months. Balfe explained, 'You can imagine how I felt, a down and out squaddie coming to the end of my war service, having been a volunteer coming from southern Ireland. Elsich was a huge brute, with no brakes at all once he got out of first gear. His former life was pulling holiday caravans on the Cumbrian Fells, but at the races he fell so often that he got used to it and used to stand grazing beside me. I got back on him twice one day at Cheltenham and three times another day to secure place money. Anyway, it was better than walking back from the top of the hill. I thought I'd get a lift and jump a few more fences.' He added, 'One day, he took such a heavy fall that he stopped breathing and they signalled for the vet and knackerman. So I took the saddle and bridle off, as I had to ride in the last. No sooner had I got the tack off, then up he gets and sets off like a scalded cat for Cleeve Hill.'

A sea of faces crowded around the parade ring to see the object of their desire. Prince Regent stood head and shoulders above the others in looks, as he did above just about every other horse in training. Starting a warm favourite at 4–7, Prince Regent, with regular pilot Timmy Hyde sitting quietly and biding his time, kept a discreet distance in arrears of the old rogue Elsich. Elsich had the distinction of leading Prince Regent briefly on the first circuit but, from then on, it was the usual day at the office for Elsich and he and Balfe went their separate ways. With the troublesome Elsich out of the way, Prince Regent proceeded to dictate the pattern of the race and coming to the second last had only Poor Flame to worry about. The race was on in earnest. Fred Rimell saw a stride and went for a big jump, but Poor Flame made another of his habitual errors and lost any slim chance they might have had of causing an upset. Prince Regent sauntered home as he liked, Hyde easing down to win by five lengths, which in truth could have been twenty-five, with Red April trailing in a respectable third, a further four lengths in arrears. But Hyde pulled no punches as he came back to meet Dreaper in the winners' enclosure. He declared, 'It took me a minute or two to beat that fellow today.'

The writing was on the wall. The Prince, like Easter Hero before him, had been to the well once too often and his best days were well and truly behind him. This was to be his only Gold Cup appearance as next season Rank attempted his Grand

National ambition again, bypassing the Blue Riband. But the Cheltenham faithful would see him again. He returned over two years later, just short of his fourteenth birthday, to maintain his unbeaten Cheltenham record in the Bibury Chase on his penultimate start. Snaffles, the sporting artist, once described Prince Regent as 'the ultimate horse' but, after the Grand National, the dream was over. There was no doubt in the minds of those close to him that he had left his best days behind during those war years. In spite of some fanatical support from the huge crowd who made sure he jumped off leading the market in the National, the welter burden of twelve stone five pounds proved to be beyond him. All Prince Regent could manage was third, having had every chance at the last.

The Prince returned to Liverpool once more, to contest the following year's Grand National, carrying even more weight. The battle-worn warrior again started a warm favourite, but the prevailing heavy ground, coupled with further over-burdening of excessive weight, meant that the Grand National was never going to suit him. Even Easter Hero in his prime hadn't been able to overcome the severity of the handicap at Liverpool in 1929. Perhaps Prince Regent's defeat was the beginning of the end for the Grand National as a 'prestige' event. Many leading figures in horse-racing today, such as David Johnson (Martin Pipe's principal owner) still regard the race as a total lottery. Would they still be prepared to risk their best horses if the prize money on offer was reduced drastically? Probably not, even allowing for the diluted nature of the present day Aintree fences. Still, stricter conditions of entry in the past few years have at least ensured a better class of animal competing in the Grand National.

People might consider Rank to have been a little optimistic or even a tad greedy when he vowed to win the Derby, Grand National and the Waterloo Cup. But that would be unfair to the memory of the man, who happily ploughed money, Kerry Packer-style, into his particular sporting quest. Completely taken with the sport, he would have been delighted to have won any of the above, though his numerous attempts on goal, more often than not, hit the corner flag. Fortunately, Rank's vow didn't include the Cheltenham Gold Cup, which brings to mind the late Tim Forster's truism: 'If you don't expect anything from your horses, then you'll never be disappointed.'

Prince Regent, if judged purely on his Gold Cup victory, was nothing out of the ordinary and certainly the horses he outclassed in the race were unexceptional. But his wartime record, taking into account the temporarily high level of Irish form – which for once included all the top performers which would normally have been sold to cross the Irish Sea – was quite exceptional. In the 1948–49 season, he was transferred to Rank's Druids Lodge establishment with a view to competing in more condition races – a sensible move in the twilight of his long career. Another veteran, the jockey Jack Moloney, who had ridden Easter Hero some twenty years back in the Grand National, teamed up with Prince Regent for his final few races in England before Prince Regent was retired following a fall at Lingfield in a race won by Coloured Schoolboy, who featured prominently in the next three Gold Cups. Winning 21 races from a total of 49 in 10 consecutive seasons, Prince Regent was the first of Tom Dreaper's many equine heroes, though his solitary notch on the Gold Cup pole will never truly reflect the high regard in which he was universally held. He should have, would have, won a fistful of Gold Cups if only he had been able to compete at Cheltenham in his prime.

Dreaper would have to wait some considerable time for his next Gold Cup winner, but it would be worth the wait.

PRINCE REGENT (1946)

b.g. 1935 (My Prince – Nemaea)
Owned by Mr J.V. Rank, trained by T.W. Dreaper and ridden by T. Hyde

✠ 1947 ✠

Ma Cherie, entirely yours Fortina.
For Britain read Siberia

One of the worst winters on record caused the decimation of the national hunt programme. The arctic conditions meant no National Hunt Meeting in March, but fortunately the most prestigious races were added to the April spring meeting, tacked on the end as an additional day. Rather ironically, Prestbury Park was bathed in glorious sunshine for the rescheduled Gold Cup day as the 12 runners moved to post. There were several newcomers in the line-up, with a few unknown quantities among them. Only Elsich dared to show his face again after the Prince Regent mauling 12 months ago. Two French-bred horses, Fabiano and a strong, good-looking chestnut entire called Fortina, were particularly interesting, both supported in an open betting contest. The well-supported favourite was Happy Home, the D.P. representative ridden by crack Irish professional Dan Moore, who would in later years carve his own niche in Gold Cup history as a trainer. Others to consider included the useful Coloured Schoolboy, and Prince Blackthorn, owned by Lord Bicester. Fortina, only a six-year-old, had been given only one outing in England prior to this race but had already clocked up four chases in his native France. He had won the Lancashire Chase impressively for his new owner, Lord Grimthorpe.

The Gold Cup race itself was pretty uninspiring. Chaka led Fortina throughout the first circuit, well ahead of the rest of the chasing pack. As they raced down the hill for the final time, Chaka weakened rapidly out of contention, leaving Fortina to take up the running. At this point it ceased to be a contest as such and Fortina, who had been travelling well for his amateur rider, Richard Black, accelerated clear of Happy Home, who never gave her illustrious owner any realistic hope of winning at any stage of the race. Prince Blackthorn, ridden by Bob Turnell, finished a further six lengths back in third. Fred Rimell, four-times champion jockey, suffered a terrible fall from Coloured Schoolboy, breaking his neck and thereby ending his riding career.

The winner, trained by Wiltshire-based Hector Christie, was to disappear from the English racing scene almost as quickly as he joined it. Being an entire and a fine physical specimen, he was soon dispatched to the Grange Stud in Fermoy, County Cork, where he replaced that remarkable stallion Cottage. Fortina went on to make a considerable name for himself as a prolific national hunt sire, responsible for two future Gold Cup winners and a plethora of top-class chasers.

This certainly was not, by any stretch of the imagination, a vintage Gold Cup. It was always going to be tough to fill the shoes of the celebrated Prince Regent. On a positive note, three of the jockeys riding in this race, Bob Turnell, Dan

Moore and Fred Rimell, would, in future years, all enjoy Gold Cup success as winning trainers.

FORTINA (1947)

ch.h. 1941 (Formor – Bertina)
Owned by Lord Grimthorpe, trained by H. Christie and ridden by R. Black

✢ 1948 ✢

Begod, 'tis Vincent O'Brien . . . and Cottage Rake!

Most trainers would tell you that to succeed in this fickle sport you need, first and foremost, a sound financial base from which to work. Then you need a good horse to put you on the map. Then understanding owners willing to pay their bills, preferably on time, and, of course, a slice of good fortune! Vincent O'Brien would be the first to admit that when he first started out on the road that led eventually to Ballydoyle and all that, he had no financial base to work from, no horses to speak of and no owners. However, necessity being the mother of invention, the young, cash-strapped O'Brien used his special brand of flair and ingenuity to create a multi-million-pound racing empire that raged like a bull for two score years and more until the Maestro, as O'Brien became known, decided he would retire graciously and give someone else a chance to have a bite of the cherry.

It didn't take that someone long to burst on to the scene. Like the Maestro before him, he seems similarly gifted and keen to break new ground in his quest for perfection. Whether Aidan O'Brien (no relation) will ever aspire to the dizzy heights of the maestro remains to be seen, but, incredibly for one so young, he's done better than most already. Michael Dickinson is another genius who springs to mind, but then he had a little help. The Yorkshire trainer who rewrote the Gold Cup record books has always acknowledged the help given to him by Vincent O'Brien when he spent precious weeks at Ballydoyle, probably getting writer's cramp from making copious notes of everything he observed while he was there. He learnt so much, watching and recording Ballydoyle life. Now recognised as a ground-breaker in America, Dickinson has completed a wonderful circle, even teaching a certain Mr Pipe a thing or two about training horses and improving facilities.

O'Brien grew up in Churchtown, Cork. His father, Dan, was a farmer who kept some point-to-pointers that young O'Brien would look after. His father died in 1943, and the farm reverted to family from a former marriage. O'Brien persuaded his half-brother, with no interest in horses, to rent him a yard and gallops. A friend put him in touch with the wool merchant Frank Vickerman, who agreed to have a horse with him. First owner secured! Vickerman had a long-range double, at huge odds, on two of O'Brien's horses for the Irish double, allowing the trainer part of the double for a massive return if both were to win. One won outright and the other dead-heated. Hey presto! Sound financial base.

O'Brien met the breeder of future speed machine Cottage Rake, Dr 'Otto' Vaughan, from Mallow, who was keen to sell him. Unable to sell him, however, he put him in training with Vincent. A few race wins later, Cottage Rake was finally sold, but the vet 'spun' him on account of supposed wind problems. O'Brien knew better, and persuaded Vickerman to part with £3,500 to buy the horse. A second vet 'spun' the horse and Vickerman changed his mind, but part-payment for horse had already been cashed by the breeder. The deal went through – O'Brien's slice of good fortune. A flagship horse and paying owner. It was early days, but the first Roman brick was in position and team O'Brien had begun.

Aubrey 'The Brab' Brabazon rode the seven-year-old Cottage Rake in his first chase at Leopardstown on Boxing Day 1946. They won by 20 lengths and would prove to be an irresistible combination, especially at Cheltenham. 'The Brab' rode two Irish classic winners, the 1948 Oaks on Masaka and the 1950 Two Thousand Guineas on Mighty Ocean, while The Rake won four races on the flat, including the 1947 Irish Cesarewitch. The Rake was appropriately named, a light-framed individual with bags of speed. The Rake was campaigned prior to the 1948 Gold Cup exclusively in Ireland and had been winning his chases impressively, that is until his final prep race at Leopardstown in February, where he fell. This blip on the record probably caused him to go off at longer odds in the Gold Cup than he should have, although he certainly didn't go unbacked by the stable at the 10–1 on offer.

The favourite on this crisp and bright Gold Cup day was Cool Customer owned by Major 'Cuddy' Stirling Stuart, the first person to try and buy Cottage Rake before he was 'spun' by the vets. Unfortunately, the Major barely had time to see his famous scarlet colours through his binoculars before Cool Customer fell at the first! At the third last, only two, Cottage Rake and Happy Home, last year's runner-up, looked to have a chance of winning and on the turn run for home the two principals were going head-to-head, neither prepared to give an inch. A titanic finish, reminiscent of the Golden Miller/Thomond II epic some years earlier, looked on the cards and the crowd weren't going to be disappointed. Martin Molony knew he had to use his charge's superior jumping to try and steal a march on the speedy Irish challenger. Gathering Cool Customer up on the inside rail for one final effort, he pinged the last in tremendous style and drove him out for all his worth up the hill. Brabazon, who had ridden a waiting race on Cottage Rake to ensure his jumping held together, met the last adequately and, landing a couple of lengths down, asked Cottage Rake to quicken up. The response wasn't instant but, as they met the rising ground, the picture began to change dramatically as Cottage Rake, now in full flight, shot past Happy Home in a matter of strides with a memorable burst of speed. The winning margin was a length and a half at the line, with the rest of the field well in arrears, Coloured Schoolboy running on to take third place.

O'Brien had signalled his arrival in no uncertain terms and it had been a race for the vast crowd to savour. Nobody could quite believe what they had just seen. O'Brien himself had been down at the final fence and didn't know that Cottage Rake's late surge had prevailed. The first confirmation he had of his great win was when the cheers went up as he entered the unsaddling enclosure. The Rake returned to Ireland to contest the Irish Grand National, with a colossal twelve stone seven pounds on his back. He finished a valiant second to the useful Hamstar. His main aim for next season would be the Gold Cup, which, fortunately for O'Brien, was postponed for a month due to frozen ground.

COTTAGE RAKE (1948)

b. or br.g. 1939 (Cottage – Hartingo)
Owned by Mr F.L. Vickerman, trained by M.V. O'Brien and ridden by A. Brabazon

✛ 1949 ✛

He's a cool customer, that Brabazon!

'The Rake' and 'The Brab' gave their growing band of supporters in England another day to remember at the 1948 King George VI Chase. The Rake's ability to use his superior cruising speed around Kempton's flatter gradients was a significant factor and he positively laughed at his rivals, which included Happy Home, who was beginning to look a shadow of his former self.

By the time The Rake returned to Cheltenham, now fully fit, after having been held up by a cold and a dirty nose, O'Brien and The Brab were looking for a Champion Hurdle/Gold Cup double. Only three of the beaten horses from last year's race were prepared to take on The Rake again, with only a disappointing six runners going to post. Gold Cup newcomer Finnure, the epitome of a typically handsome Lord Bicester chaser, and last season's disappointment Cool Customer were expected to give the odds-on favourite most opposition. In a race that panned out in similar fashion to his first Gold Cup win, The Rake had only the pride of Yorkshire, Cool Customer, to beat as they headed for home. Upsides Cool Customer at the second last, The Rake was out-jumped and an upset looked very much on the cards, as Cool Customer showed no sign of stopping. Over the last, the champion was still a length or so behind and as the two brave horses settled down to fight it out up the hill and, once more, the response from The Rake to The Brab's urgings wasn't immediate. The Brab used all his experience to coax a final burst of speed and they edged into the lead with a hundred yards to go. The Irish contingent roared as The Rake passed the line two lengths to the good. It was a performance that encapsulated the horse's great courage and breathtaking speed, which his rider used to perfection to gain unlikely victories from the jaws of defeat.

What next for the dual champion? Surprisingly, defeat in the King George. Finnure, although not in the same parish at Cheltenham, had improved steadily through the season and a pull of eleven pounds was enough to see Lord Bicester's gelding win by three-quarters of a length. The slow pace of the race and the heavier ground were given by The Brab as reasons for the odds-on favourite's defeat. Nobody could argue with the logic, but the turnaround in form was enough to make Finnure's connections believe that they had a serious contender for the champion's crown come March. O'Brien knew otherwise.

COTTAGE RAKE (1949)

b. or br.g. 1939 (Cottage – Hartingo)
Owned by Mr F.L. Vickerman, trained by M.V. O'Brien and ridden by A. Brabazon

68

✠ 1950 ✠

Caught in Molony's flytrap? Not likely!

Although the last two Gold Cups had effectively turned out to be two-horse wars, albeit exciting ones, there was no way to predict this before these races. This year was very different. Cool Customer was sidelined with a leg injury and so this was effectively a two-horse race from the outset – barring accidents. The few connections brave enough to take on the big two with their third-raters would have had a struggle on their hands to have beaten even old Elsich. The race would undoubtedly be a tactical affair and Martin Molony, Lord Bicester's jockey, must have been confident that he held the whip hand. After all, he could dictate the pace of the race, putting the champion at a disadvantage once more. It had worked at Kempton, why not here? The O'Brien camp were looking for their second consecutive Champion Hurdle/Gold Cup double as The Brab, on board Hatton's Grace again, had already won the hurdling crown for the second year running. It was a close call in the market on the off, but The Rake went off as marginal favourite.

As expected, the race was run at a crawl – possibly even slower than The Brab could have expected. Forced to take up the running going down the far side of the course for the final time, The Brab suddenly upped the tempo, giving The Rake a crack down the shoulder for good measure. The champion strode into a six-length lead, catching Molony unawares. The race was effectively over at that point and the result never in doubt, as Finnure struggled to close the gap. In fact, the gap grew and what had been billed as the toughest Gold Cup challenge so far turned out to be the easiest of his three wins; The Brab had made sure of that.

A serious leg injury sustained at home later in the year meant that The Rake would miss the following Gold Cup. Not surprisingly, considering his age, he lost that vital edge in speed over his rivals and was never raced at the highest level again. Their exploits had already been immortalised in this Irish verse:

> Aubrey's up, the money's down,
> The frightened bookies quake,
> Come on, my lads, and give a cheer,
> Begod, 'tis Cottage Rake.

But just how good was Cottage Rake? Opinion differs. O'Brien has always maintained that The Rake would have been a match for any Gold Cup winner, declaring, 'If any Gold Cup winner could have beaten him, it would only have been by the smallest of margins.' Martin Molony summed up his feelings about Cottage Rake when we spoke in Dublin last year. 'Great horses are able to carry weight, good ones can't. Cottage Rake, although he won three Gold Cups, was never able to give weight away like Arkle or Prince Regent could.' Molony is well qualified to make an accurate assessment of Cottage Rake's ability, having been in the frame for all of the three Gold Cups that Cottage Rake contested – and won. He and Vincent O'Brien have been firm friends since they were children; I'm sure they would both have a chuckle over their difference of opinion!

Cottage Rake made his last racecourse appearance in December 1953 at Wolverhampton, with Dick Francis in the saddle, having been transferred to England during the spring to see out his racing days with Gerald Balding, father of current trainers Toby and Ian. Cottage Rake's three successive Gold Cup wins were the springboard for an incredible sequence of continued success for O'Brien, which included further Gold Cup glory. His haul of eight festival winners in 1958 is a record that will surely stand for ever. Within a year, he effectively switched codes, continuing the sort of results that really did have those bookie chappies quaking in their boots.

COTTAGE RAKE (1950)

b. or br.g. 1939 (Cottage – Hartingo)
Owned by Mr F.L. Vickerman, trained by M.V. O'Brien and ridden by A. Brabazon

✤ 1951 ✤

Molony magic

Following another wet winter, which extended through to the spring, yet again a national hunt meeting was badly affected. The programme for the first day was just about completed, in appalling conditions, before the stewards took the inevitable decision to abandon the rest of the meeting. But the thousands who had braved the incessant rain to witness Hatton's Grace and National Spirit, both pitching for a record third win in the Champion Hurdle, were not to be disappointed. Tim Molony drove the eleven-year-old Hatton's Grace, trained by Vincent O'Brien, to win a third consecutive championship.

The impact of postponing the Gold Cup until late April had a devastating effect on both the quality and quantity of the eventual field, which was reduced to a mere six. The most significant absentee was the expected favourite, the classy six-year-old chestnut Arctic Gold, owned by the American Jock Whitney. Arctic Gold, who headed the market for the Grand National, was just one of numerous fallers in the early part of the Aintree race, which was dubbed by the press of the day as 'The Grand Crashional' or the 'ninepins National'. Only three horses completed the course, from a starting line-up of no fewer than thirty-six. Fully expected to be the natural successor for Cottage Rake's vacant throne, Arctic Gold must have been a bitter disappointment to his wealthy owner. Indeed, he never did face the Gold Cup starter at Cheltenham.

Of those who stood their ground come April, the Cheltenham specialist Silver Fame, trained by George Beeby, stood head and shoulders above the others, at least on all known form. He was duly installed as 6–4 favourite on the day, though he was not to have things all his own way: the Cheltenham faithful would be treated to one of the most exciting finishes since Golden Miller's epic duel with Thomond II in 1933. Although he was now a twelve-year-old, Silver Fame certainly hadn't lost any of his speed, despite campaigning regularly for nine seasons, winning more than half of his forty-eight races including, significantly, eight times around Cheltenham. He was a real 'park' jumper, standing well back from his fences and just skimming the top. His owner, Lord Bicester, was blessed with two other top-class chasers around that time, namely Finnure, last season's Gold Cup second, and Roimond, runner-up to Russian Hero in the 1949 Grand National. It was only fitting that such a grand supporter of national hunt racing was finally rewarded with a top prize.

Other Gold Cup challengers included the Aintree specialist Freebooter, a fine stamp of a chaser who had been at his most impressive winning last season's Grand National by 15 lengths. However, in total contrast, his record at Cheltenham was truly abysmal, never having won a race there, despite having numerous opportunities to do so. A well-backed second favourite at 3–1, Lockerbie was no mean performer either and had narrowly beaten Silver Fame at Manchester in March, though on revised terms of nearly a stone and on Silver Fame's favourite course he realistically had little chance of maintaining his superiority. Speaking about the horse many years later, his trainer, Capt. Neville Crump, felt that his charge was probably over the top for the season by the time the race was run and hadn't been able to do himself justice. The royal runner Manicou had surpassed himself when winning the 1950 King George VI as a five-year-old in the hands of Bryan Marshall, beating none other than Silver Fame in receipt of only eight pounds. But his form was beginning to tail off this season and he had been well beaten in a moderate race at Lingfield only days before the meeting. The Queen (then Princess Elizabeth) and her mother were present to see their horse perform, but it was unlikely that Manicou's downturn in form was about to change here.

On a glorious day, so very different from a month earlier, the six runners jumped off with Lockerbie taking up the early running and the Horris-trained Greenogue, the complete outsider of the sextet, breathing down his neck. The latter took up the running after almost a circuit and Manicou was the first to cry enough, after making a desperate blunder on the far side. An entire, Manicou trailed in a well-beaten last and would never manage to recapture anything like 'classic' form again (after three more seasons of recurring unsoundness he was retired to stud in Sussex). Freebooter was the next to find the increasing pace too hot to handle, as Lockerbie regained the lead and piled on the pressure. His supporters must have had high hopes of a first northern victory in the race, but Martin Molony and Glen Kelly knew otherwise. Asking their mounts for maximum effort at the last, which they jumped in unison, they began to forge clear on either side of Lockerbie and steeled themselves for a battle royal up the hill to the line. It was nip and tuck throughout the final climb, but yards before the winning-post, Silver Fame, with Molony using every ounce of his seemingly-limitless strength, began to edge ahead in the dying strides, to lift the Cup for his proud owner. The gallant J.V. Rank-owned Greenogue had been beaten by the official margin of a short head – a decision that was to be disputed for many years after. However, the judge's decision was final and Silver Fame became the first twelve-year-old to win the Blue Riband and duly completed the second leg of an historic Champion Hurdle/Gold Cup double for the Molony brothers, in course record time.

Molony, speaking at the Dublin Gold Cup celebrations in 1998, had no doubts which chaser had a special place in his heart. He confirmed, 'Without a shadow of doubt, Silver Fame was the greatest I ever rode. It was quite an achievement by the horse, when you consider he was twelve years old when he won his Gold Cup. He was at his best around Cheltenham, winning nine races there throughout his long career.' Martin Molony was elegant and fearless in the saddle and, but for two factors, would have appeared more than once in the roll-call of Gold Cup-winning jockeys. First, he had the misfortune to come up against Aubrey Brabazon and the brilliant Cottage Rake, three times trailing in their wake in successive Gold Cups between 1948 and 1950. Second, unlike his brother Tim, he steadfastly refused to leave Ireland and link up with a powerful English stable on a permanent basis. A natural lightweight and an extremely versatile rider, Molony rode extensively on the flat, winning all the Irish Classics, before going on to finish third in the 1951 Epsom Derby. As fate would have it, the young Molony would never have another opportunity to add to his Gold Cup tally. Only a matter of months later, he suffered a life-threatening fall while riding at Thurles, which put an immediate end to his riding career. His late brother Tim, champion jockey here for five consecutive seasons from 1948 to 1952, once said of his brother, 'Martin had velvet hands. Horses always galloped and jumped well for him. He had wonderful patience, was a superb judge of pace and his sense of balance was always perfect – he was the greatest of them all.' A fitting tribute from an equally brilliant horseman.

SILVER FAME (1951)

ch.g. 1939 (Werwolf – Silver Fairy)
Owned by Lord Bicester, trained by G. Beeby and ridden by M. Molony

✣ 1952 ✣

D.P. in seventh heaven

With Silver Fame now beginning to show the effects of having fought one battle too many, there was much speculation concerning which of the younger generation of chasers would succeed to his chasing crown. One horse whose performances had earned rave reviews was Mont Tremblant, Dorothy Paget's impressive young novice. As a four-year-old, the chestnut son of Gris Perle had already won on the flat and over hurdles in his native France. It didn't take long before he and his year-younger half-brother, the massive Lanveoc Poulmic, came to the attention of D.P.'s network of agents and duly found themselves under the expert wing of Fulke Walwyn, one of the greats of national hunt racing.

During his early career in the saddle, Walwyn had been three-times champion amateur and turned professional shortly after winning the 1936 Grand National on Reynoldstown. 1936 proved to be quite some year for Walwyn, as he was then asked to team up with none other than Golden Miller. Walwyn certainly knew how to ride Aintree, finishing a highly creditable second on The Miller in the two-and-a-half-mile Becher Chase at Liverpool – some achievement considering The Miller's growing aversion to the place. However, an injury that season put paid to any chance of keeping the ride on Golden Miller and indeed worse was to follow. A serious fall at Ludlow left Walwyn with a fractured skull and unconscious for a month. He recovered, but his riding days were over. Setting up as a trainer at Delamere, Lambourn, he managed a number of early successes before war broke out. Inevitably, Walwyn's efforts to rejoin the Army were brushed aside on medical grounds. Having bought Saxon House stables in 1944, Walwyn secured his first trainers' championship in the very next season and, with the added bonus of six horses sent to him by Dorothy Paget, a second trainers' title was duly achieved. His biggest training feat had been winning the 1947 King George with Rowland Boy and with the sort of ammunition that D.P. could provide, Walwyn began an onslaught on the major prizes that Vincent O'Brien would have been proud of.

Mont Tremblant had graduated seamlessly from novice to handicap company and had given weight and a beating to a useful bunch of handicappers at Kempton in February. In contrast, both the established star Silver Fame and the disappointing Arctic Gold had done nothing to enhance their credentials for the forthcoming Gold Cup, having both been beaten in a minor Leicester chase in January. Arctic Gold hadn't managed a win in three starts and it was looking increasingly as though his unfortunate experience in last season's National, where he fell and crashed through the rails, had left its mark. On the other hand, Freebooter had enjoyed a minor revival in his fortunes, winning four times in the early part of the season, albeit in fairly moderate company. Despite this marked improvement, he had suffered a recent defeat by his old rival Silver Fame and, as ever, had shown all his usual deficiencies on a park course. Quite inexplicably, weight of money kept him as favourite both in the ante-post lists and on Gold Cup day itself, despite the presence of the likes of Silver Fame, Greenogue, Mont Tremblant and the O'Brien representative, Knock Hard. Knock Hard, despite some erratic performances, had a touch of class and was backed accordingly, in spite of the prevailing heavy ground being against him.

Glen Kelly set out in customary fashion on Greenogue to make the running ahead of his 12 rivals and kept up a cracking pace until mid-way through the second circuit, by which time Freebooter had already made his exit as the field began to close on last year's runners-up. Despite major problems with the tack, Shaef was still in contention, along with the six-year-olds Mont Tremblant and E.S.B. As they turned for home, an Irish roar went up as Knock Hard began to close menacingly on the leaders. However, any hopes of an Irish victory were dashed at the second last where the bonny chestnut crashed out of the race, to leave his jockey, Phonsie O'Brien, cursing his bad luck.

Mont Tremblant, who had been travelling better than anything else throughout the race, paddled through the last before bounding up the hill. In behind the leader, E.S.B. was still in with every chance of making the frame, but was a spent force when he crashed out at the final fence. His turn would come at the expense of Devon Loch at Aintree, but for now it was left to a young Fred Winter, performing miracles aboard Shaef, to finish some ten lengths behind the impressive winner. Galloway Braes, Lady Orde's fine young chaser, ran on well in the closing stages to be a never-nearer third (he would be ever-present in future Gold Cups, without ever looking like winning).

There were a number of positives to come out of the race. To illustrate that true camaraderie wasn't simply the preserve of the weighing room, it transpired that rival trainers, at least in those less cut-throat days, were also prepared to help each other out, especially at difficult times. I can't imagine too many trainers falling over each other to offer Martin Pipe the use of their gallops if deepest Somerset were to freeze over suddenly. Hearing that Mont Tremblant's Gold Cup preparations were being continually thwarted by frozen gallops at Lambourn, Bill Wightman offered Walwyn the use of his gallops at Upham in Hampshire, which had been largely unaffected by the prevailing arctic conditions. This must have been like manna from Heaven for the grateful Walwyn. If there was ever a trainer who deserved even greater success than he actually achieved, it was surely Wightman. As we will see, this gentle man, who survived the horrors of life in a Japanese prisoner of war camp, would surely have won at least a brace of Gold Cups, given the right sort of ammunition. In the entire history of the Gold Cup, there has surely never been a horse less physically suited to the rigours of Cheltenham than Wightman's beloved Hallowe'en, famously described by his regular pilot, Fred Winter, as 'a bouncy little blanker, all backside and heart'. Yet it was this dual King George-winning 'little blanker' who would figure prominently in the next four Gold Cups, without ever getting his head in front.

Dave Dick, a six-footer and the latest in a long line of Paget jockeys, had proved himself to be a top-class rider, his strength in the saddle being a key factor in his many big race successes. He had certainly come a long way since winning the Lincoln some eleven years earlier, as a pint-sized apprentice with George Lambton, and was renowned for being one of the more colourful characters of the time.

The Jack 'Towser' Gosden-trained Shaef, meanwhile, enjoyed the distinction of being the first grey ever to be placed in the Gold Cup. Enormous credit for this must go to his jockey Fred Winter, who could have taken the easy option of pulling up after Shaef's bridle had been dislodged following a bump crossing the water jump on the first circuit. But such thoughts would have been alien to someone as determined and single-minded as Winter. Literally holding on to Shaef's head for the rest of the race, he managed to cajole his partner to such effect that the gelding ran the race of his life. Inexplicably, greys haven't fared a lot better in the Gold Cup since then – with one very notable exception, that is. Although Stalbridge Colonist's two post-Arkle placings were creditable efforts, it would take Desert Orchid's unforgettable surge up the hill in 1989 to make the ultimate breakthrough.

Mont Tremblant, the last of D.P.'s seven Gold Cup winners, would be the first of many Walwyn heroes to grace Cheltenham for the next three decades and his victory was only the third for six-year-olds in the race, following that of Golden Miller and Fortina. Hopes were high that this could be the next great Paget champion. However, a cruel catalogue of injuries put a stop to any such thoughts and it was soon clear that the imposing chestnut with the white blaze lacked The Miller's incredible robustness. Although further Gold Cup success eluded Mont Tremblant, he did manage a gallant second in the 1953 Grand National under a welter burden and recorded a memorable win in The Mildmay of Flete two years later.

Knock Hard, carrying the hopes of Ireland, had his detractors even before his fall at the second last, having done the same thing in a similarly strong position in the King George VI on his only previous visit to England. His jockey, Phonsie O'Brien, was adamant after the race that, 'he was cantering at the time and would have won by fifteen lengths, but for slipping going into the fence'.

Vincent O'Brien was convinced that, in many ways, his horse was more of a high-class horse on the flat than over jumps. After all, hadn't he won the Irish Lincoln by no less than five lengths in 1950? Knock Hard would also have taken the Irish Cesarewitch the previous year had Herbert Holmes not gone so early and been caught by his less-fancied stable-companion Hatton's Grace, the triple-champion hurdler also owned by the Keoghs. Despite his obvious shortcomings over fences, Knock Hard undeniably oozed class. O'Brien's talents would be well and truly put to the test with this particular inmate, but if anyone could be relied upon to unlock the key to him, it was the maestro himself.

MONT TREMBLANT (1952)

ch.g. 1946 (Gris Perle – Paltoquette)
Owned by Hon. D. Paget, trained by F. Walwyn and ridden by D.V. Dick

✢ 1953 ✢

Knock Hard enough and the door will open

Vincent O'Brien and Knock Hard were a pretty daunting combination. Ask any bookmaker, or maybe ex-bookmaker, still alive to tell the tale from the early O'Brien period. Staving off bankruptcy must have been the order of the day if you were ignorant of his capabilities, as most people were in the embryo days of the O'Brien operation, just after the war.

Knock Hard, arriving hot on the heels of both Cottage Rake and Hatton's Grace, must have made it much more difficult for O'Brien to confuse the enemy – but he tried mightily hard anyway. Sometimes the bookies got lucky. The Irish Cesarewitch involving Knock Hard and Hatton's Grace would be one case in point, in terms of the stable's financial involvement. However, pilot error is not something that I imagine O'Brien tolerated too often, hence the reason he employed the very best throughout his long career. I suppose you could say O'Brien and Piggott were a pretty daunting combination, too! But having a horse like Knock Hard to go to war with must have given the Churchtown trainer the versatility he needed to throw bookmakers off the scent. It might not have worked all the time; one look at the O'Brien betting ledger and the entries against Knock Hard would probably have made most bookmakers at the time cringe.

Knock Hard's owner Harry Keogh also liked a bet and none more so than on his own horses. Where better to have them than with a trainer like O'Brien, who was always prepared to back his own judgement, if the price was right? The price was definitely right when Knock Hard won the Irish Lincoln, simply because O'Brien had run him in a novice chase at Naas only two weeks before. 'Few would believe that a horse that had just run over fences could win a Lincoln' was O'Brien's view on the matter.

Was it Knock Hard's versatility that helped him to be able to cope with such a variation in demand? In truth his reverting to the flat was probably made easier when you take into account the trainer's assertion that 'Knock Hard had no natural aptitude for jumping.' Despite this, Knock Hard still managed to win eight chases throughout his career. In the Great Yorkshire at Doncaster, where he gave weight and a beating to Teal, the 1952 Grand National winner was undoubtedly on top-class form. However, the biggest win of his career would come soon after another abortive attempt at a gamble with him on the flat, this time in England. Knock Hard had been touched off in the Manchester November Handicap by the Derby third, Summer Rain.

There can't have been another horse in the 1953 Gold Cup line-up that would have finished within two furlongs of Summer Rain over the mile and a half trip. However, winning the Gold Cup was never going to be easy for Knock Hard, especially after he took fright in the King George VI Chase at Kempton, slipping on landing, which knocked his confidence. He was still suffering when he was beaten at Leopardstown giving weight to Mariner's Log, another of Lord Bicester's classy performers (who would re-oppose in the Gold Cup ridden by a youthful Pat Taaffe, the first of his many Gold Cup rides). O'Brien, concerned that all was not well with Knock Hard, called out a Dublin vet to check the horse over. It transpired that he was found to have a heart problem that could cause him to drop dead at any time, without warning. The decision was taken to continue campaigning Knock Hard – with the agreement of the jockey, who would be told the exact prognosis and the dangers involved. Tim Molony, particularly fearless and having ridden the horse to his impressive Doncaster win, didn't bat an eyelid.

So to Cheltenham on a misty and cold day, with the cream of steeplechasing, 12 lining up to do battle. The opposition included the current champion Mont Tremblant, as well as Mariner's Log, Rose Park, Hallowe'en and Teal. The public had latched on to Hallowe'en, following his superb win in the King George VI at Kempton, and he was sent off the 5–2 favourite. The race was no spectacle – the mist that hung across the course, particularly on the far side, saw to that. As the leaders came out of the mist with three to go, E.S.B. was marginally ahead of Mont Tremblant, Galloway Braes and Rose Park, with no sign of Knock Hard. Rose Park, unquestionably going like the winner at this stage, unshipped Tommy Cusack at the second last. But Knock Hard, having been under pressure and seemingly getting nowhere, suddenly took hold of the bit and made up a lot of ground towards the two leaders, who were beginning to tread water. A mighty leap at the last sealed it for the Irish challenger, with Hallowe'en, having struggled as ever coming down the hill, running on in grand style to finish a brave five-length second. Teal had injured himself when making a mistake at the water, sadly rupturing a bowel in the process; despite valiant efforts to operate and save him, he relapsed and was put down.

Knock Hard became his trainer's fourth Gold Cup winner in six years, but this was the last display of real brilliance. He returned to defend his crown next year, but the heavy conditions would be very much against him.

KNOCK HARD (1953)

ch.g. 1944 (Domaha – Knocksouna)
Owned by Mrs M.H. Keogh, trained by M.V. O'Brien and ridden by T. Molony

✢ 1954 ✢

Cusack compensation

Just for a pleasant change, Cheltenham managed to escape the worst of the terrible snows that threatened to engulf the local area. There had been a number of meetings lost in previous weeks and although there was never any real danger of the Festival not taking place, the ground was pretty desperate.

Incredibly, the first six home in last year's Gold Cup were all back again to take their chances, with varying degrees of optimism from their connections. Mont Tremblant, having won impressively at Sandown, was fully expected to take full advantage of the prevailing conditions, which were very much in his favour. It can only have been loyalty money from the Irish contingent that almost forced Knock Hard down to second favourite. Surely the burst of speed that he had shown on the fast ground last year would be blunted in the gluepot conditions here? Galloway Braes, Alec Kilpatrick's King George VI winner and fast-ground specialist, went for a walk in the market as connections must have been in two minds to even run. Four Ten, a giant bay gelding with a bold blaze to match, had won last season's National Hunt Handicap Chase in impressive fashion. The eight-year-old, formerly run in point-to-points, was locally trained by John Roberts, whose father Ben had previously trained at Kinnersley, before the Rimells. Four Ten had run six times prior to Cheltenham and had won three times, all his wins achieved with Tommy Cusack in the saddle. Hallowe'en was making his third appearance in the race, but without his usual jockey, Fred Winter, who was sidelined with a broken leg. Hallowe'en's price of 100–6 reflected the fact that he had struggled to find his form all season.

Lady Orde's Galloway Braes made the running for more than a circuit before coming to grief six out. Mont Tremblant appeared on the scene full of running as they headed down to the third last. The complexion of the race had changed a fence later as the favourite's promising run had petered out and it was left to Mariner's Log to take the lead, with Four Ten coming through with a strong run on the outside under Cusack to challenge over the last. An enormous roar went up from the locals in the crowd as Four Ten began to stride clear up the hill to win by four lengths. He had proved that he could handle any type of ground and it was impossible to jib his win. Knock Hard had never really got in contention, basically getting stuck in the mud.

There was no happier man after the race than Tommy Cusack. A late replacement for Bryan Marshall in last year's Gold Cup, he felt that Rose Park would have won last year if they hadn't fallen at the second last, so this unexpected win provided more than adequate compensation for him. Cusack, from Waterford, worked for some interesting trainers in his time, initially apprenticed to Senator J.J. Parkinson at the Curragh. After winning races on the flat, he became too heavy and moved to England to join Steve Donoghue, who trained at Epsom. Cusack also enjoyed considerable success, winning eight times on Lady Stalbridge's Red April.

Four Ten was sired by Blunderbuss, who had been bred by Lord Howard de Walden, who only raced him once as a two-year-old. Four Ten was home-bred by his owner Alan Strange, a dairy farmer from Dorset, who rode in point-to-points and went on to train under permit a few years after this memorable success. He had been hunted with the South Dorset and had taken part in four point-to-points and one hunter chase at Buskfastleigh, before being switched to John Roberts.

FOUR TEN (1954)

b.g. 1946 (Blunderbuss – Undue Praise)
Owned by Mr A. Strange, trained by J. Roberts and ridden by T. Cusack

✣ 1955 ✣

Gay Donald – Gold Cup hero
and Napoleon's best friend

She couldn't win a race herself, but Pas de Quatre's record as a brood mare is still unique in terms of producing two Cheltenham Gold Cup winners. Her subsequent rise to fame was about as unlikely as her forty pounds price tag as a yearling in 1939 – her breeder was none other than Beckhampton-based champion flat trainer Fred Darling. The fact that he was prepared to accept such a low bid from neighbouring Wiltshire farmer Harry Frank spoke volumes about the financial straits facing breeders in England at that time, with no major sales taking place. Even the likes of Darling were forced to offload at bargain basement prices.

Frank's new acquisition was broken in by Bob Turnell, who took the feisty filly out hunting, reporting that she had a distinct habit of ploughing through the odd fence, a trait her second son would copy, at times with disastrous consequences, throughout his illustrious career. Put into training with Alec Kilpatrick, she competed a number of times over fences at Cheltenham without getting her head in front and Frank decided to breed from her and sent her to a little-known Gloucestershire-based stallion, Gay Light. In 1946, Pas de Quatre managed to foal unaided out in a paddock at Frank's farm near Crudwell and the colt foal, who would become known as Gay Donald, damaged an eye at birth, with the resultant clouding of a pupil for life. Gay Donald was subsequently sold on very cheaply as a four-year-old to Yeovil trainer Jim Ford, on behalf of one of his owners, Mr P.J. Burt, another Wiltshire farmer. Ford moved his training operation to Cholderton in Wiltshire. His new base, Park House stables, had already enjoyed much success as a racing stable through the exploits of the celebrated Percy Woodland. Woodland was a former champion national hunt jockey who trained a number of top-class chasers in the 1930s, all renowned for being well schooled and supremely fit.

Gay Donald had won eight chases prior to the 1954–55 season, but, like the majority of the nine runners, had suffered an interrupted preparation, affected by the appalling winter weather that had gripped the country for the month prior to Cheltenham. The National Hunt Meeting didn't escape the problems either, with the first day of the meeting postponed and the Gold Cup being the only event to survive the re-arranged Thursday.

Last year's winner Four Ten went off as favourite, having won three of his last four races. But he had struggled to win them and there were others believed to have every chance of winning. Gay Donald, it must be said, wasn't one of them, having been beaten out of sight in the King George VI Chase at Kempton. 1953

Grand National winner Early Mist was well supported by the Irish, despite only having run in a hurdle race in January. All in all, it seemed a tricky contest to weigh up, with any number in with a chance. It didn't turn out that way, however.

Gay Donald, ridden by Royal jockey Tony Grantham, set off in front at a rate of knots, considering the treacherous conditions. Allowed to dictate, he pulled clear of the others and they never looked like getting to him. Despite ploughing through the last two fences, clearly getting tired, he was still far enough in front to hold on for an unlikely victory at odds of 33–1, ten lengths ahead of the ultra-consistent Hallowe'en. This win was rubbished as being a fluke by the experts of the time, but nine days later Gay Donald proved himself to be in truly outstanding form, this time giving Mont Tremblant weight and a beating at Sandown. Although he contested two further Gold Cups, he never recaptured the same level of form.

Many years later, a long-retired Gay Donald was back in the spotlight where he belonged. While Ryan Price was cutting a dash at Cheltenham ensuring another veteran of the turf, What A Myth, was doing his bit for Help the Aged, Gay Donald was spending his time hurtling around Salisbury Plain, being filmed for a BBC television play, *Rainbird* – playing Napoleon's charger! Only a small part, of course.

GAY DONALD (1955)

b.g. 1946 (Gay Light – Pas de Quatre)
Owned by Mr P.J. Burt, trained by J. Ford and ridden by A. Grantham

✢ 1956 ✢

Limber up, and put those turnips down!

Not for the first time in the Gold Cup, there was considerable support for a northern-trained horse, the only problem in 1949 being that Cottage Rake had spoiled the party and come out of the clouds, to pull the race out of the fire. Teal had even got badly injured in the 1953 race, just as he was beginning to bustle up the leaders.

Would this year be any different? Limber Hill, the impressive King George VI Chase winner, had posted the best form all season and was backed as if defeat was out of the question. He was a giant of a horse, not dissimilar in size and racing background to Four Ten. He had raced in point-to-points and had also won the National Hunt Handicap Chase. The nine-year-old had been a strong favourite for some time, even in the ante-post market. His trainer, Billy Dutton, rode Tipperary Tim to finish alone in the 1928 Grand National. He was regarded as one of the shrewdest operators around and his Malton yard one of the most versatile, housing arguably the best long-distance chaser in Britain, as well as the top five-furlong sprinter, Pappa Fourway – at the same time. Injuries to major players around Christmastime had robbed the race of much of its quality. Mont Tremblant and Gay Donald had broken down badly, the latter a very disappointing loss considering his performances since winning last year's Gold Cup.

Limber Hill's owner, John Davey, had bred the horse and named it after his farm in north Lincolnshire. The Roman-nosed gelding was a bit idiosyncratic. When he was back at his owner's farm, he would wander around the fields, uprooting turnips and tossing them over his shoulder as he went along! Strangely, his dam Mindoon had been mated to a carthorse the year before she produced Limber Hill in an attempt to breed a heavyweight hunter – on the grounds that she had been absolutely useless. This was a move of sheer desperation by Davey. Could he follow Cottage Rake and be only the second ever to win both the King George VI Chase at Kempton and the Cheltenham Gold Cup?

Racing had been severely curtailed prior to Cheltenham due to a freeze-up, which meant Limber Hill and others didn't have a prep race prior to the big race, though this would disadvantage others more than Limber Hill, who was reckoned to be a better horse fresh. His jockey, Jimmy Power, was a top-notch pilot who rode a considerable amount for Ripon-based Bobby Renton, riding Freebooter to win the 1950 Grand National.

The novice Cruachan, a talented front-runner, took over on the second circuit from Four Ten, who had taken the field along at a crawl. Power was biding his time on Limber Hill, content to play late, waiting until the second last where he slipped Limber Hill into overdrive, swept past Cruachan in an instant and set off up the hill, chased by Frenchman René Emery on the unconsidered Vigor. Limber Hill was simply too good for the others and won by a comfortable four lengths from Vigor and the gallant Hallowe'en, re-united with Fred Winter and finishing in the frame for the fourth time in a row, a fantastic achievement from an eleven-year-old with considerable mileage on the clock.

Limber Hill injured his back attempting to win his second King George in December and was never the same horse again, finishing well down the field on his second and final Gold Cup appearance in 1958, with Tim Molony in the saddle. Incredibly, he never won another race, in three seasons of trying.

LIMBER HILL (1956)

ch.g. 1947 (Bassam – Mindoon)
Owned by Mr J. Davey, trained by W.P. Dutton and ridden by J. Power

✣1957 ✣

From little acorns . . .

This particular Festival roared into life from the outset with a popular and significant win for Mandarin, the Fulke Walwyn-trained French-bred, in the Broadway Novices Chase. A popular win because Walwyn had gone through every emotion imaginable trying to teach Mandarin to jump properly – but it had all been worth it now. A significant win because Mandarin's next visit to the Festival winners' enclosure would be five long years away, though definitely worth the wait.

This was also a special year for a man who wore a multitude of hats, but not one of them, officially at least at the time of his greatest triumph, a trainer's hat. Ivor Herbert's name will never appear in the record books against Linwell, winner of the 1957 Gold Cup, although he continued to train the horse, in all but name, at his Cadmore End base in the Chilterns. Racing's rulers at that time concluded that his activities as a racing journalist, writing for a London newspaper, precluded him from training horses. So the licence was transferred to head lad Charlie Mallon, who had worked in a similar capacity for Hector Christie, another Gold Cup-winning trainer back in 1947 with Fortina.

Linwell, or Floral Tribute as the bay gelding was known in 1953, came from horse dealer Paddy Quinn's Tipperary base. Herbert acquired the small bay gelding from Quinn in a private deal, on behalf of his friend David Brown of Aston Martin and tractor fame. Brown was master of the South Oxford Hounds and wanted to win their point-to-point. This would be seven hundred and fifty pounds well spent. Herbert took the ride in Linwell's first point-to-point and the partnership fell at the first, although his next run, a placed effort, was more encouraging. Herbert then pulled off a bit of a masterstroke, employing Michael Scudamore, a fine horseman from a farming background who had come through the amateur ranks to became a much sought-after professional, both on-course and off. Scudamore had few peers when it came to teaching a young horse to jump. Some horses he worked with presented a greater challenge than others, Mandarin being a case in point. But it was he who managed to perfect Linwell's jumping, a vital ingredient that would guarantee Linwell's place at the top of the chasing tree in future years.

Herbert knew all about Linwell's superb jumping pedigree, which included numerous winners on the dam's side, and endeavoured to improve on it. In return for vital tutelage, Scudamore was given the chance to build a partnership with Linwell where it mattered most – on the track – winning six races in that first year. A superb victory over the highly-rated northern mare Kerstin in late 1956 meant Linwell had now announced his intentions as a live Gold Cup contender. Exciting times lay ahead for connections of the talented son of Rosewell, an Irish classic winner.

Linwell's prep race for the Gold Cup was at Kempton and Herbert was happy with his performance, behind Pointsman on a course deemed unsuitably sharp. Linwell loved Cheltenham and had won four times there already, which must have given Herbert considerable hope come the big day.

Kerstin, Linwell's cousin through their dams being half-sisters, went off joint-favourite at 6–1, despite falling in her prep race, the Great Yorkshire Chase. Pointsman was the other joint favourite in a very open market with E.S.B. and Sir Ken, the former champion hurdler, bracketed together on 7–1. Gay Donald, the only former Gold Cup winner in the field of 13, was 11 years old and past his best. Linwell looked a generous price at 100–9, especially taking into account his impressive Cheltenham record.

Rose Park set off at a good pace, considering the soft ground, with Michael Scudamore holding Linwell up towards the rear of the field. Coming to the third last, Kerstin and Linwell made their moves simultaneously to challenge the long-time leader, with Pointsman going easily in behind. Over the second last, Linwell put in a fine leap, taking a length out of Kerstin as they landed. Kerstin sprawled on landing, interfering with Pointsman. Linwell jumped the last in front a length clear and maintained the advantage over Kerstin all the way up the run-in. It had been a masterful display of tactical awareness from Scudamore, bringing Linwell through with a long, steady run to put the issue beyond doubt over the last with the minimum of fuss.

Linwell had announced his arrival at the top in no uncertain fashion. Herbert had more faith in the horse than he dare admit, certainly in print! But his belief in Linwell had already been totally justified and, barring accidents, the future looked rosy. It was highly likely that Herbert would be returning to the Cheltenham stage for a number of years to come, with a serious chance of emulating one or two of the greats in jump racing. The little Irish acorn was threatening to be that big oak tree – all he needed was to get a rub of the green. He didn't – not at Cheltenham, anyway.

LINWELL (1957)

b.g. 1948 (Rosewell – Rubia Linda)
Owned by Sir David Brown, trained by C. Mallon and ridden by M. Scudamore

✦ 1958 ✦

Revenge is sweet for the fair Kerstin

Linwell's defence of his Cheltenham crown began in earnest with the new Hennessy Gold Cup at Cheltenham in November – the first ever sponsored race. This meant a clash with Mandarin, the sponsors' darling, at the horrendous disadvantage of no less than sixteen pounds in the weights (Linwell, not over-big, was asked to bear no less than twelve stone two pounds). Weight stops trains, but it nearly didn't stop brave Linwell, who did everything in his powers to fight off the favourably weighted 'little Frenchman', but went down by only three lengths, fighting back in fine style up his favoured hill.

That tremendous tussle took its toll on Mandarin, who apparently spent two days in his stable feeling the effects of the epic battle. It looked for all the world as though this would be Mandarin's year. Another big prize came his way when he went on to land the King George VI Chase, this time giving seven pounds and a length beating to that good yardstick Lochroe, trained by Peter Cazalet, with the mare Kerstin back in third. The racing public grew to love Mandarin for his courage and he was now being touted as a serious Gold Cup challenger, reflected in the ante-post lists which now had Mandarin only a point behind Linwell, the 3–1 favourite to retain his Gold Cup crown.

There looked to be a useful novice coming through the ranks in the form of Polar Flight, a seven-year-old who had made eye-catching improvement in the hands of George Slack, beating none other than Linwell at Newbury, admittedly in receipt of nearly a stone. It would have been dangerous to read too much into this defeat, though, as Herbert was bringing Linwell slowly but surely to the boil in readiness for Cheltenham in March. Polar Flight had the Grand National as an option, but after being allotted a crushing eleven stone seven pounds in the weights, the sensible decision was taken to go for Cheltenham Gold.

It had been an exceptionally wet winter, which would suit Linwell come Cheltenham, although it looked for a time as if a couple of dry weeks were going to produce good ground, a considerable worry to many, not least Linwell. As if on cue, as Cheltenham approached, the frosts and snow arrived, particularly bad up north. A snowstorm broke over the course on Wednesday afternoon, but Gold Cup day went ahead as planned. Despite the Irish having no runner in the Gold Cup, they were to win a record eight races over the three days!

Mandarin took over as favourite of the nine runners on the day, followed by Linwell, Polar Flight, Gay Donald and Kerstin. It was to be a race full of surprises. Kerstin had taken the lead after four fences and just as the race was beginning to take shape, it suddenly became much less of a contest, as Mandarin and Linwell crashed out of the race at the eighth last. Mandarin made a dreadful mistake, screwing badly sideways and causing Linwell major interference on the landing side of the fence, catapulting Scudamore out of the saddle in the process.

With the principals gone, Polar Flight was the next to almost exit, dragging his hind legs through the water, losing many lengths. Gay Donald looked as though his chance to repeat his efforts of three years ago had come, but no sooner had he flattered to deceive, he was swallowed up by Kerstin, ridden by a young northern jockey, Stan Hayhurst. Polar Flight was by now back at full steam and closing on the mare. After a battle royal over the final two fences, Kerstin showed slightly the better turn of foot to win by half a length and go one better than last year. It was the second time in three years that the Gold Cup was heading north, to Northumberland to be precise. Incredibly, Kerstin recorded exactly the same time as that of his cousin Linwell last year, and, like her cousin, had been bought privately in County Tipperary. Her trainer Verly Bewicke had been a decent amateur rider before the war and served with the Northumberland Hussars. Young Kerstin was to contest the next two Gold Cups without ever looking like repeating her success. By the time she retired, she had won one hurdle and eleven chases and went on to breed three winners, including the useful Fashion House, winner of fourteen races before sadly breaking a leg in 1972.

KERSTIN (1958)

br.m. 1950 (Honor's Choice – Miss Kilcash)
Owned by Mr G.H. Moore, trained by C. Bewicke and ridden by S. Hayhurst

✢ 1959 ✢
Roddy good show

When it rains, it pours . . . and it seemed to pour all winter. Thirty-eight meetings had been lost to the weather by February. Ironically, this year the Festival had been brought forward to the first week of March in search of better weather and Sod's law dictated that this brainwave coincided with simply another belt of incessant driving rain. I can't see the current Cheltenham Steeplechase Company having any plans to change dates again – it could mess up half of Ireland's industry, possibly for weeks!

It was to prove to be another great week for the Irish following on from last season's rout of the English. They managed to win the inaugural Champion Chase with the speedy Quita Que and recorded six wins from the sixteen races. However, unlike last season, they had two Gold Cup challengers of some distinction. First, there was the Vincent O'Brien-trained Saffron Tartan, the ante-post favourite who bore all the hallmarks of a typical O'Brien champion. Second, and not far behind in ability and in the ante-post market, was Roddy Owen, a strongly-built handsome bay gelding, trained at Newbridge, County Kildare.

Unfortunately, Saffron Tartan had to be withdrawn on the morning of the race, having coughed at exercise. This unexpected turn of events meant that Taxidermist, the winner of both the Whitbread and the Hennessy last year, was suddenly catapulted to favourite. Amateur-ridden by John Lawrence, now better known as Lord Oaksey, Taxidermist had beaten Kerstin in the Hennessy victory, but he had a habit of getting behind in his races, and it was doubtful that he would be able to get away with doing that in the prevailing mudbath.

The new course, which was supposed to have been utilised for the first time at the Festival meeting, was simply unraceable and the stewards had no choice but to switch the race back to the old course, which was in a marginally better state.

Kerstin and Linwell were back in opposition for the third year running and Pas Seul, a six-year-old trained by Bob Turnell, had shown himself to be a most precocious type, with a few idiosyncrasies thrown in for good measure. Roddy Owen, bought as an unbroken five-year-old, was owned by Lord Fingall, who rode as an amateur over jumps before the Second World War – in glasses! He won the Military Cross in the First World War and showed his prowess in the saddle by winning the 1930 National Hunt Chase on Sir Lindsay. The bay was particularly well-named, after 1892 Grand National-winning jockey Captain Roderick Owen, one of the finest amateur riders of all time, winning over two hundred and fifty races, despite a totally unpredictable character. The equine version certainly seemed of kindred spirit.

It was generally believed that the nine-year-old Roddy Owen would probably have won the 1958 King George VI Chase had he not been brought to a virtual standstill four out. In the circumstances, he only went down by a head in a driving finish with the brave Lochroe, but he had subsequently disappointed in the Leopardstown Chase. His regular jockey, 'Bunny' Cox, generously offered to stand down and suggested Bobby Beasley to the trainer for the ride in the Gold Cup, opining that Beasley would probably have a better chance of winning on Roddy Owen.

The trainer in question was Danny Morgan, Gold Cup-winning jockey and nephew of Frank Morgan, who trained Ballinode to set the Irish ball rolling at Cheltenham, carving his own niche in Cheltenham history in 1959 by becoming the first person to ride and subsequently train a Gold Cup winner. His riding career had been quite special. Apprenticed to Basil Jarvis, D.J. (as he was known) rode and won on the flat and had the distinction of riding for three kings and winning for two of them, Edward VIII and George VI. Morgan then switched to the winter game and rode Morse Code to glory for Ivor Anthony in 1938, beating the great Golden Miller, his only reverse at Cheltenham. Incredibly he never finished out of the frame in any of his eight Gold Cup rides from 1934 to 1942. He eventually turned his hand to training in 1948.

Taxidermist, who had drifted dramatically in the final exchanges, still clung on to favouritism, marginally ahead of Roddy Owen and Linwell, now ridden by champion jockey Fred Winter. In the race itself, young 'Taxi' fell five out still in contention, but the race looked there for the taking as Bill Rees riding Pas Seul came down to the last cantering over his rivals. Whether Pas Seul was distracted or simply crashed through the last through pure inexperience will remain a mystery, but he not only got himself on the floor but all but brought Linwell to his knees. He in turn hampered Lochroe as he landed over the last and it took all of Winter's skill to keep the partnership intact and get Linwell going again as quickly as possible. In the meantime, Roddy Owen, at least four lengths down on Linwell jumping the last, with prospects of third place at best, found himself with a clear run on the far side. Beasley got to work on Roddy Owen and he responded in great style, powering through the mud up the hill with the unlucky Linwell trailing him by five lengths. Winter had managed to reduce the deficit to three lengths nearing the line but Roddy Owen lasted out in brave fashion.

Beasley, from possibly the greatest family of pedigree Irish horsemen in the history of the sport, would in time become a victim of his own success. The '60s lifestyle of a cavalier band of jockeys that embroiled the naïve Beasley turned out to be a contributory factor in his downward spiral, which would eventually lead to the loss of his job as stable jockey at Uplands and his facing up to the stark reality of being an alcoholic. To his immense credit, Beasley returned from the mire to the Cheltenham winners' enclosure after a spell of 15 years. He plundered his second Gold Cup, teaming up with his friend Pat Taaffe in his new guise as a trainer, riding the redoubtable Captain Christy – generally regarded as one of the greats of national hunt racing, despite his lunatic tendencies.

Reflecting on Roddy Owen's triumph, most observers believed he was one of the luckier winners of the Gold Cup, as Pas Seul seemed to be travelling like the winner when he came to grief. It would have been a close run thing between Roddy Owen and Linwell had the latter not suffered any interference. Roddy Owen, given an inspired Beasley drive, might well have pipped Linwell anyway.

But we'll never know, or will we? It would be quite something if, in the twenty-first century, we can somehow recreate these sort of 'what if' situations with a computer simulation or virtual reality machine and apply a more scientific approach to solving these 'mysteries'. Wouldn't it be great, for example, to know what would have happened if Tied Cottage hadn't knuckled on landing in the 1979 Gold Cup? With the level of technological progress reached since the very first Gold Cup, I don't think it would be expecting too much for this to become reality, so long as losing connections don't expect a retrospective change in the actual result! However, on a more serious level, it might even help with stewards' inquiries. Certain stewards seem to need all the help they can get – some of the decisions that have been made over the years beggar belief, particularly the ones that have been sensibly reversed at Portman Square weeks later. It might help to pacify aggrieved connections, but does nothing to redress the balance for the losing punter.

RODDY OWEN (1959)

b.g. 1949 (Owenstown – Desla's Star)
Owned by Lord Fingall, trained by D. Morgan and ridden by H. Beasley

✝ 1960 ✝
Justice prevails

'Too much money . . . too soon'. An appropriate epitaph for the Hon. Dorothy Wyndham Paget. Dead at the age of fifty-four, forty-three of her years had been spent in pleasing herself. She became a millionairess at the age of eleven . . . that was her tragedy. Poor little rich girl! That phrase might have been written for her. Her glory? Mostly reflected. She chose the Turf as her playground and, by chance, became associated with Golden Miller, one of the greatest horses of all time . . . We shall remember her as the bulky, Glastonbury-booted figure which appeared on the racecourse surrounded by a retinue of servants. We shall reminisce about her bad manners, enormous appetite and extraordinary clothes. And we shall miss her!

The Sporting Life, 1960

The tone of this piece upset many people, especially those few close to her who knew a very different person from the one described above. It has to be said that it was rather unusual for a trade newspaper to take such a vitriolic stance, but then you either loved her or hated her. Was the final offering of 'And we shall miss her!' an afterthought, an attempt at irony or simply sarcasm? There is no doubt she was far more charitable towards the needy than most people were prepared to believe; she wasn't the type to shout her generosity from the rooftops. However, her eccentric behaviour certainly did nothing for her public image. Nevertheless, her impact on horse-racing generally was huge. Had she been lost to racing in her prime, it would have been something akin to the Maktoums pulling out of racing *en masse* and without warning in the new millennium. It wouldn't have been just the racing industry that would have suffered from such a loss, as a few bookmakers might not exist today but for the wayward nature of her gambling habits.

The 1960 Gold Cup turned out to be an open-looking affair as the Festival approached, with no one horse excelling through the season. Pas Seul, in particular, had been up to his usual tricks, falling in the Hennessy and blundering away his chances in numerous other races, including the King George VI Chase. But connections knew that after last season's fall with the Gold Cup at his mercy they had a potential Blue Riband winner in Pas Seul. A half-brother to the 1955 Gold Cup winner Gay Donald, Pas Seul had been bought by Bob Turnell as a yearling for six hundred pounds, on behalf of John Rogerson, a stockbroker, farmer and Senior Steward of the National Hunt Committee in this Gold Cup year. Pas Seul's career over fences had got off to an inauspicious start, falling twice in his early races before proceeding to win three chases without compromising on his jumping. Undoubtedly, Pas Seul had more talent than his illustrious half-brother and Turnell believed his stable star to be 'too brave for his own good'.

Bill Rees, son of 'Bilby' Rees and nephew of the great pre-war jockey Fred Rees, had been in the saddle 12 months earlier, and had the dubious pleasure again here. With his record of failing to complete, it was hardly surprising that Pas Seul didn't go off favourite, with Kerstin and Roddy Owen back to try and win a second Gold Cup. However, favourite on the day was the exciting novice Knightsbrook, the impressive winner of two important chases, the Emblem and the Great Yorkshire.

In the race itself, Kerstin took her 11 opponents on from the start, with Stan Hay-hurst trying to run them into the ground and, for a time, looking like he might succeed. As they rounded the final bend, Kerstin appeared to be going better than Roddy Owen, Pas Seul and the diminutive Lochroe, the latter now a twelve-year-old, competing in his fourth Gold Cup. With the favourite never going at any stage, Kerstin still led at the second last but looked as though she was coming to the end of her tether. Pas Seul's supporters had grown accustomed to expecting one or two blunders from him and he didn't disappoint here. Fortunately, Rees, who knew him better than anybody, sat tight and gathering him up set off down to the last together with Lochroe, moving past the tiring Kerstin. Meanwhile, Roddy Owen began to stay on menacingly in behind Kerstin, with three still in with a serious chance at the last.

Pas Seul came to the last full of running and Rees, mindful of last year's fall, decided to sit quietly and just let him pop. Lochroe, with young David Mould in the saddle, got away much the faster of the two, with a fine leap at the last. In behind the leaders, an exhausted Kerstin fell right in front of Roddy Owen, almost bringing the champion down. Beasley somehow managed to stay in the plate on Roddy Owen, but had lost all chance of winning. Up ahead, it looked as if Lochroe was finally going to tame the hill, but Rees had ridden a canny race on Pas Seul and, meeting the rising ground, began to ask Pas Seul to lengthen his stride. Ahead of him, Mould had given Lochroe a wonderful ride and the brave Lochroe kept pulling out a bit more for him. Sadly, it was never going to be enough, as Pas Seul strode majestically past him with a hundred yards to go, quickening in the style of the classy performer that he was.

The new champion Pas Seul had been at his best here and, according to his trainer, should have won back-to-back Gold Cups if he hadn't been doped by intruders at Ogbourne Maisey two days before the 1961 Gold Cup. He recovered, but it was a testament to the toughness of the horse that he was able to take part in the next Gold Cup at all.

In the twilight of his career, Pas Seul was still disregarding fences, even at Aintree! Asked to give weight all round in the 1964 Grand National, by which time the eleven-year-old gelding was well past his best, Pas Seul went straight through the twelfth fence, moving the whole frame of the fence and pushing out the bottom – and still he never fell. His jockey Dave Dick couldn't quite believe what Pas Seul had done, and after the race described the almost comical scene. 'He was on the floor the other side of the fence, with me still sitting on him, but he never turned over. When I stepped off him, he was sitting there like a dog on the floor – he'd knocked himself out!' Old habits . . .

PAS SEUL (1960)

b.g. 1953 (Erin's Pride – Pas de Quatre)
Owned by Mr J. Rogerson, trained by R. Turnell and ridden by W. Rees

✛ 1961 ✛

Saffron Supreme

Vincent O'Brien thought the world of Saffron Tartan when he trained him for a syndicate led by Colonel Guy Westmacott. Saffron Tartan had been earmarked as a future champion since winning a division of the Gloucester Hurdle at Cheltenham in 1957 and looked equally good the following season as a novice chaser, before illness and respiratory problems forced O'Brien to put him away for the season. Saffron Tartan returned to chasing with three solid wins, which had his trainer and half of Ireland believing that it would be only a matter of time before he would win the Gold Cup. O'Brien, on the verge of turning his attentions exclusively to flat racing, decided to go for gold straight away with the handsome eight-year-old. He was heavily backed to become the trainer's fifth winner in the race – despite the presence of the most recent Gold Cup winners, Kerstin and Linwell.

However, Saffron Tartan was found to be coughing on the morning of the 1959 race and O'Brien had no option other than to withdraw the favourite. Found to be still suffering from the virus that had affected him so badly earlier in his career, he was subsequently hobdayed and sent to England to be trained by Don Butchers. Butchers had been a fearless jockey before becoming a trainer in 1949. Six years later, his good friend Gay Kindersley bought Priam Lodge in Epsom and persuaded Butchers to train there, which he did, successfully under both codes.

Saffron Tartan, despite his problems, retained his superb turn of foot and the decision was taken to revert to hurdles, for the time being at least. He proved his class over the smaller obstacles, finishing a fine third in the 1960 Champion Hurdle, won in record time by Paddy Sleator's Another Flash. Back over fences later in the year, he won the King George in fine style on a course which undoubtedly would have suited his speed and suspect stamina. Butchers chose to run him in a two-mile chase at Sandown for his final Gold Cup prep race, but this backfired, Saffron Tartan taking a rare tumble.

Bookmakers were well aware of Saffron Tartan, a much better horse on the prevailing fast ground, and took no chances. Winter's renowned strength in the saddle made for an irresistible combination. As the tapes went up, Saffron Tartan went off a well-supported 2–1 favourite, with Pas Seul second in at 10–3. Winter was hoping to secure his first Champion Hurdle/Gold Cup double, having already won the hurdles championship with Eborneezer for Ryan Price. Mandarin led until four out, where a challenging Pas Seul, putting in one of his trademark howlers, somehow managed to find a leg, but lost lengths in the process. Winter chose this moment to inject some pace into the race and booted clear. Frenchman's Cove and Mandarin found the pace too hot, leaving Saffron Tartan out in front and galloping on strongly down the hill. Meanwhile Dave Dick had managed to get Pas Seul back into contention, and chasing the leader, the two began to pull right away from the others. Over the second last, Saffron Tartan was patently going the better and jumped the last with a three-length lead. Dave Dick, using all of his famed strength to great effect, tried valiantly to bridge the gap, but, try as he might, it was to no avail. Winter had kept just enough in reserve to hold off the persistent Pas Seul by a length and a half, with Mandarin getting his second wind, staying on stoutly up the hill to finish three lengths back in third. After the race, Winter explained that a few yards from the last, he had felt his horse almost collapse, desperately tired from his exertions. He added, 'I was very glad to get to that winning post. I never thought we would make it.'

Butchers became disillusioned with racing and in 1966, rather bizarrely, left to work for a local butcher in Kent. Sadly, within the year he suffered a heart attack and died. Saffron Tartan had been the first horse to be placed in a Champion Hurdle and go on to win a Gold Cup. But there would be no repeat performance.

SAFFRON TARTAN (1961)

br.g. 1951 (Tartan – Kellsboro Witch)
Owned by Col. G.R. Westmacott, trained by D. Butchers and ridden by F. Winter

✣ 1962 ✣

Confucius, he say Mandarin

At the beginning of the 1961–62 season, Fred Winter had accepted a retainer to ride for Fulke Walwyn, with the proviso that as well as honouring his existing commitments to Ryan Price, he could also maintain his links with the champion, Saffron Tartan. Unfortunately, Saffron Tartan would never have the chance to return to Cheltenham to defend his title – a leg injury which didn't respond to treatment ended his racing days in the autumn of 1961 – leaving Winter free to partner little Mandarin. That particular autumn had also started in frustrating fashion for Winter, with a broken collarbone. He was forced to sit out the valuable Hennessy Gold Cup and watch crack Irish jockey Willie Robinson take over on the sponsors' horse. Mandarin, as usual, battled his way to victory, leaving Winter with mixed emotions; he was choked at missing out on a big race winner, but at least he could look forward to riding Mandarin, despite the bonny French-bred being very much in the twilight of his career.

It didn't seem possible that the eleven-year-old, with all the injuries and ailments that had beset him over his eight seasons at Saxon House, could still continue competing and succeeding at the highest level for so long. His enthusiasm alone paid a tremendous compliment to the skills of his trainer. Winner of two King Georges in 1957 and 1959 and now a dual Hennessy winner, he did seem to be as good as ever, winning all five races this particular season. Walwyn knew he would need to have Mandarin at his best if he was going to have any chance of winning that elusive Gold Cup at his third attempt. He had run a creditable race in defeat last year, without ever looking like overhauling the two principals.

It was no surprise that the classy Pas Seul had been installed as ante-post favourite. He still headed the market on the day of the race, but only just, as both Mandarin and Fortria, representing Tom Dreaper, came in for plenty of late support. Mandarin led briefly over the first few fences, before one of the rank outsiders, Cocky Consort, took over the running. Pas Seul, running in his fourth consecutive Gold Cup, headed the northern challenger and jumped the ditch on the hill in front. Pat Taaffe riding Fortria made his challenge as Pas Seul weakened out of contention, with Mandarin moving up strongly to challenge on the leader's inner. Jumping the final fence, Mandarin was still half a length behind the Irish raider, but he showed true grit to battle bravely past the year-younger Fortria.

Mandarin returned to the noisiest reception there had been at Cheltenham for many a year. Winter spelt out post-race exactly how they had won. 'Mandarin was well off the bit going to the water second time round. Jumping the final ditch just behind the leaders, he was going nowhere, but when I gave him a smack, he took off. We got a great run down the hill. As Fortria pulled out wide, I got through on

Jockeys outside the old weighing room at Prestbury Park, March 1932
FROM THE LEFT: Horsefall (the gateman, wearing bowler hat), Farnham Maxwell,
Len Lefebve, William Parvin, Tim Hamey, Arthur Wendby, Bob Everitt,
Monty Smyth, William Payne, Arthur Smith, Bill Gurney, Jack Moloney,
Danny Morgan, Tommy Morgan, Dick Rees, Tommy Cullinan, Georges Pellerin,
Keith Piggott (almost hidden), Gerald Hardy, Billy Stott, Staff Ingham, Billy Speck,
Jack Mason, Eric Foster, William Ransom

ABOVE: a last-fence battle. Golden Miller and Thomond II, 1935 Cheltenham Gold Cup

RIGHT: the Honeybourne Steeplechase, Cheltenham, 16 November 1962. It was Arkle's first race in England, which he won by twenty lengths

Mill House (G.W. Robinson) leading the winner Arkle (P. Taaffe)
at the second-last fence, 1964 Cheltenham Gold Cup

What A Myth (P. Kelleway) after winning the 1969 Cheltenham Gold Cup

ABOVE: the last fence. L'Escargot (T. Carberry) and French Tan (P. Taaffe), 1970 Cheltenham Gold Cup

RIGHT: trainer Fulke Walwyn, photographed in 1973 at Saxon House, Lambourn

ABOVE: the 1974 Gold Cup. Captain Christy (H. Beasley) and The Dikler (R. Barry) at the last fence

LEFT: The Dikler going to the post (1974)

Abandoned! Gold Cup Day 1978. This view of the
old stands was taken from the members' lawn

Celebrating the 1978 Piper Champagne Gold Cup, which was won by Midnight Court.
Trainer Fred Winter holds high the Gold Cup with owner Mrs Olive Jackson to his left.
In the bowler hat, behind Fred Winter, is Lord Vestey

The last fence of the 1979 Cheltenham Gold Cup. Alverton (J.J. O'Neill), the eventual winner, and (no. 21) Tied Cottage (T. Carberry), who fell on landing

Little Owl (A.J. Wilson), winner of the 1981 Cheltenham Gold Cup, being led into the winners' enclosure

Silver Buck (R. Earnshaw) winning the 1982 Tote
Cheltenham Gold Cup from Bregawn (G. Bradley)

Bregawn's connections with their trophies. On the left, owner J. Kennelly,
with trainer Michael Dickinson standing next to jockey Graham Bradley

his inside. Taking off just behind him at the second last, that was when I knew we'd win.' Mandarin's owner, Mme Peggy Hennessy, enthused, 'It may sound banal, but this is the greatest day of my life. I have kept horses in training over here for ten years with only one objective – to win the Gold Cup.'

But it didn't end at Cheltenham, not just yet for Mandarin and Winter, who was obviously keen to repay Mme Hennessy the compliment of one last win, in her own back garden, *chez* Auteuil. It was an unforgettable swansong in Paris, Mandarin beating the best chasers in France on the tricky figure-of-eight course, on unsuitably boggy ground, with the handicap of a broken bit and damaged tendon to match. Not to mention Winter feeling physically sick with violent stomach cramps and grogginess. Even Hans Christian Anderson would have struggled to dream this one up. Mandarin could never be accused of taking the easy way out. As we will see, he might not have been the best of Fulke Walwyn's talented army of chasers, but he was certainly the trainer's personal favourite.

MANDARIN (1962)

b.g. 1951 (Deux pour Cent – Manada)
Owned by Mme K. Hennessy, trained by F. Walwyn and ridden by F. Winter

✢ 1963 ✢

The Big Horse with the big reputation

I don't imagine Fulke Walwyn was much of a surfer, not having the time or inclination to do anything that would take him away from his beloved horses, but he certainly was riding the crest of a wave in those heady days of the early '60s. There was so much equine talent at Saxon House that if his string had to suddenly be split around the various yards in Lambourn, each and every one would have been guaranteed a star performer. Few could contemplate facing a new season without a Mandarin to lead the team – those that couldn't, or wouldn't, admit to this would only be fooling themselves. Walwyn didn't have that problem. Mandarin's successor, Mill House, was already *in situ* and proved to be extremely precocious, in stark comparison to the gallant Mandarin who, for all his achievements, needed time and the full range of Walwyn's skills to realise his potential.

How fitting it was then for Walwyn to have two champions, such opposites, who dovetailed so perfectly into that two-year period that, when at their best, nothing could live with either of them. Nothing, that is, until a juggernaut came hurtling down the Cheltenham hill to flatten Mill House, supposedly in his prime. The fact that Pat Taaffe, at the wheel of that juggernaut, had in fact schooled and ridden Mill House in his formative days back in Ireland doesn't help to ease any reflection on the rapid fall from grace that the Walwyn star would suffer. If it were only that simple. Was there a chink in the armour that Taaffe knew about to the exclusion of everyone else? The answer would have to be 'no'.

When Taaffe found out that Mill House had been transferred from Syd Dale's Epsom yard to Saxon House, he actually wrote to his friend, Willie Robinson, enthusing, 'You will soon be on the best horse in Britain, and quite possibly the world!' 'The Big Horse', as he became known, didn't seem to have any visible chink in his armour and his form seemed bullet-proof. Certainly nothing could live with him, especially now that his owner Bill Gollings had switched him to Fulke Walwyn. Perhaps the sheer size of the beast – well over seventeen hands – would ultimately have the biggest bearing on his change of fortunes. That he had had his problems by the time of his defence of the Gold Cup crown is a factor that could, quite conceivably, have made his future nemesis appear even more chilling. For now though, his win as a six-year-old was to match any winning performance witnessed for many years.

To achieve that win, Mill House would have to overcome, along with his eleven opponents, a considerable spell off the track. With Britain in the grip of an icy winter that would last from late December through to early March, Walwyn, along with everybody else, simply had to do the best he could in the circumstances. Fortunately, Mill House had been kept busy prior to this particular freeze-up, one or two jumping errors contributing towards a shock Kempton reverse which was sandwiched between two impressive victories at Sandown.

Fortria, runner-up 12 months earlier behind Mandarin and Mill House's closest rival in the betting, was expected to give Mill House a good run for his money, despite the ground and the fact that he had been hobdayed. Apart from Frenchman's Cove, who had been a proven performer at the highest level, and Duke Of York, who would benefit from Fred Winter's strong handling, the others were a poor bunch. Robinson took the bull by the horns from the word go and ran the opposition into the ground, ground much softer than Fortria would have liked. Taaffe, to his credit, at least tried to bridge the gap on the clear leader, but his response was very limited on the day. Mill House waltzed home to victory, easing down to win by ten lengths.

His wealthy owner picked up twenty-five thousand pounds in bets alone, with the promise of more to come if his pride and joy could repeat the dose 12 months later. The seven and a half thousand that Gollings had paid for the then four-year-old with a solitary Naas hurdle win to his name was beginning to look very good value. One question was on everyone's lips – is this the next Golden Miller? A number of good judges thought so. He was young enough and the manner of his win had evoked inevitable comparisons with the greats. He seemed to have the physique and all the attributes necessary to become one of them. However, in 12 months' time it was unlikely he was still going to have things all his own way. Arkle, equally as impressive, landing the Broadway Novices Chase on the opening day, was going to be aimed at the Gold Cup and Mill House would have to produce the goods once more or be found out. Even at this stage, the 1964 Gold Cup was being looked upon as a straightforward head-to-head battle, such was their perceived superiority over the rest of the opposition.

Fortunately, their adoring public wouldn't have to wait until the Gold Cup to see them take each other on. The Hennessy Gold Cup at Newbury in November was to be the scene of their first showdown. Few were disappointed with the outcome and even fewer were prepared to believe that the winner wouldn't go on to confirm the form, on better terms, in the forthcoming Gold Cup.

MILL HOUSE (1963)

b.g. 1957 (King Hal – Nas na Riogh)
Owned by Mr W.H. Gollings, trained by F. Walwyn and ridden by G.W. Robinson

Big problems for The Big Horse?

30 November 1963, and Hennessy Gold Cup day had arrived. England's champion was set to give five pounds in weight to 'Tom Draper's nice prospect' – the novice that had waltzed away with the usually competitive Broadway Chase – so what was all the fuss about this Irish upstart?

Arkle had been reared and broken at Dorothy Paget's Ballymacoll Stud and Tom Dreaper knew the family well. He had trained the dam, who was very speedy and recommended the horse to Anne, Duchess of Westminster, who bought him at Goffs, Dublin, as a three-year-old for one thousand, one hundred and fifty guineas. Not over-big and initially slow to mature, he was now held in the highest regard. Dreaper brought him to England to contest his first steeplechase, the Honeybourne Chase at the 1962 Mackeson meeting, which he won effortlessly by 20 lengths, before he returned for the Broadway, the novices' championship.

It wasn't exactly David and Goliath, although the excited crowd that had flocked to the Newbury paddock to drool over The Big Horse couldn't be blamed for thinking of the mouth-watering clash in those terms. Could he be felled with a stone? Surely even a cannonball fired at close range wouldn't upset the giant's stride pattern. After all, hadn't he already shaken fences down to their very roots, yet galloped on, oblivious to the fact that he was defying a lifetime of jumping logic? This was raw power at its most latent and about to be unleashed in the dreary mist of an autumn afternoon in Berkshire.

He had already proved himself at Cheltenham and just in case anyone dared to think of his Gold Cup rout as a flash in the pan, he flashed again at Newbury, as if to let his rival know: 'Move over, you'll have your day, but not when I'm around.' Little did supporters of Mill House know that this would be his last hurrah over Arkle, who would soon be kicking Mill House et al. well and truly out of the way, *en route* to his own Gold Cup glory.

The eager Newbury crowd cheered as the tapes went up and favourite Mill House set off in front, gaining ground at every obstacle. Four fences from home, Pat Taaffe, stalking the leader, decided this was the time to close up and apply some pressure on the leader, almost joining issue. Three out, Taaffe kicked Arkle into the fence. Standing right off it, he over-jumped and slipped on landing, sprawling on all fours and losing all momentum in the process. Mill House, meanwhile, had flown, winging in by eight lengths, leaving the unconsidered Happy Spring to beat the hapless Arkle for second place, both trailing in The Big Horse's impressive wake.

The Dreaper faithful were left scratching their heads, pondering what might have been, but for that crucial mistake. For the Walwyn camp, it was now full steam ahead for Cheltenham and total euphoria for the champion's legion of supporters. With the King George VI Chase and a Gainsborough Chase, despite a bad mistake at the last, in the bag at prohibitive odds against poor opposition in relatively effortless style, it looked plain sailing for The Big Horse, primed for more Gold Cup indulgence – of the Cheltenham kind. After all, who could stop him now?

The postmortem into Arkle's performance at Newbury brought about an interesting tactical review. Never again would Taaffe, by his own admission, try and kick Arkle into a fence. Arkle had become such a fast and economical jumper that he simply didn't need any additional encouragement from the saddle – so much so that he felt that they could now concentrate on using the devastating finishing kick, that they knew the horse possessed, to best advantage.

On the run-up to Cheltenham, the Irish were still pouring fortunes on Arkle, disregarding the Hennessy form, making him their Festival banker. Arkle had been mopping up at home in Ireland, proving himself to be in good nick for the battle ahead. Both camps were talking a good fight, with tactics openly discussed on television by the two jockeys, neither at all bothered about revealing their race tactics ahead of the big day, such was their belief in their respective partners. How things have changed. I cannot imagine Tony McCoy and Mick Fitzgerald sitting down cosily, either individually or together, in a television studio to give their fellow professionals the benefit of their tactical plans. If they ever were to, you could be sure to ignore it anyway – it would only be a smokescreen put up to confuse the enemy!

Only four lined up for the Gold Cup from a dozen entries back in January, with Pas Seul and King's Nephew making up the numbers. Pas Seul, now an eleven-year-old, ridden by Dave Dick, was a 50–1 shot – an incredible reflection on the slump that the 1960 winner was currently in and the superiority of the two fancied runners. Mill House went off the 8–13 favourite, ahead of Arkle at 7–4.

Both looked ready to run for their lives. As good as his word, Robinson took up the running and dictated matters from the outset. Arkle was going well within himself and travelling sweetly for Taaffe as they played cat and mouse for the first two miles of the race, albeit at a fast pace. The other two runners were already struggling to keep up and were left to play for third place, barring mishaps up front. With both seemingly going well within themselves with four to go, Robinson made a concerted effort to shake off the attentions of his stalker, who was still going ominously well and not making any semblance of an error, jumping with tremendous speed and efficiency. However, from here in, the writing looked to be on the wall for Mill House as Arkle cruised up effortlessly to within a length of the leader as they came down to the third last, Taaffe sitting quietly in that rather odd upright way of his. Robinson actually gained some ground here with a prestigious leap that would have shaken off lesser rivals – but not Arkle. Although not as extravagant, he met it in his stride and soon closed up again as they began to turn the final bend, less than a length separating them.

Straightening for home, Mill House was already under pressure and looking one-paced as Taaffe decided now was the time to put some distance between them. Robinson had already gone for his whip and the response was minimal. The champion was a beaten horse with two to go as Taaffe asked Arkle to quicken up on the run to the second last. In the blink of an eye, the new leader was three lengths clear of a floundering Mill House as they approached the last. With the gap between them ever widening, it was only a matter of negotiating the last safely for Arkle to record a memorable win. Meeting the final fence on a perfect stride, Taaffe gathered Arkle up and he strode clear to win comfortably by five lengths from his great rival, who struggled on, albeit at a respectable distance, never looking likely to bridge the gap with the winner.

Arkle had smashed the course record by four seconds and as the two horses stood together, with their jockeys shaking hands in the aftermath of the race, it appeared that the winner was looking down on The Big Horse. Arkle was displaying his habit of holding his head aloft, rather stag-like, in total contrast to Mill House who seemed to have the world on his shoulders, head bowed as he waited patiently for Robinson to point him towards the unsaddling enclosure.

Fulke Walwyn would offer no excuses, graciously acknowledging the winner's wonderful talents. 'At Newbury, Mill House won terribly easily, you know. I think Arkle made the most fantastic improvement between November and the following March.'

Significantly, nearly twenty-five years later, at the Gold Cup celebration in Dublin, Willie Robinson recalled the day his dreams of winning back-to-back Gold Cups went up in smoke. He admitted, 'I knew Arkle was something special, but Mill House did have his problems at that time – he may not have been at his best.'

What exactly were these problems and what did he mean by 'he may not have been at his best'? There was something about Robinson's words that didn't quite gel with Walwyn's post-race statements, extolling the perceived improvement made by Arkle. I have never subscribed to the pathetic fallacy that one horse can break another horse's heart, as Mill House's capitulation has been so often described. Surely a physical problem wouldn't have been beyond the realms of possibility?

It goes without saying that Walwyn was genuinely shocked at Mill House's defeat, but he was not the type of person to make excuses on behalf of his horses. Certainly, with Mill House, for two seasons defeat had rarely come into the equation, so the trainer's reaction was perfectly understandable in the circumstances. That said, it wasn't the done thing for racing journalists of that time even to consider questioning a highly respected trainer such as Walwyn about the wellbeing of a beaten horse, never mind a vanquished Gold Cup favourite. After all, with less than a week to go before the Gold Cup, Walwyn had told Richard Baerlein of *The Observer*, in a Gold Cup feature, that he could not imagine Mill House being beaten.

The apparent discrepancy between jockey and trainer made me ponder if indeed something had been wrong with Mill House in that first Gold Cup which hadn't come to light until a much later date. I can't imagine any journalist, at least not one that wanted to remain in work during in the Arkle era, daring to stand up and question the worth of Arkle's achievement. Suggesting that Arkle had beaten nothing more than a couple of handicappers and not one but two distinctly below-par former Gold Cup winners in Mill House and Pas Seul would have been almost a hanging offence!

In January 2000, Robinson revealed to me what exactly had come to light concerning Mill House's wellbeing and also expanded on his view of that first significant Gold Cup meeting between the two titans of racing. Robinson explained, 'Mill House had leg problems after the Hennessy win in November 1963, but he got over them. He was a horse that took a fair bit of getting fit and his last run, prior to Cheltenham, had been in the Gainsborough Chase at

Sandown in mid-February. Unfortunately, the Gold Cup came a bit too soon for him after that race and we could have done with more time in-between.' I wanted to know if Mill House on 1964 Gold Cup day had felt anything like the horse that he had partnered to glory as a six-year-old only twelve months earlier. Robinson was quite adamant about this. 'No, he didn't give me anything like the same feel against Arkle. They were two great horses, but there should never have been more than necks and head between them in a race.' Robinson continued, 'Much later in his career, Mill House took a heavy fall at Ludlow in 1968. He had suffered back trouble for years before this fall, but the problems were always considered to be of a muscular nature. They turned out to be more serious and were only discovered when he was taken to Newmarket's Equine Research Station, where he underwent a spinal operation. It was discovered that vertebrae in his back were fused together in two different places, which I was told could have been affecting him for many years, especially if pressing against nerves, which would have been a very painful condition.'

According to expert opinion in this field, fused vertebrae can be caused in racehorses by trauma over a number of years and can remain subclinical – in other words, to a degree not detectable by usual clinical methods. Such back problems can remain underlying and only surface in pressure situations. This revealing new slant on Mill House's possible wellbeing, basically through ignorance of the facts at the time, might well have explained Mill House's dramatic fall from grace. His superior jumping skills had always been one of Mill House's great assets, but any underlying problem with his back would have caused this strength to become a weakness, which it clearly was in his Gold Cup defeat in 1964. This might also explain why Robinson's assertion of 'heads and necks only' between the two protaganists became a matter of five lengths in their first Gold Cup meeting.

By the time he met Arkle again in the 1965 Gold Cup, Mill House's condition must have clearly deteriorated, in direct contrast to 'Himself', who was going from strength to strength, with twenty lengths now between the two rivals.

If the necessity for that back operation had come in the earlier stages of Mill House's career, we might well have been treated to some real battles between the two Gold Cup winners. Had Mill House's ongoing leg problems diverted attention away from his chronic back problems? Even nowadays, discovering fused vertebrae remains one of the most difficult areas to detect, as heat-seeking scanning equipment will show up merely muscular and ligament problems and not deep-rooted spinal problems, which require a general anaesthetic before they can be detected.

As it was, with Mill House effectively out of the equation, Arkle ruled the roost, toying with his opposition in the style of a champion.

ARKLE (1964, 1965)

b.g. 1957 (Archive – Bright Cherry)
Owned by Anne, Duchess of Westminster, trained by T.W. Dreaper and ridden by P. Taaffe

1966 and all that

Pat Taaffe had his own ideas about what Arkle would have done had he been allowed by his owner to grace Aintree with his presence. But one thing is certain, Arkle would never have got away there with the sort of blunder that he made at the eleventh fence on St Patrick's Day 1966 during his bid for his third consecutive Gold Cup. The shamrock pinned to his brow band barely moved as he chested the fence with an almighty thump that reverberated around the packed stands. Yet he hardly broke stride. If ever there was an example of perfect balance and harmony between man and horse faced with potential disaster, this was it. For me, only one incident has ever come close to mirroring that extraordinary moment – Desert Orchid's dive through the final fence at Fairyhouse *en route* to a memorable Irish Grand National victory in the hands of Richard Dunwoody. It must have shocked Sir Peter O'Sullevan, too, for as he gathered his thoughts to explain what had just happened, his voice perceptibly changed mid-sentence, adding a touch of Cary Grant to proceedings. There was nothing deliberate or affected about it, and I have not noticed it in any other O'Sullevan race commentary. But it added to the mystery of the moment that Arkle should, according to the laws of gravity, have fallen. 'Another complete circuit – ooooh! And he barely took off at that one, he just looked at it and ignored it – and how he got the other side . . . well, you should have heard the gasp from the crowd here, it looked as though he wasn't going to jump at all. He just ignored the fence completely, and how he got the other side is a mystery.' It was one of those defining moments in racing history and, to be frank, it was the most exciting thing about the race.

Even Arkle must have been getting bored with the lack of opposition and probably spent too long staring at the crowd, losing vital concentration. Taaffe made sure his partner didn't make the same mistake next time round. His starting price of 1–10 said everything about his superiority over his four opponents, who simply had a private battle for second place. One of them, Hunch, had taken a fatal fall three out and David Nicholson's mount, Snaigow, was in such a state of exhaustion that he could barely make it over the line.

With the fickle English weather then playing havoc with Arkle's plans, the decision was made to put him away for the season. He returned for the Hennessy, looking to repeat his victory in the race 12 months earlier. However, vital work had been missed due to a cut picked up schooling over hurdles and he was caught near the finish, trying to give two and a half stone to that useful grey, Stalbridge Colonist. It was back to winning ways at Ascot three weeks later in nothing more than a workout, before the fateful King George VI at Kempton that would end his career.

Frost caused the King George VI to be put back a day and six others lined up, with the dubious pleasure of taking on a fit champion. Arkle wasn't jumping with his usual fluency and on the second circuit made a mistake at the open ditch, clipping the guard rail. Woodland Venture took full advantage of Arkle's mistake and closed up on the leader, Terry Biddlecombe seeming to have plenty of horse under him. However, Woodland Venture over-jumped at the second last and crumpled on landing, seemingly handing the race to Arkle, well clear of the others at the time. But he met the last all wrong and it suddenly became very hard work for Taaffe. Jeff King riding Dormant, a distant second at the last, seized his chance and powered past Arkle as the line approached. Arkle was painfully lame as he stood waiting to be unsaddled and Taaffe knew that this was a serious injury. Arkle had broken down and x-rays showed that he had cracked a pedal bone inside his hoof. It required delicate surgery to save him, but he recovered sufficiently to give at least some hope that he would resume his career. Come the autumn of 1968, those lingering hopes were quashed by the Duchess's announcement that October that Arkle would never race again and he spent his retirement years at the Duchess's farm at Bryanstown, near Maynooth, County Kildare.

However, by the spring of 1970, rheumatism had set into the leg that had been operated on and towards the end he could barely stand. Rather than have him suffer continuous pain, his owner took the only option open to her and Arkle was put down at the age of 13. A premature end to the only horse, at least in the twentieth century, that had a realistic chance of overhauling Golden Miller's record five wins.

With this missed opportunity in mind, there is more than a little irony about the result of the 1969 Gold Cup, that ties in neatly with all the conjecture that raged prior to Arkle's injury. Arkle, then nine years old and having won three Gold Cups already, would realistically have had to win the next three Gold Cups in order to break Golden Miller's record. The 1969 renewal was in fact won by a contemporary of Arkle, the veteran What A Myth, notably 12 years old at the time of his Gold Cup victory. Without wishing to disparage the valiant efforts of the Ryan Price-trained chestnut, it is very likely that if Arkle hadn't been injured, he would have won again that year, possibly achieving the record in the process. One thing's for sure, it didn't happen and we can only ever speculate about what might have been.

ARKLE (1966)

b.g. 1957 (Archive – Bright Cherry)
Owned by Anne, Duchess of Westminster, trained by T.W. Dreaper and ridden by P. Taaffe

✠ 1967 ✠

The lull before the snail

So the Arkle years came to an abrupt and unexpected end, flinging the Gold Cup door unexpectedly wide open in 1967. Mill House, almost inconceivably still only rising ten, would be back again to take on all comers, but he would need to be back to his very best to have a serious chance of regaining his crown.

In the aftermath of Kempton, the whole of Ireland was hoping that Flyingbolt, another of the Dreaper Rolls-Royces, would be a ready-made substitute for Arkle. He had almost stolen Arkle's thunder at Cheltenham, winning the Two Mile Champion Chase by fifteen lengths, before going close the following day in the Champion Hurdle, finishing a gallant third, beaten less than four lengths by Salmon Spray. To be as close as that to achieving an almost impossible double spoke volumes for the amazing versatility of the huge chestnut and it was hardly surprising that he was one of Tom Dreaper's favourite horses. At one time, the Irish handicapper had Flyingbolt a mere two pounds behind Arkle, although this assessment surprised many people, including the man who rode them both. The late Pat Taaffe recalled in his autobiography, *My Life – and Arkle's*, 'I am sure that there was at least a stone between them,' adding, 'Over two miles, of course, it would have been a very much closer thing, but Arkle would still have won.'

Unfortunately, by the end of the year, things also went very wrong for Flyingbolt, who followed up his Cheltenham heroics by winning the Irish Grand National, giving upwards of forty pounds to a field of useful handicappers. He was subsequently found to be suffering from a rare viral infection which affected his withers and limbs. The illness would prevent Flyingbolt from ever contesting a Gold Cup.

So it was left to Dreaper's third string, the nine-year-old Fort Leney, to fill the void left by Arkle and Flyingbolt. A top-class performer in his own right, despite being officially rated some twenty-five pounds behind Arkle, he had been diagnosed earlier in his career as suffering from intermittent heart trouble. Fortunately, the condition never caused a problem in his races and Taaffe always maintained that he never rode a horse that battled like Fort Leney in a finish. A 15-length victory in the Leopardstown Chase would ensure that the bay son of Fortina headed the market come Gold Cup day, with the English challenge led by Lady Weir's grand stamp of a horse, What A Myth.

The spring-like weather had dried the ground out considerably, which would go against Ryan Price's chestnut. Terry Biddlecombe partnered Woodland Venture for his boss Fred Rimell and, although unfancied in the betting, the champion jockey knew that, but for tipping up at the second last, he would have been sitting on a King George VI Chase winner. The all-action grey Stalbridge Colonist, ridden by former champion Stan Mellor, had his supporters, and rightly so. He was capable of harrying any horse out of a race, even the great Arkle, so could never be left out of calculations. With Pat Taaffe and Willie Robinson on the sidelines through injury, Peter McLoughlin and David Nicholson were given a chance to take over on the fancied horses.

Unfortunately, it was to be a red-letter day for neither jockey. Fort Leney almost crashed out at the second fence and was never sighted afterwards. Mill House seemed to be going well enough for Nicholson, until both he and Woodland Venture made a hash of the fence that would be the last second time round. Lucky to survive that mistake, Mill House was still in the lead coming to the final open ditch when he clipped the top and slithered to the ground, leaving Woodland Venture in the lead much earlier than Biddlecombe would have preferred. From the back of the field What A Myth was beginning to stay on under a typically vigorous ride from Paul Kelleway. Meanwhile, Biddlecombe had nicked a couple of lengths on his pursuers but, as he turned into the straight, Stalbridge Colonist began to close him down, the diminutive grey picking up in fine fashion for Mellor. Neck and neck over the second last, it seemed only a matter of time before Stalbridge Colonist would take it up and record a memorable win. He might have headed Woodland Venture over the last, but Biddlecombe got a fantastic response from his partner. Lengthening all the way up the rising ground, Woodland Venture, under a superb drive from Biddlecombe, simply refused to give in and held on to win by three-quarters of a length. What A Myth finished in great style to be a never-nearer third, on ground that clearly didn't suit.

Woodland Venture was owned and bred by Somerset farmer Harry Collins, who had been advised by his friend Harry Dufosee, breeder of the runner-up, to send his mare Woodlander to the sire Eastern Venture. Woodland Venture was the result of that mating and it was also Dufosee who suggested the ex-point-to-pointer should go to a 'proper' racing yard, such as the Rimells at Kinnersley. The combination of the bold-jumping Woodland Venture, only a seven-year-old, and the fearless Biddlecombe looked sure to dominate future Gold Cups. But it wasn't to be. Woodland Venture missed the following season completely through injury and never contested another Gold Cup. In the summer of 1969, Woodland Venture was found dead in his owner's paddock. A postmortem revealed internal haemorrhaging as the cause of death.

WOODLAND VENTURE (1967)

b.g. 1960 (Eastern Venture – Woodlander)
Owned by Mr H. Collins, trained by T.F. Rimel and ridden by T. Biddlecombe

✢ 1968 ✢

Leney's all heart, but look out for the snail trail

Normal service was resumed at Cheltenham once more, with the Dreaper and Taaffe combination coming up trumps for their fourth win in five years. In truth, it had been a trying season for national hunt racing in Britain, following a serious outbreak of foot-and-mouth disease in October. All racing was cancelled from the end of November for approximately six weeks, which meant no King George VI Chase. The restriction of movement on horses stabled in those infected areas was lifted only days before the National Hunt Festival.

Nevertheless, there were one or two decent prospects coming through the ranks to challenge the more established stars and Bob Turnell had high hopes that The Laird would emulate Pas Seul by winning the Gold Cup as a seven-year-old. The attractive brown gelding had been impressing in recent weeks, winning the Gainsborough Chase by a length and a half from Mill House who, it must be said, was having one of his poorest seasons, having fallen twice already. Things weren't going to get any better for the old warrior Mill House.

There had been considerable doubts concerning the participation of Fort Leney because of the unusually hard ground. However, the rains came just in time for the Irish raider and he took his place among the disappointing field of only five runners. Mill House, reunited with his old ally Willie Robinson, went straight for the jugular from the off, running with the sort of zest that he had shown for David Nicholson in the 1967 Whitbread. Still going well going out on the final circuit, he reached the open ditch after the water and simply ignored it, giving Willie Robinson a nasty fall on the other side of the fence. Mill House's not wholly unexpected departure could have left Pat Taaffe with a slight dilemma, not wanting to be left in front too early. He needn't have worried on that score, as Jeff King rousted The Laird up to challenge.

In behind, Terry Biddlecombe, having taken over from Stan Mellor on Stalbridge Colonist, now had his chance to frank that form. He began to ask for an effort from the brave grey and the response was immediate, closing right up on the two leaders as they approached the third last. Only a length separated all three as they approached the second last, where Biddlecombe did well to stay in the saddle, losing vital momentum which would probably cost him any chance of winning. The Laird looked to be going like the winner coming to the last, but the canny Taaffe had kept a little bit up his sleeve and, landing upsides at the last, began to get down to work on Fort Leney, in his own inimitable, arm-waving style. Two lengths down with one hundred yards to go, King galvanised The Laird into one last-ditch effort, which would have succeeded in another twenty yards. But Fort Leney, brave as a lion, kept finding a bit more and stuck his neck out to hang on by a fast-diminishing neck. The unlucky Stalbridge

Colonist had battled his heart out to finish only a length behind at the line.

There was a certain irony about the manner of Taaffe's victory. He had been criticised for his 'amateurish-looking' riding style for twenty years, yet here he had beaten one of the strongest finishers, Jeff King. It would have been a joy to see Jeff King ride against the likes of Peter Scudamore and in particular Tony McCoy. Both King, and indeed Bobby Beasley, seemed to have the ability to get a horse, even a reluctant one, running and jumping for them without any great effort. Although King never became champion jockey, his name is usually one of the first mentioned when his contemporaries are asked to name the best jockeys of their era.

Fort Leney's win here had been his first on British soil and his consistency won him 14 of his 27 races. Unfortunately, he broke down badly at Fairyhouse in November and never raced again, returning to his owner's Oxfordshire Stud, where he survived until the ripe old age of 26. Fort Leney was the last of Tom Dreaper's incredible five Gold Cup successes over a period of some twenty-two years. Dreaper might only have wanted to train around thirty horses at Greenogue at any one time, but nevertheless he produced a constant flow of top-class performers, year after year. Like all great trainers, his attention to detail was a crucial factor in his success: his tried and tested method of schooling his horses on a regular basis, believing this to be a prerequisite for realising potential and afterwards maintaining it, paid dividends for him. It obviously worked – a glance at the Dreaper record tells its own story. Apart from the five Cheltenham Gold Cups, he won no less than ten Irish Grand Nationals and every Gold Cup on offer in England, at least once. In 1975, having already handed the reins to his son Jim following ill health, he was able to enjoy seeing Jim follow in his footsteps by winning the Gold Cup with Ten Up. He died a month later a proud man.

There had been another Irish performance of note earlier in the week, L'Escargot winning a division of the Gloucestershire Hurdle. In two years, he would be lining up in Gold Cups – and winning them. But for now, he continued to mop up as a top-class hurdler in the capable hands of one of Ireland's best trainers, Dan Moore.

FORT LENEY (1968)

b.g. 1958 (Fortina – Leney Princess)
Owned and bred by Col. J. Thomson, trained by T.W. Dreaper and ridden by P. Taaffe

✛ 1969 ✛

What a way to bow out

Heavy ground was the order of the day for the whole of the National Hunt Festival, in stark contrast to the previous season. It had been the same story throughout the entire winter whenever racing did take place – which wasn't very often, with almost a hundred meetings lost to frost, snow and flooding.

Cometh the rain, cometh the man and when conditions demanded strength in the saddle and an unquenchable spirit, Paul Kelleway was the sort of jockey you wanted on your side. One of the hard men of the weighing room, Kelleway knew What A Myth like the back of his hand. He won the 1966 Whitbread Gold Cup on the giant chestnut and came third, beaten by less than three lengths, in the 1967 Gold Cup on ground that was clearly not soft enough. But could What A Myth possibly turn back the clock and become only the second twelve-year-old chestnut to win the Gold Cup, following Silver Fame's sterling efforts for Lord Bicester back in 1951?

In his favour, What A Myth was trained by a man who seemed capable of just about anything – or so racing's rulers thought anyway! Captain Ryan Price had, in his time, come through a number of scrapes with the authorities. The Captain, as he was known, had been disqualified from training in February 1964 for the rest of that season because of his handling of Rosyth, winner of the Schweppes Trophy. Banned in true kangeroo court fashion because, according to the Captain, 'It is a crime to improve a horse and a far bigger crime to win too many races.' What A Myth was among the horses forced to leave the Captain's historic Sussex base of Findon temporarily in 1964, but within three years Price had bounced back to win two further trainers' titles to add to the two he had won pre-Rosyth.

What A Myth had become one of the stable stalwarts, but was generally considered to be just short of top-class. A greater problem seemed to be that he had lost his way over the past two seasons, since his Gold Cup third. In fact, at the beginning of the season the Captain had advised the owner, Lady Weir, that it would be a good idea to try to rekindle her horse's enthusiasm by sending him hunting with the Quorn in Leicestershire. He showed enough in two hunter chases prior to the Festival and, guaranteed his favoured bottomless ground, was given the green light to take his chance.

The fancied runners include Playlord, winner of the Great Yorkshire Chase and the horse that put Gordon Richards on the map as a trainer. Joint-favourite with The Laird on the day was Domacorn, an ex-point-to-pointer, formerly trained by Harry Dufosee and recently switched to Kinnersley. Switched back to fences from hurdles, the strongly-built, almost black novice had been a revelation in recent weeks, winning on the soft at Ascot and Newbury. He thoroughly deserved his place at the head of the market, although he was still inclined to take the odd chance at his fences.

In an eventful race, one of the outsiders, Dicky May, brought down The Laird at the eighth fence. It wasn't long before Stalbridge Colonist, back running his third and final Gold Cup, came to grief at the tenth. Clearing four out, Kelleway decided to take the bull by the horns and test his rivals' stamina, setting What A Myth alight coming down to the third last. What A Myth responded to his rider's urgings and began to stretch clear on the turn for home. Using the chestnut's long loping stride to great effect and coming to the second last, the leader had only Domacorn to worry about. Again, Kelleway kicked his willing partner into orbit from outside the wings of the fence. At this point, Domacorn blundered badly and almost lost Terry Biddlecombe out of the back door as he struggled to recover his balance. Crucially, he lost his whip in the process and it took the jockey vital seconds to get the partnership going again. Kelleway asked his old friend for one final effort at the last, which they cleared in good style to hold on in fine style from Domacorn by a length and a half, with Playlord plugging on a distant third.

That mistake at the second last probably cost Domacorn his chance of gaining Gold Cup glory and it also ruined owner Bryan Jenks's chances of a remarkable treble at the meeting, having won two earlier races with Normandy and Coral Diver.

It had been a brave performance from horse and jockey and What A Myth was immediately and deservedly retired after the race. Paul Kelleway, who died in April 1999 from cancer, was a man of many words – including a few unprintable ones! After going on to win two consecutive Champion Hurdles teaming up with Bula, he went on train at Newmarket with great success on the flat. He became known as 'Pattern Race Paul', mainly because of his fearless attitude towards aiming his horses at the best races, even when it appeared on the book that they had very little chance. An example of typical Kelleway wit was his famous description of Newmarket in winter, succinctly summed up in just one word – Siberia. They broke the mould with P.A. Kelleway.

WHAT A MYTH (1969)

ch.g. 1957 (Coup de Myth – What A Din)
Owned by Lady Weir, trained by H.R. Price and ridden by P.A. Kelleway

✛ 1970, 1971 ✛
The Snail on the Festival roundabout

One name you can be sure that everyone remembers from the Cheltenham Festivals of the early '70s is L'Escargot. He didn't do too badly at Aintree either, interrupting the winning sequence of a certain Grand National institution. However, even if the chestnut had finished stone last in every one of the 60 races he actually contested, he would have always been guaranteed a following. As it was, his moniker matched his breeding, but belied his fleet of foot. He was a seriously talented horse – do all winning snails train on Guinness?

Dan Moore's charge had speed to burn as a youngster and proved it on his first Festival visit in 1968, winning the equivalent of the Supreme Novices' Hurdle, known then as the Gloucester Hurdle. He was still showing his paces eight Festivals later, running a highly creditable fifth in the Two Mile Champion Chase – his prep race for Aintree! L'Escargot was bought for three thousand guineas at Ballsbridge by Tom Cooper of the British Bloodstock Agency (Ireland) on behalf of Raymond Guest, the millionaire American Ambassador to Ireland. Larger than life, Guest was no stranger to success, as Larkspur had won him the 1962 Derby and Sir Ivor had followed up in the 1968 Derby, both trained by Vincent O'Brien. Guest, a keen sportsman himself, naturally wanted to emulate Dorothy Paget by taking all three 'majors' and turned to Moore – who, by coincidence, had significant links with D.P. during neutral Ireland's racing through the war years – to do the necessary. A classic case of Dan's your man. In fact, Moore had gone within a whisker of winning a Grand National himself, as a jockey. Riding Royal Danieli, he just lost out in a driving finish to a young Bruce Hobbs on the American-owned Battleship. So it was a bit of a retrieval mission anyway for Moore himself, as much as satisfying Guest's almost carnal desire to pillage jump racing's crown jewels.

So Moore set about educating the young snail with attitude. L'Escargot was in luck. A young jockey had rejoined Moore's Fairyhouse yard in 1961 and it was he who would partner the chestnut gelding in the majority of his races over his ten seasons of combat. Tommy Carberry had been twice champion flat apprentice before he returned to the Moores, where he had learnt to ride as a schoolboy some years earlier. Moore's stable jockey at that time was Willie Robinson, but he was soon to leave to join Fulke Walwyn. Within a year, Carberry, at only 21, was made Moore's stable jockey. In time, he would become his employer's son-in-law, marrying daughter Pamela and starting the Carberry dynasty that would end the century with a family victory in the 1999 Grand National.

The four-year-old L'Escargot had been broken in and was prepared for a bumper at Navan in February 1967, ridden by a little-known English amateur, who had been learning the ropes with Dan Moore and who would go on to train with great success in Newmarket. That amateur was Ben Hanbury, who won that initial bumper and partnered him again to his second win later in the year.

L'Escargot was switched to hurdles and Carberry began to cement their illustrious partnership, the season's highlight being the Cheltenham win. After being hobdayed the following season in order to rectify a wind problem, L'Escargot won impressively at Leopardstown prior to returning to Cheltenham to contest the 1969 Champion Hurdle. At his best when the mud was flying, he was the only horse backed to beat Persian War, but couldn't trouble the champion, finishing a remote sixth. Switching to fences less than three weeks after Cheltenham, L'Escargot began competing against more experienced performers at Fairyhouse and was not disgraced when beaten by Kinloch Brae, the impressive Cathcart Chase winner at Cheltenham.

L'Escargot showed that this new sphere would be his forte as he followed up with two useful wins in the space of two weeks, before the ebullient Guest decided it was time for L'Escargot to have a crack at two top races in America, a fortnight apart. He duly obliged in the first of the two races, at Belmont Park. Unfortunately, there were problems with L'Escargot for the second. Dan Moore's wife, Joan, remembers the time all too clearly. 'Checking L'Escargot over the night before the race, we discovered he was lame. We tried everything but it was a lost cause as far as the race was concerned. He was as right as rain within twenty-four hours and I can still remember the feeling of dread having to tell Mr Guest that his horse was unable to run. Not the most tolerant of men, he was actually quite a frightening person to confront, especially with such bad news. What made it worse was that we were in America, in his back yard. I remember he was not best pleased!'

That setback clearly didn't put Guest off too much, though, as L'Escargot was back to Belmont Park in the autumn, finishing a creditable third before returning once more to Ireland to continue novice chasing. Guest was keen to see L'Escargot run in the Gold Cup, though taking an easier option would have made more sense at this stage of his development. In all the chestnut's races throughout the build-up to Cheltenham there was cause for serious doubts about him seeing the trip out. However, nothing would deter Guest, although Moore would have preferred to take in the Two Mile Champion Chase or a two-and-a-half-mile race instead. L'Escargot had won twice, including a good effort to win the Wills Pemier Chase Finala at Haydock, but, in truth, he hadn't set the world alight up to this point. To say a Gold Cup challenge was optimistic at this stage of his career was an understatement and his odds of 33–1 totally reflected this.

The main Irish Gold Cup challenge was expected to come from Kinloch Brae, a seven-year-old owned by Anne, Duchess of Westminster. He had looked more than useful against decent opposition, but the acid test would be at Cheltenham. Trained by Edward O'Grady's father, Willie, he had won the Gainsborough Chase at Sandown, giving five pounds and a ten-length drubbing to none other than The Laird, a useful yardstick, although possibly past his best. The English challenge was headed by the seven-year-old Spanish Steps, owned and trained by wheelchair-bound Edward Courage. Spanish Steps had run away with the novice's Gold Cup at the last National Hunt Meeting and vied for Gold Cup favouritism with Kinloch Brae. Another young top gun to consider was The Dikler, an ex-point-to-pointer bequeathed to Mrs Peggy August in her uncle's estate. The Dikler would become a Gold Cup standing dish, running for the next seven years consecutively

– more than any other in the entire history of the Gold Cup. The seventeen hands, hard-pulling bundle of energy was causing quite a stir wherever he went, with his devil-may-care style of running that was guaranteed to raise the pulse.

This would be Pat Taaffe's tenth and final Gold Cup in a remarkable career in the saddle that was shortly to come to an end before training beckoned. Taaffe was to bow out here on another Irish raider, French Tan, Kelso Stewart's strapping eight-year-old who had been busy rattling up an impressive hat trick. Among his latest victims at Ascot was none other than the veteran Flyingbolt, the former Dreaper star returning from injury and now trained by Ken Oliver in Hawick.

It promised to be a wonderful renewal, but somehow the race itself didn't quite live up to expectations. Titus Oates, the King George winner, led for well over a circuit with Timmy Hyde tracking him on board the favourite Kinloch Brae, who was jumping like a buck and thoroughly enjoying himself. As they went down the far side for the final time, Hyde must have thought that he would follow in the footsteps of his father, who had steered the magnificent Prince Regent home back in 1946, and complete a unique father and son double. However, Taaffe had other ideas and took Hyde on at the third last, the fence which has changed the outcome of so many Gold Cups! Kinloch Brae found the sudden attentions of French Tan too much to bear and crashed to the ground, leaving French Tan ahead of L'Escargot, with the rest of the field well in arrears. There wasn't much between the two leaders over the last two fences, if anything French Tan landed marginally in front, but it was L'Escargot who got away from the last the quicker and despite hanging towards the stands side, Carberry was always holding Taaffe on French Tan. L'Escargot ran on well to win by a length and a half, despite putting his head slightly in the air – a habit that would stay with him throughout his career. Spanish Steps plugged on to take third, without ever looking like getting into the race.

Twelve months later, L'Escargot, The Dikler and Herring Gull apart, faced a totally different field with Kinloch Brae and French Tan both out injured. Kinloch Brae had developed leg trouble and had been sent to Toby Balding in England, who only managed to get one run into the ante-post favourite, the John Bull at Wincanton in late February. He managed to win the race, but unfortunately finished lame and his season was over there and then. Spanish Steps never got as far as the declaration stage, as the Courages managed to mix up his name with that of another horse in their stable, having submitted their Gold Cup entry to Weatherbys! Dan Moore, after a mainly frustrating season of falls and disappointments with L'Escargot, had finally managed to recapture some of the chestnut's better form with a promising third under top weight at Leopardstown in February. He would be cherry-ripe for the Gold Cup and was bracketed on 7–2 with Leap Frog and Into View.

Little did he know it, but Fred Winter's disastrous run with Gold Cup favourites would begin here. The Uplands challenger, Into View, had looked a useful tool, having beaten the new Dreaper hope, Leap Frog, at Ascot over a shorter trip. The eight-year-old, unplaced in the Champion Hurdle two years earlier, would have his stamina tested to the full over the Gold Cup trip, particularly on the prevailing dead ground. Leap Frog had followed in L'Escargot's footsteps and won this season's Embassy Premier Chase Final at Haydock. Still only seven years old, Leap Frog was flying high here, but had struck up a good partnership with his young jockey, Val O'Brien. A third Irish challenger was the talented mare Glencaraig Lady, another second season chaser and not unfancied behind the principals at 7–1.

A depleted field of only eight faced the starter and it was the Francis Flood-trained mare that made the first decisive move in the race. Jumping with rare gusto, she had the majority of her opponents in trouble with four to go. Coming to the third last still full of running, Glencaraig Lady crashed to the ground, leaving her jockey Bobby Coonan wondering what might have been. Much as with Kinloch Brae 12 months ago, her departure left two horses clear of their field. But this time, it was L'Escargot in front, with Leap Frog his only challenger. Carberry always knew he had plenty in hand on his less experienced rival toiling in his wake and pushed L'Escargot out to a famous victory by ten lengths with The Dikler a further 15 lengths behind in a remote third.

Carberry, speaking about the race in Dublin some thirty years on, recalled, 'L'Escargot was without doubt the best horse I ever rode. He won every chase that he could when he came to England and his second Gold Cup win was much easier than the first, he won it quite smoothly.'

Moore would have L'Escargot back in good shape for the hat trick bid next season, a chance to emulate the mighty Arkle. There was no doubting the standing of the home of national hunt racing in Arthur Moore's affections. It was a place of inspiration for him. In the *Irish Horseman* in the early '70s, he enthused, 'Ever since I went to Cheltenham as a spectator to watch the tremendous race between Golden Miller and Thomond, Cheltenham has been my ideal racecourse. I have always had wonderful luck there, which has continued down through the years.' Sadly, bearing in mind the saga of Tied Cottage, a quick look in a future Moore's almanac would have told him that any continuation of the Cheltenham luck was about to come to an abrupt end.

L'ESCARGOT (1970 AND 1971)

ch.g. 1963 (Escart III – What A Daisy)
Owned by Mr R.R. Guest, trained by D.L. Moore and ridden by T. Carberry

✛ 1972 ✛

The Winter years

The beaten favourite for the 1971 Gold Cup, Into View, had set the Uplands ball rolling. For the next seven years, that ball careered out of control, as the destiny of the Gold Cup seemed to revolve year after year, almost exclusively, around the fortunes of Uplands – the Upper Lambourn yard of one F.T. Winter.

It had been eight years since the former champion jockey had taken the plunge into the often frustrating world of training hurdlers and steeplechasers. If anyone could make a go of it, it was Fred Winter. It didn't take the iron man of jump racing long to carve out a new career at Uplands. Andrew Sim in *English Racing Stables* describes the former flat racing yard's amazing transformation under Winter.

> When Winter first moved into the yard, in the summer of 1964, it was a mess but, characteristically, Uplands' new guvnor could see that, underneath the weeds and the broken glass, lay a potentially top-class training establishment. After all, just next door, on a similarly sized plot of land, was one of the most successful jumping yards of the time, Saxon House, the source of Fred Winter's great Gold Cup triumph on Mandarin, and from where, only a few months earlier, Fulke Walwyn had sent out the great Team Spirit, to win the Grand National. Incredibly, the very next year, Winter's fledgling team trumped the exploits of 'over the wall', as the lads nicknamed Saxon House, with the performance of the American horse, Jay Trump, in the 1965 Grand National. The rest is jumping history: after winning the National again the next year with Anglo, Winter went on to collect just about every top prize in the calendar and established Uplands as the leading National Hunt yard of its day. It is an unlikely setting for such honours. Although Fred Winter expanded Uplands' capacity to sixty boxes, in comparison with the great training establishments of the flat there is nothing which sets the yard apart from the ordinary (apart, that is, from that intangible atmosphere, which comes from association with great sporting success). Like all the other yards in Upper Lambourn, there is very little space for manoeuvre and few private facilities.

A quick glance at entry 625 in the timeless 1972 *Horses In Training* reads like an equine *Who's Who* of jump racing. Nestling opposite the entry for W. Clout, Chantilly, lies the list of 43 horses under the watchful eye of Winter. Clout is a word that springs to mind when you study the endless list of owners at the bottom of the Winter page, headed by none other than the Duke of Alburquerque and ending with Mr and Mrs E.H. Vestey – both owners, as you would expect with a stable like Uplands, linked with Aintree and Cheltenham. Sonny Somers might have been only a spring chicken of ten, but the class of performer further down the Uplands list is staggering. Into View apart, the names roll off the tongue, even nearly 30 years on – Crisp, Bula, Pendil, Killiney and last, but definitely not least, Lanzarote. Some became champions, others failed gloriously, but all were major Uplands players and fuelled the hopes of Gold Cup success over the coming years.

In November, despite a comfortable win over Kempton's easy three miles, Fred Winter decided that Into View would miss the Gold Cup this season, believing that the doubtful stayer wouldn't be good enough to take on his likely representative, Crisp. Bula had already won his second Champion Hurdle under Paul Kelleway and now it was the turn of Richard Pitman to see if he could add the first sponsored Gold Cup, by Piper Heidsieck, to Crisp's two-mile Champion Chase win at the Festival last year. The near seventeen hands gelding had been bred by his owner, Sir Chester Manifold, in Australia and had already captured the hearts of jumping enthusiasts across the world, winning the Melbourne Cup Chase and the Carolina Hunt Cup at Camden before joining Winter.

Crisp had been the ante-post favourite back in November, but the Irish had punted Leap Frog heavily to go one better this year and he was as low as 3–1 at one stage over the winter. Nevertheless, by the time they reached the post, Crisp was back at the head of the market with L'Escargot, bidding for a hat trick of wins in the race, at 4–1 with Leap Frog. The Irish had a third contender in Glencaraig Lady, a tough little mare, barely sixteen hands high, who had been unlucky in the two previous Festivals, falling on both occasions, latterly in the previous year's Gold Cup when still only seven years old. The mare had been plagued by training problems throughout her career, having chipped a bone in her knee on only her second start in a Dundalk bumper (this floating chip was never operated on, but necessitated hours of walking and trotting at home). She had been bought cheaply, for only eight hundred guineas, in a private sale by trainer Francis Flood, champion Irish amateur on numerous occasions when assisting Paddy Sleator, who had trained the 1960 Champion Hurdle winner, Another Flash.

Fred Winter decided that because of the prevailing soft ground, Crisp would be held up to get the trip. Unfortunately, Crisp resented the restraining tactics that prevented him from running his usual bold race from the front. He still had a slim chance with two to go but the damage had been done and he sulked to finish a well-beaten fifth. He was to show his flair and courage at Aintree the following year, a race that he will be remembered for as much as Red Rum snatching it in the shadow of the post.

In one of the best finishes for years, The Dikler led over the last, ahead of Glencaraig Lady, with the hope of the West Country, Royal Toss, trained by wholesale butcher Tim Handel and ridden by Nigel Wakley, coming with a strong late challenge. Glencaraig Lady gradually pegged The Dikler as the huge gelding began to roll around in front. With Royal Toss gaining on the mare as the line approached, she hung on to her narrow lead in gamest fashion to win by three quarters of a length from Royal Toss and The Dikler, separated by only a head at the finish.

The mare, a daughter of Fortina, broke down yards from the line and subsequently never ran again. Her jockey Frank Berry, only 20 years old and on his first visit to Cheltenham, had given the brave mare a memorable ride and had shown the utmost coolness under pressure. Surviving a stewards' inquiry and an objection to the winner by Nigel Wakley, Glencaraig Lady was declared the winner. The stylish Berry had shot to fame by winning the Irish St Leger for the President of Ireland, on Giolla Mear, before weight necessitated a switch to the jumps. Glencaraig Lady went straight to the paddocks, but passed on to her progeny not one iota of her brilliance and indeed suffered many barren years.

GLENCARAIG LADY (1972)

ch.m. 1964 (Fortina – Luckibash)
Owned by Mr P. Doyle, trained by F. Flood and ridden by F. Berry

✣ 1973 ✣

The horny problem of Pendil

It is strange to think that Pendil, the undisputed king of the Uplands chasers and odds-on favourite for the 1973 Gold Cup, had, less than four years earlier, been an ordinary hurdler doing the rounds of the northern circuit. It sounds like he was quite at home at the Macdonalds', especially as they trained on a farm! A whippet-like bay, with a pair of small horns on his forehead, he probably wasn't even anything special in their six-horse stable in Wetherby. He won an egg-and-spoon hurdle at Catterick before being snapped up by Fred Winter at Ascot Sales. Transformed at Uplands, Pendil won six hurdles in his first season and continued in the same vein over fences, taking the Arkle Chase at the previous season's Festival. He looked every inch the part, brushing opponents aside with a sort of swagger in the manner of an equine John McEnroe, with the talent and temperament to match. He had beaten The Dikler comfortably in the King George VI at Kempton and he then showed his versatility a month before Cheltenham by thrashing some top-class two-milers at their own game, namely Tingle Creek and Inkslinger. His next outing, back at Kempton, was a formality and he looked nailed on to take the Gold Cup and was backed accordingly.

Over the wall at Saxon House, Fulke Walwyn was double-handed with two veritable giants of jump racing, The Dikler and Charlie Potheen, a failed point-to-pointer who had blossomed into a talented if totally unpredictable character since arriving at Lambourn. Terry Biddlecombe had been booked to ride Charlie Potheen and with stable jockey Barry Brogan having left to return to Ireland due to ill health, a strong jockey was needed for The Dikler. Biddlecombe suggested Ron Barry, then current champion jockey, and the new partnership was formed.

Eight runners went to post with Pendil a very warm favourite at 4–6, ahead of the two Walwyn runners. As expected on the fast ground, Charlie Potheen set a blistering gallop from the start, with Pitman attempting to settle Pendil as best as he could, aware that his partner had never been the Gold Cup distance before. Over the third last and coming round the final turn, the leader began to send out distress signals and conversely Pendil came through swinging on the bridle, full of running. As he fell away, Charlie Potheen hung as usual to his left, interfering with The Dikler, as Ron Barry weaved through to make his challenge. Pendil sailed over the penultimate fence and quickened a couple of lengths clear on the run to the last. With Pendil pricking his ears, Pitman chose to steady him and not risk going long at the last. In hindsight, it was probably a decision that cost him the race. Although he cleared the last adequately and at least three lengths clear, Pendil had lost vital momentum, which gave The Dikler the chance he needed. Barry went for broke at the final fence and The Dikler responded with a fantastic leap and, landing running, began to reel the leader in. Halfway up the run-in, Pitman realised the danger coming on his left and frantically tried to urge Pendil to quicken one final time. With his stick flailing like a windmill, Pitman did all he could in the circumstances but Pendil had hit a brick wall of sound that now surrounded him as he neared the line. Pendil seemed to freeze momentarily and The Dikler, finishing like the proverbial tank, gained the advantage some twenty yards from the line and held on in a finish of bobbing heads to gain the most unlikely of victories by a short head.

The Dikler had thoroughly deserved his win in his fourth Gold Cup appearance, which could so easily have been his second victory in the race, many observers believing that he could easily have won last year's race if Barry Brogan hadn't gone for home as early as he did. Probably more incredible than this victory was The Dikler's record of seven consecutive Gold Cup appearances, which will stand forever. He might not have been the greatest Gold Cup winner of all time, or even his own era, but he was certainly one of the most exciting to watch – and probably ride!

L'Escargot had run in his fourth consecutive Gold Cup and looked to be finished as a top-class performer. But there was life in the old dog yet, as he proved at Aintree, finishing a fine second in 1974. Incredibly, when he ran in the Two Mile Champion Chase in 1975, it would be his eighth successive Festival appearance, and although he came fifth, L'Escargot proved the range of his ability by crowning a fantastic career by going on to win the Grand National, beating the hat trick-seeking Red Rum at the ripe old age of 12. He was retired immediately by his proud owner.

Ron Barry will always be remembered for the fantastic ride he gave The Dikler here, a race he would never have been allowed to ride nowadays, with stricter medical supervision, quite rightly now the order of the day. Barry, from County Limerick and tough as old boots, was intent on taking his chance, whatever the pain. In a strange way, the injury might have helped secure the unlikely victory, as he found himself having to let The Dikler, the epitome of a hard puller, have his head as soon as the race commenced. The talented ex-point-to-pointer settled as he never had before and the rest is history. I bet Richard Pitman still shakes his head in disbelief, if he can bring himself to watch the race video at all. It didn't seem possible that Pendil could be beaten as he cleared the last. The Uplands Gold Cup hoodoo wouldn't end – as least not yet.

THE DIKLER (1973)

b.g. 1963 (Vulgan – Coronation Day)
Owned by Mrs D. August, trained by F. Walwyn and ridden by R. Barry

✚ 1974 ✚

Captain, my Captain

Ever the realist, Fred Winter, when asked how good Pendil was before his narrow defeat, had declared, 'You don't believe you have a horse good enough to win Gold Cups – you have got to wait until it's over before he has proved it.' Winter could do no more than have Pendil in great shape for another crack at the Blue Riband. He had only been beaten a whisker in course record time and was again unbeaten in the run-up to Cheltenham, having twice thrashed The Dikler in recent months, latterly in the King George VI at Kempton, beating his rival from 'over the wall' by no less than 32 lengths.

Uplands might well have been double-handed in the race but for the fatal fall of their star novice, Killiney, at Ascot in April. The seven-year-old, known as 'The Gentle Giant', had been quoted as low as 7–1 for this Gold Cup after he had routed the opposition in the three mile Tote Champion Novices' Chase, his eighth win on the reel over fences. So Pendil had his chance to prove himself, on the day an even stronger odds-on favourite than he had been 12 months ago.

They were a few days to remember, not only for the racing but also for the weather, which was glorious for the time of year. Basking in sunshine, the first-day crowd enjoyed the opening day Champion Hurdle win for Lord Howard de Walden, with his home-bred Lanzarote, giving Richard Pitman the chance of landing a famous double for Uplands. The Dikler was back again to cross swords with Pendil and was joined by his stable-companions, Charlie Potheen and Game Spirit. The latter, owned by the Queen Mother, was ridden by Terry Biddlecombe, who was looking to complete a memorable last day in the saddle by going out in a blaze of glory on a royal winner. The Irish had high hopes for their novice Captain Christy, ridden by Bobby Beasley. An unruly individual in his early days, Captain Christy was ridden in early hurdle races by his eccentric owner Major Joe Pidcock, who won only once in six attempts on his pride and joy, even getting run out with on one occasion at Limerick. He was then switched to Pat Taaffe for a hefty ten thousand pounds. Not surprisingly, he was dubbed a 'Jekyll and Hyde' character by the English press, which was a pretty accurate assessment of his rather in and out performances. Even Pat Taaffe used to struggle to keep him on an even keel at home – Captain Christy actually managed to hospitalise three of Taaffe's work-riders during one of his mad spells. Reformed alcoholic Bobby Beasley, former stable jockey at Uplands, then entered the equation and, with the headstrong gelding now in very strong and capable hands, they struck up an instant rapport, which would ultimately give Beasley hope that he could achieve another Gold Cup success after a yawning 15-year gap.

It was a strange race which revolved around the dramatic fall of the 100–1 outsider High Ken at the notorious downhill fence three out. Pendil, said by

Pitman to be 'simply cantering at the time', was in the wrong place at the wrong time and was brought down. Whether it is a case of being clever with hindsight, you can't be sure, but both jockeys that went on to fight out the finish have since professed they were fearful of tracking High Ken, particularly coming down to that tricky fence. Perhaps that was the difference between Bobby Beasley and others: the best know instinctively where to be in a race, reducing the risks. Captain Christy looked all over the winner from that point and would have won easily but for a monumental blunder of Captain Christy proportions at the last. Fortunately, Beasley knew what to expect there, too, sitting tight and recovering to power past The Dikler up the hill to win by five lengths going away.

Although he wasn't sure at the time, Pitman would be back to try again next year, but not riding Pendil. He broke down badly prior to Cheltenham, but made a brief and successful comeback two years later. With a third attempt at the Gold Cup very much on the cards, he injured himself, slipping and damaging his neck on the way to the gallops. The decision was made to retire the unlucky Pendil.

Captain Christy had become the first novice to win the Gold Cup since Mont Tremblant 22 years earlier. He was exceptional; his record over hurdles proved that he was top-class in that sphere, too – he might well have been the first horse to do the Champion Hurdle/Gold Cup double. Beasley blamed himself for giving his mount too much to do in the 1973 Champion Hurdle, getting involved in the race far too late, yet finishing a close third, beaten only just over three lengths by Comedy Of Errors.

Captain Christy was to return a strong favourite for the Gold Cup in 12 months' time, in an attempt to emulate L'Escargot. He did look an outstanding prospect to go on and achieve at least another win in the race, possibly more. Some of his supporters at the time believed that he had the potential to become even greater than Arkle – blasphemous thoughts indeed.

Despite the disappointment over Pendil, Winter at least had the satisfaction of ending the season as leading trainer, amassing some eighty-nine winners with prize money of over a hundred thousand pounds. Fulke Walwyn was second in the trainers' table on the sixty-five mark. Uplands would have their dual former champion hurdler Bula to try and break the Gold Cup sequence.

CAPTAIN CHRISTY (1974)

b.g. 1967 (Mon Capitaine – Christy's Bow)
Owned by Mrs J.M.A. Samuel, trained by P. Taaffe and ridden by H. Beasley

✢ 1975 ✢

Hellcatmudwrestlers' paradise

In the light of some impressive performances in recent years, this particular renewal, as a spectacle, was a bit of a disaster. Noah came, parked his ark, and went after the first race. Even the horses came into the paddock two by two! Pat Taaffe noted in his memoirs, 'If I have one dream it is that one day, I shall school and train an Arkle of my own.'

Even Arkle would have struggled to excel in the conditions that faced Captain Christy and the seven other unfortunates – well, six, in fact. On paper there was only one horse that would positively revel in the sloppiest mudbath in living memory and that was Ten Up. The eight-year-old bay gelding was certainly no stranger to Cheltenham, having won last season's Sun Alliance Chase on good ground. Ten Up was clearly adaptable and didn't need to have it hock deep to produce the goods at top level, but he preferred it when the mud was flying. Trained by Jim Dreaper, who had taken over at the helm at Greenogue, Ten Up had been bought as a three-year-old by Dreaper senior for five and a half thousand guineas at Goffs for Anne, Duchess of Westminster. Jim Dreaper had ridden Ten Up to victory on his racecourse debut and the headstrong Ten Up proved to be an extremely slow learner when switched to fences as a six-year-old. Dreaper had been appalled by the novice's inability to fence properly and set about the task of schooling Ten Up, in the best Greenogue tradition. His Sun Alliance win had confirmed him as a potential Gold Cup winner and the conditions on Gold Cup day tipped the scales firmly in his favour. He had already beaten one of the Uplands runners, the American horse Soothsayer, at Ascot in February by no less than 25 lengths, in atrocious conditions.

Captain Christy had already shown that he would struggle in heavy ground, having been a well-beaten fourth in the Leopardstown Chase. With Bobby Beasley retired from the saddle, he was now partnered by Bobby Coonan, the Irish champion jockey. Despite his patent dislike for heavy ground, Captain Christy was still allowed to go off the 7–4 favourite, just ahead of Ten Up at 2–1, with Bula next in the betting at 5–1. John Francome had ridden Bula in all his races this season and Richard Pitman chose to ride the outsider of the two, Soothsayer. Bula had won three of his four races so far this term.

Tommy Carberry had virtually no choice but to let Ten Up bowl along at his own pace, knowing that there was no point trying to fight the hard-pulling bay. He soon had most of the field in trouble and it was only Bula and Soothsayer that managed to stay with him as they approached the second last. Ten Up made a semblance of a mistake here, which let Bula take a very narrow and momentary lead. At the last, both Bula and Soothsayer had virtually ground to a halt, neither getting high enough, mainly through sheer exhaustion, while Ten Up met the last in his stride and was powering up the hill through a sea of mud to score easily by six lengths from Soothsayer, who just got the better of an equally tired Bula, to finish a brave second.

Dreaper, recently looking back on Ten Up's victory, reflected, 'Guts won the day and I'm certain the horse was never the same again after it.' It had been a slog, but a significant one for connections. Anne, Duchess of Westminster became only the second person after Dorothy Paget to win a Gold Cup with different horses and Jim Dreaper became the first second generation to train a Gold Cup winner. It had been a tremendous Festival for him generally, landing two other races and ending the meeting as top trainer, at only 24 years of age. Poignantly, Ten Up's Gold Cup triumph was witnessed by a very proud Tom Dreaper, who died only a month later.

Captain Christy, who managed to pull himself up here, ended his career on a high note later in the year in the 1975 King George VI Chase at Kempton, thrashing Bula, in course record time, by a staggering 30 lengths. However, tendon trouble meant that he would never race again. Come March, a beaten, but not bowed Bula, would return in pole position on better ground to try and win that missing trophy for Uplands and, at the same time, become the first horse to achieve the unique and equally elusive Champion Hurdle/Gold Cup double.

TEN UP (1975)

b.g. 1967 (Raise You Ten – Irish Harp)
Owned by Anne, Duchess of Westminster, trained by J.T. Dreaper and ridden by T. Carberry

✛ 1976 ✛

Frolicking on the firm

Absenteeism. Nobody likes it, least of all when it messes up the most coveted race in steeplechasing, especially on Gold Cup day itself. The Irish challenge, already depleted by the absence of Captain Christy through injury, was further reduced on the morning of the race when Jim Dreaper was forced to withdraw Ten Up, one of his three Gold Cup entries. Ten Up had been one of the leading fancies for the race throughout the winter, but had begun to break blood vessels. He had been allowed to run in Ireland, having been injected with a coagulant, but here at Cheltenham, the stewards informed him that if he administered the medication prior to the race then the horse would be liable to disqualification. Amid much shaking of heads, Ten Up was duly withdrawn on the day and, to rub salt in the wound, Dreaper was fined one hundred and twenty-five pounds for his action.

Although numerically Dreaper still had a say in proceedings, it was pretty clear to those in the know that his chance of winning the race had virtually gone, despite Brown Lad vying for race favouritism with Bula. Second string and former Irish National winner, Colebridge, was nothing out of the ordinary and Brown Lad, who had scooted up in a hurdle at last season's mudfest, was never going to be as effective on the prevailing fast ground.

Bula had been running his usual brave races, without setting the world alight. After being blown away by Captain Christy at Kempton on Boxing Day, he had been given some confidence-restoring outings and had come through with the minimum of fuss. The fast ground was thought to be very much in Bula's favour and it was hardly surprising to see him go off a marginal favourite over Brown Lad. There was a yawning gap in the betting to Colebridge, with Fred Rimell's smart novice, Royal Frolic, heading the others.

Royal Frolic had started the season rated some forty-three pounds below Bula, but had been improving all season – so much so that his trainer was particularly bullish about his chances pre-Cheltenham and made the decision to run, despite his owner, Sir Edward Hanmer, hedging and keen to wait another year. Knowing that the owner was desperate to have a runner in the Gold Cup, Rimell's diplomatic skills were put to good use. Rimell put it to the owner, then 82 and not getting any younger, that it might not be prudent to wait too long for his horse to strike for gold. The shrewd Rimell knew it wasn't a vintage year and his bold jumping seven-year-old bay had as good a chance as any in the field. I don't know if Sir Edward Hanmer was superstitious, but I don't suppose any horse has ever won the Gold Cup carrying the dreaded number 13 cloth, especially with only 11 runners in the race! It didn't seem to affect Royal Frolic's fortunes in the race – far from it.

Glanford Brigg, one of the rank outsiders, took the field along at a cracking pace for much of the way, with Royal Frolic and Colebridge coming to challenge six out. With four fences to go, Royal Frolic jumped into the lead under his stylish young rider John Burke and began to stretch the field on the run to the third last. Jumping with great zest, Royal Frolic bounded clear on the turn for home and never looked in any danger from that point. Francome's attempts to get Bula into the race proper were done no favours as the favourite made a crucial error at the third last fence and petered out from that point. It was left to Tommy Carberry to produce a storming run on Brown Lad, whom he had ridden with great care on conditions that the gelding must have hated.

Royal Frolic was positively spring-heeled at the last and was kept up to his work by his jockey to score impressively by five lengths. It had been the start of a wonderful month for Fred Rimell, after Rag Trade gave him his fourth Grand National winner, completing the very rare Cheltenham Gold Cup/Grand National double in the same season, albeit with different horses, a feat last achieved by Vincent O'Brien back in 1953. Following Fred's untimely death in 1981, Mercy Rimell took over the Kinnersley helm, having been her husband's assistant ever since Fred took out his first licence to train after the war. Fred had won just about every top-class race at least once, in many cases more than once: the Grand National on four occasions, the Cheltenham Gold Cup twice and the Champion Hurdle twice. For decades, Rimell winners had flowed from Kinnersley like the proverbial stream and Mercy upheld that tradition with considerable aplomb, with star performers such as champion hurdler Gaye Brief and his full-brother, Gaye Chance, the champion stayer. She decided to retire in 1989 and Kinnersley hasn't been the same since.

For the fifth time in six years, Uplands had supplied the Gold Cup favourite, only to have every single one beaten. Winter groaned after the race, 'I've got a feeling about this race – like Gordon Richards had about the Derby.' Unfortunately, things were not going to improve for him. Not yet, not for a couple of years anyway.

ROYAL FROLIC (1976)

b.g. 1969 (Royal Buck – Forward Miss)
Owned by Sir E. Hanmer, trained by T.F. Rimell and ridden by J. Burke

✛ 1977 ✛

Micko and his Lad

Surely Lanzarote could be the one to break the Gold Cup hoodoo for Uplands? Certainly, trainer and jockey were making encouraging noises about Lord Howard de Walden's former champion hurdler. In a television interview before the race, neither could hide their almost total belief in the novice. He had the least experience over the bigger obstacles of any runner in the entire history of the Gold Cup, yet possibly the greatest jockeys in jumping history stood side by side telling the world they all had Lanzarote to beat, with one proviso, or rather 22, to be jumped before victory could be claimed. Winter, refreshingly frank, opined, 'I suppose he has a good chance as Bula ever had really. He's not as experienced as Bula, but he's very intelligent and I think, in fact, he jumps his fences better than Bula did in his younger days. Barring accidents, he must win – I can't see anything to beat him. If it wasn't for the bogey me, he's odds-on, isn't he?' Francome agreed. 'His only problem on the day will be the fences. If he jumps well he'll hack up. I think this will be the easiest winner of the Gold Cup we've seen for a long time.'

Lanzarote had only had the three runs over fences, four if you count the pseudo fences he came up against in his first run in November, finishing fourth in the Colonial Cup in Camden, South Carolina. He completed three wins in his next three races, culminating in a superb crushing of a decent field in the Reynoldstown Chase at Ascot.

There is no doubt, despite his inexperience, that he deserved his place in the line-up. He probably had most to fear from the Irish challenge of favourite Bannow Rambler, from Davy Lad, two years younger than Lanzarote and the former point-to-pointer from 'over the wall' at Lambourn, the veteran Fort Devon.

The meeting had started with pretty disastrous consequences for Winter, when Bula fell heavily in the Champion Chase, having been brought back in distance from the Gold Cup. Bula had damaged a shoulder so badly that after three weeks of trying to save him, he had to be put down – a tragic end to a wonderful horse. In the Gold Cup it was left to another Irish challenger, Tied Cottage, to take the running at a blistering pace, considering the atrocious ground. As they approached the ninth fence, Lanzarote, in fourth place at the time, cleared the fence but slipped on landing, breaking his near-hind, bringing down Bannow Rambler in the process. Peter Jones, now the chairman of the Tote, was helping racing photographer Ed Byrne at the very fence where Lanzarote came to grief. Jones, along with many others, admitted to 'shedding more than a few tears when the vet put him down, mercifully very quickly'.

With the first and second favourites out of the race, Tied Cottage continued to bowl along in front, Tommy Carberry blissfully unaware of the carnage behind him. At the sixth last, old Fort Devon departed the race and the Bob Turnell-trained Summerville began to close up on the leader. Two fences later, Tied Cottage made his only error of the race, handing the lead to Summerville, who appeared to be going best of all at this stage. In behind, Dessie Hughes appeared to be struggling to get Davy Lad into the race at this point, but the seven-year-old was notoriously lazy and connections knew he would stay on well in the ground, having won in the glue-pot conditions at the Festival two years earlier. Clearing the third last, Summerville looked sure to break Jeff King's duck in the race, as he appeared full of running, ahead of the long-time leader Tied Cottage tiring in behind. However, moving stealthily into contention behind the two leaders and finally responding to Hughes' urgings, Davy Lad began to mount a decisive challenge. Over the second last, Summerville was still in front and still travelling when he began to send out distress signals. Davy Lad and Tied Cottage swept past him on the run to the last and Davy Lad produced a superb leap from nowhere to seal it there and then. He plugged on to score by six lengths, with a further twenty back to Summerville.

After the race, Summerville was hopping lame – he had broken down on his near foreleg after jumping the penultimate fence. He soldiered on bravely, but King knew that his chance had gone and had nursed him home to an unlucky third. His jockey always maintained that he would have won with his head in his chest, but King seemed destined never to win the Gold Cup. After the horrors of the ninth fence and the dreaded screens, you couldn't have had more of a contrast in the winners' enclosure, with Davy Lad's beautiful owner, Ann Marie McGowan, holding up the Gold Cup – the first horse she had ever owned!

Davy Lad's unlikely victory was appropriately achieved on St Patrick's Day, but it had been a Festival to forget for Winter, with both his former champion hurdlers lost in action. Winning trainer Mick O'Toole, a flamboyant character, was no stranger to classic success. He had won the Oaks with Marjone back in 1965 – the greyhound Oaks at Harringay! He bought Davy Lad as an unbroken three-year-old for five thousand guineas on impulse at Goffs one day because he always wanted a horse by David Jack as he was friends with the two brothers the sire was named after! Davy Lad's Festival win in 1975 had sparked off an amazing run of Festival success for the Kildare trainer, enjoying at least one Festival winner every year for the next six. O'Toole always knew that he had something decent and backed his horse with some confidence, having a speculative ante-post punt of five hundred pounds at 50–1 on Davy Lad. His many Festival winners usually resulted in wholescale gambles.

Jockey Dessie Hughes's record at the Cheltenham Festival over the years was also second to none. His subsequent victory on Monksfield in the second of that brave horse's Champion Hurdle wins, two years later, would remind many onlookers of the brilliant ride that Hughes had given the sometimes reluctant Davy Lad. This Festival proved to be a particularly happy hunting ground for Hughes, who won three races. In his time he also won three Arkles, the Sun Alliance Hurdle twice and a Champion Chase. Hughes has been a trainer for over 20 years and his son Richard looks like he has inherited his father's talent and horsemanship. Joe McGowan, who bought the winner as a present for his wife, was one of the luckiest owners ever to set foot in Cheltenham. Parkhill and Hartstown have given him the grand total of four Festival wins from three horses, with fortunes gambled on Hartstown.

Davy Lad broke down the following season and was forced to retire as an eight-

The 1986 Tote Cheltenham Gold Cup. Dawn Run (J.J. O'Neill) leads
Run And Skip (S. Smith-Eccles) on his way to becoming the first
horse to win both the Gold Cup and the Champion Hurdle

Jonjo O'Neill and Mrs Charmian Hill receive their trophies from The Queen Mother

Jimmy Fitzgerald (left) and Barney Curley in the racecourse car park, Gold Cup Day

The 1988 Tote Cheltenham Gold Cup, which was won by Charter Party. No. 7 is
Forgive 'N Forget (M. Dwyer) and no. 10 is Kildimo (G. Bradley)

Desert Orchid after winning the 1989 Cheltenham Gold Cup,
with owner Richard Burrough and lass Janice Coyle

D.L. Jones (left) and Tim Hamey, local jockeys who both won early
Cheltenham Gold Cups. Davy Jones rode Red Rower to victory in 1945
and Tim Hamey rode Koko to win in 1926

Owner/trainer Sirrell Griffiths receives the 1990 Tote Cheltenham Gold Cup from
The Queen Mother after Norton's Coin's 100–1 win. On the left is Lord Wyatt
of Weeford and behind Griffiths, in the bowler hat, is Captain Miles Gosling,
then chairman of The Steeplechase Company

Trainer Jenny Pitman, with the three joint-owners of Garrison Savannah, winner of the
1991 Gold Cup, receives her trophy from The Queen Mother

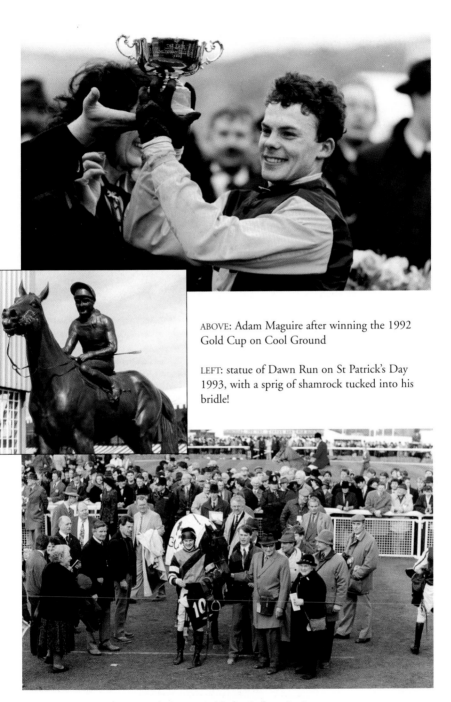

ABOVE: Adam Maguire after winning the 1992 Gold Cup on Cool Ground

LEFT: statue of Dawn Run on St Patrick's Day 1993, with a sprig of shamrock tucked into his bridle!

Mark Dwyer and Jodami after winning the 1993 Tote Cheltenham Gold Cup

Last fence at the 1994 Cheltenham Gold Cup. The Fellow (A. Kondrat), who won the race, leads Jodami (second) on the left and Young Hustler (third) on the right

Norman Williamson jumps for joy from Master Oats, winner of the 1995 Cheltenham Gold Cup

ABOVE: Imperial Call (C. O'Dwyer), winner of the 1996 Cheltenham Gold Cup, clears the last fence

LEFT: Lord Vestey, the chairman of The Steeplechase Company, makes a retirement presentation to David Nicholson

Mr Mulligan after winning the 1997 Gold Cup.
Tony McCoy salutes the crowd in the winners' enclosure

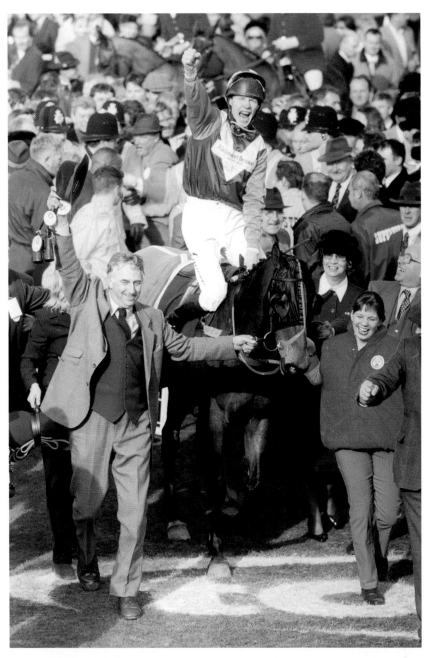

See More Business and Mick Fitzgerald are led into the winners' enclosure
by joint-owner Mr Paul Barber after the 1999 Tote Cheltenham Gold Cup

year-old, spending his final years at the McGowan stud near Fairyhouse. He suffered from arthritis and was put down in 1984.

DAVY LAD (1977)

b.g. 1970 (David Jack – Château)
Owned by Mrs J. McGowan, trained by M.A. O'Toole and ridden by D.T. Hughes

✝ 1978 ✝

Poetry in motion and definitely born lucky

16 March 1978 and Gold Cup day. Some things are simply meant to be – ask John Francome. His prayers the previous night must have been answered in no uncertain fashion, with a freak snowstorm suddenly hitting Cheltenham overnight and causing the abandonment of the final day of the Festival. From a purely selfish point of view, Cheltenham was the last place he wanted to be given the media hullabaloo that he could have expected to face, having been interviewed by Racecourse Security at Prestbury Park the night before who asked him to explain the nature of his relationship with his friend John Banks, the wealthy bookmaker.

The abandonment also turned out to be good news for Uplands, where Francome had spent an apprehensive morning riding out. With the Gold Cup now moved to the mid-April meeting, the stable's hopeful, Midnight Court, would have a far better chance as ground conditions would very likely be more suitable. It was high time that the Fred Winter run of bad luck in the Gold Cup came to an end. Could this be the horse to do it?

Midnight Court joined Uplands as a five-year-old, having won two hurdles and a bumper race in his native Ireland. Fred Winter, on one of his previous buying trips to Fenloe, had sat on him and been suitably impressed, having watched him being schooled. Tom Costello had suggested to Winter that the young bay, by Ascot Gold Cup winner Twilight Alley out of a winning mare by Umberto, a Knights' Royal Stakes winner, would make up into a decent performer over fences, with the proviso that he would always need decent ground. How prophetic his words would turn out to be, come Gold Cup day on 12 April.

The first time Midnight Court ran for Fred Winter was in a two-and-a-half-mile hurdle at Chepstow. Stable jockey John Francome recalls, 'The whole of Uplands (had) fortunes on him and he simply trotted up.' After another successful foray over hurdles, beating the useful Approaching at Newbury, Winter decided to switch his impressive Irish import to the larger obstacles. Midnight Court, after an inauspicious start over fences, having fallen and been brought down on his first two starts, knuckled down to the job at hand. He won a novice event at Sandown before signing off for the season with a very creditable second in Ascot's Heinz Chase behind the useful Commandant, who looked the likely winner before the welter burden of almost twelve stone took its toll.

Francome had no doubts about Midnight Court's qualities. 'He would do just what you wanted, settled well in a race and was a very good, clever jumper. Although he was prone to getting in close, he was neat in front and if you asked him to stand off at a fence, he had the class to do that too.' As a six-year-old he took the SGB Chase at the Berkshire course in December, making it four wins from four runs in his second season chasing.

Leading up to Christmas, Midnight Court had been installed as Gold Cup favourite at around 5–1, with the veteran Fort Devon a point longer. The latter, an evergreen twelve-year-old chestnut, was a failed point-to-pointer who was subsequently sold to America. Fort Devon redeemed himself, winning the 1976 Maryland Cup, before returning to England to join Fulke Walwyn at Saxon House. A disappointment when falling in last season's Gold Cup, he nevertheless bounced back to form in the hands of Bill Smith, finishing a neck to Bachelor's Hall in the Hennessy Gold Cup, giving a stone to the younger horse. Successful in all three of his other chases that season, he was clearly expected to get his revenge on Bachelor's Hall.

A great favourite with the public, Fort Devon went off a well-supported 2–1 favourite, with Midnight Court at 5–2. The favourite led approaching the final turn, with Royal Frolic pressing him on his outside. Coming into the straight, Fort Devon hung to his right, allowing Francome to slip Midnight Court through a gap on his inner, from which point he accelerated towards the final fence. Many lengths behind the leader at the last, Royal Frolic, having misjudged his take-off, took a crashing fall, almost landing on his jockey. Fort Devon had broken a blood vessel and was allowed to come home in his own time. Brown Lad, the hope of Ireland, finished a creditable second, seven lengths adrift at the line.

In the circumstances and on unsuitably fast ground, Jim Dreaper must have been delighted with the veteran Brown Lad's performance. His best chance of Gold Cup glory had undoubtedly disappeared with the abandonment back in March, when ground conditions were eminently more suitable to the evergreen mud-lover. Midnight Court's win ended a lean spell for Lambourn trainers – their first Gold Cup in fifteen years since the glory days of Mill House. Francome was, as ever, poetry in motion on the winner. Finally, the end of the Gold Cup hoodoo, that interminable wait that Uplands had suffered for so many years, with so many fancied runners beaten, was over. Five Cheltenham Gold Cup winners would pass through Tom Costello's hands, beginning here with Midnight Court. There was also the small matter of four Hennessys, three King Georges, two Mackesons and two Irish Grand National winners. The master of Fenloe's motto is 'break them, make them into jumping horses and sell them'. It's a motto that obviously works very well.

MIDNIGHT COURT (1978)

b.g. 1971 (Twilight Alley – Strumpet)
Owned by Mrs O. Jackson, trained by F.T. Winter and ridden by J. Francome

✛ 1979 ✛

The Northern Lights in sparkling form

A couple of years ago, a Habton Grange insider, who preferred to remain nameless, described the merits of Peter Easterby in the *Racing Post*. 'Peter has been a genius with horses. He is a stockman at heart and has the stockman's eye. He would never get bogged down in endless blood tests or weighing horses . . . he looks at a horse, makes his judgement and then goes to work. He doesn't get through much cotton wool with them either. He's a hard man – much tougher than Mick – and can't stand people who try to flannel him. But every double-barrelled southern assistant trainer should be made to spend a year with either of them. If they stayed the course they would learn enough to last a lifetime.' Having spoken to Peter a few times, who would often happily speak on son Tim's behalf, when previewing races for the *Sporting Life*, I have to say I found him pretty straightforward and easy enough to deal with, unlike a few trainers I could mention.

One senior trainer was particularly monosyllabic towards everybody at 'The Life', allegedly because we had reported details, many years ago, of some damage that had been done deliberately to his car, apparently by somebody who had a grudge against him. Others were simply rude. I remember calling Newmarket trainer Mick Ryan one morning to ask him what the plans were for a particular horse in his yard, now that the owners had been warned off by the Jockey Club well into the millennium. His reply was short and not so sweet. 'Fuck off!' and slam went the telephone. Understandably, some trainers tend to get on better with some hacks than with others, but there was always an element of trepidation involved when ringing either Josh Gifford or David Nicholson. On one occasion, I remember calling the Duke to find out a bit more about a young 16-year-old jockey based at Jackdaws Castle who had been making a bit of a name for himself. The Duke seemed pleasantly surprised that I was making this inquiry and, asking me to hold the line, he duly went off in search of the lad. Ten minutes must have passed and a breathless Duke returned to the phone, apologising for the delay – he had been unable to find the lad in question, Richard Johnson. I thought then this youngster must be a bit special as I couldn't see too many busy trainers wandering around looking for one of their youngest recruits. I should have backed him there and then to win the jockeys' championship one day, McCoy willing. The Duke's actions that day told me something about his character and I had to smile when I heard him, on the verge of retirement, speaking with Mike Cattermole on the Racing Channel about his desire to help young people to come through. Like father, like son.

Alverton and Night Nurse, the two Easterby challengers for the 1979 Gold Cup, were both archetypal Easterby horses – tough, uncompromising and versatile. Night Nurse had already shown himself to be above average over the bigger obstacles, what you might expect from a dual champion hurdler with the size and scope to make a top-class steeplechaser. Alverton was another fine example of the dual-purpose horse that Easterby excelled with. Totting up all the wins at the end of Alverton's career makes interesting reading: as many races won on the flat as over jumps, twenty-two in all, including two as a two-year-old. He had already won both on the flat and over hurdles before he broke down on both forelegs in February 1974. He was fired and, after being sidelined for almost eighteen months, he returned to the fray and continued his winning ways under both codes. After establishing himself as a leading handicapper on the flat, second in no less a race than the Ebor at York and winning no less than seven times that season, he made the natural progression to fencing. He was a natural and in his novice season he won his only four races, culminating with a gutsy win in the 1978 Arkle Chase.

Alverton had been ridden by the newly crowned champion jockey Jonjo O'Neill from Cork, who had a record of one hundred and forty-nine wins, for two of his unbeaten four outings. This season, O'Neill would be in the plate for all seven of Alverton's races – a partnership that would flourish as the season progressed.

After running with immense promise against young guns Silver Buck and Diamond Edge, Alverton got back to winning ways at Haydock less than two weeks before the Gold Cup itself and dropped like a stone in the ante-post market in the final days, following a number of withdrawals which changed the ante-post market considerably. With the likes of ante-post hot favourite and King George winner, Gay Spartan, forced to pull out through injury at the eleventh hour, it began to look very promising for Alverton. There were other absentees, too: the last two Gold Cup winners, Davy Lad and Midnight Court, and the new hope of Ireland, Jack Of Trumps. This promised to make life a bit easier for Alverton and the 13 others, who ran in the sort of conditions that Davy Lad and Gay Spartan would have revelled in, and that Midnight Court hated.

Night Nurse was allowed to take his chance after a succession of wins that had been brought to an end by the very promising Silver Buck, one of many Dickinson horses with a big future, in a memorable encounter at Haydock. Both these classy novices would remain top-class steeplechasing prospects. But, for now, Night Nurse's inexperience as much as anything else told here.

Alverton went off a 5–1 joint favourite with last year's runner-up, the veteran Brown Lad, with Night Nurse and Gaffer a point longer in the most open betting market for years. Gaffer, trained by Fulke Walwyn, had run Gay Spartan to two lengths in the Jim Ford Challenge Chase at Wincanton on his last run and was reputed to be possibly the best Saxon House chaser since Mill House. But he didn't shine here, reportedly pulling muscles in his neck after making a blunder at the fifth last.

The race itself was run in a mixture of snow and driving rain on already very soft ground, making it a severe test of courage, ideal for the likes of Alverton and Tied Cottage. Unusually in a championship race with this number of runners, at the final bend into the straight it was already down to a two-horse war, as Tied Cottage had burnt off all challengers, bar one very important one – Alverton. Tied Cottage still seemed to be full of running as the two approached the last and to his outside O'Neill had Alverton in overdrive. Tied Cottage, still a fraction ahead, knuckled on landing – according to O'Neill, 'having caught a glimpse of us out of the corner of his eye' – and the race was over. The tremendous leap put in by Alverton at the last might well have been enough to seal victory anyway, as he was probably the more determined of the two in a battle, but there are thousands of Irish people who might disagree with that view. Tied Cottage didn't deserve to fall. It wasn't through exhaustion, just bad luck.

For O'Neill, it was his first major 'classic' win since his arrival in England in 1973 to ride for Gordon Richards and his strength, skill and determination, particularly in a finish, became legendary. Twice champion jockey, the challenge of taming the famed Cheltenham hill would always appeal to the never-say-die O'Neill attitude, which he put to such good use over the years. The best was yet to come for O'Neill. Despite his numerous and serious injuries, O'Neill would go on to cement his place in national hunt history and he would need all of those special qualities in his subsequent battle for his own life. He has a refreshing honesty about him too, readily admitting that he felt he should have won the 1979 running of the Champion Hurdle on Sea Pigeon, but he more than made up for that on this Gold Cup day.

Peter Easterby would provide the backbone of the northern challenge at the Festival for many more years, his 'classic' successes sparked off by the flying hurdler Saucy Kit back in 1967. The Easterby urge to train began to develop in earnest in the late '40s when he assisted his uncle Walter before moving on to spend some three years assisting Weyhill-based Irishman Frank Hartigan, a hard task master and a great trainer, during which time Easterby rode in point-to-points. Easterby inherited the family farm, Habton Grange, and set about building up his string. There had always been horses around the place as Easterby's father used to deal in horses, a tradition eagerly continued as he built a reputation second to none in the art of buying and selling horses, often in the dual purpose, Alverton mould.

The Grand National beckoned for the well-handicapped Alverton, a certainty if he stayed on his feet with only ten stone thirteen pounds – a year later he would have been given probably a stone more. In the race itself, things seemed to be going like clockwork, with Alverton travelling like the winner. It looked a formality as the field approached Becher's Brook second time round. Tragically, Alverton must have then suffered a heart attack, as he most uncharacteristically ploughed straight into the bottom of that most unforgiving fence and was dead before he hit the ground on the other side. Sadly, though already a champion, nobody will ever know whether he would have finished the job and emulated Golden Miller. Would he then have been hailed a great horse? Somehow, I think he would. There are those who will always try to devalue his Cheltenham victory, but you only beat the horses that run on the day. What is inescapable is the fact that he was truly as hard as nails and gave his all in the driving snow, where others, possibly more talented, cried enough. He had downed the next Gold Cup winner in all but name. Tied Cottage surely paid the ultimate compliment to the brave Alverton. I rest my case.

ALVERTON (1979)

ch.g. 1970 (Midsummer Night – Alvertona)
Owned by The Snailwell Stud, trained by M.H. Easterby and ridden by J.J. O'Neill

✢ 1980 ✢

Gypsies, pigs and a lean machine?

If ever there was a horse that deserved to go down in the record books as a Gold Cup winner, it was Tied Cottage. He was desperately unlucky to crumple at the last when challenged by Alverton in the 1979 Gold Cup and his supporters must have wondered at times over the next 12 months if the ageing son of Honour Bound was beginning to lose his touch. Would he ever return to the sort of form that would worry the likes of Silver Buck, Jack Of Trumps and Diamond Edge? Dan Moore had worked the oracle with any number of horses over the years, but after eight defeats with only two placings, even the genial Moore must have wondered if he could rekindle the fire within his stable star. As it turned out, the outcome of the Gold Cup would be of no surprise to ardent Moore followers but the events surrounding the weeks to follow this renewal beggared belief.

With Cheltenham just around the corner, Moore cleverly pitched Tied Cottage in at Naas a fortnight before the 1980 Gold Cup, on yielding ground over a painfully inadequate two miles. How form books have improved in 20 years! 'Ran poorly: needs longer distances' is about as minimal as you get in terms of useful information. Although this particular run would never have been intended as anything other than a glorified racecourse gallop, I dare say Tied Cottage ran up to stable expectation. The more pertinent of Tied Cottage's form lines would have included a reasonable King George run on Boxing Day, where he finished a distant fourth behind old adversaries Silver Buck and Jack Of Trumps on unsuitably fast ground. A better effort followed that Kempton run, admittedly on his more favoured heavy ground, chasing home the eventual Gold Cup favourite Diamond Edge at Sandown in February.

Meanwhile, a smart young West Country challenger in the shape of Master Smudge had been progressing on the right lines throughout the season. Master Smudge, one of only two horses in training for Somerset permit holder and haulage contractor Arthur Barrow, had already won at the Festival, winning the 1979 Sun Alliance Chase in impressive fashion, with the likes of Silver Buck among the 16 opponents trailing in his wake. Master Smudge's background and how Barrow came to buy him is quite unique in the history of the Gold Cup, and pretty remarkable by any standards. Master Smudge's breeder, Henry Radford, based near Ilminster, had been distinctly unimpressed by the latest produce of his very ordinary mare, Lily Pond II, and he passed on the diminutive 'coat-rack', as Barrow was later to describe Master Smudge, to some passing gypsies in exchange for an undisclosed amount of whisky. Local pig farmer John Tarr then bought the gelding from the gypsies for seventy-five pounds, having seen the chestnut when driving past the gypsies camped on the side of the road near Martock. At this point, Barrow entered the equation, collecting some of Tarr's pigs to go to market. Barrow spotted Master Smudge across a field and he recalls, 'I fell in love with Master Smudge the moment I saw him. I drove my lorry into the farmyard and he came galloping over to me. I just had to have him, although he wasn't the best of lookers – I bought him because of the way he moved.' A lot of haggling and three hundred and twelve pounds later, the unbroken two-year-old bag of bones was his. It was probably the best deal Barrow had ever done in his life, though unbeknown to him at that time.

A confirmed mudlark, Master Smudge, despite having run consistently well all season, hadn't actually managed to get his head in front. Finishing runner-up in February to Diamond Edge in the Jim Ford at Wincanton, beaten twelve lengths at level weight, doesn't tell the whole story. He was in close contention at the fifteenth when he parted company with his regular jockey, Richard Hoare. Swiftly remounted, he ran on in fine style to prove his utter gameness. Heavy ground at the Festival would hold no terrors for Master Smudge, who sluiced home in similar conditions last year.

The race itself was a catalogue of disasters for some of the fancied runners. John Francome rode the classy Border Incident. He recalled, 'He was very talented but also a very difficult horse to get right because of injury. This particular day we had him right and we were absolutely cruising in behind, when we tipped up at the fourth last. I remember Jonjo (O'Neill) having a laugh at my expense as he came past me on Jack Of Trumps. The last laugh was on him, though, as he promptly fell off himself at the next!'

Tied Cottage and Tommy Carberry had taken the lead from the off and stayed there. Master Smudge ran on stoutly into second place, having made an early blunder that cost him a lot of ground. Old Mac Vidi, a sprightly looking fifteen years young, ran the race of his long life for Devon permit holder Pam Neal, to become the oldest horse to be placed in a Gold Cup. Surely no horse will ever match Mac Vidi's wonderful effort.

The twist to this Gold Cup tale came three weeks later and coincided with the Grand National meeting. The Moores, at Aintree, were informed by the Irish Turf Club that there had been traces of theobromine, a prohibited substance, found in Tied Cottage's post-race urine sample. Extensive investigations revealed that contaminated feed had come from soya beans that had travelled in a cargo hold that contained traces of cocoa, the source of the contamination. Not only was Tied Cottage disqualified, but so were Mick O'Toole's runners at the Festival, both trainers using the same supplier for horsenuts. Chinrullah had won the Queen Mother Champion Chase and finished fifth in the Gold Cup the following day. No blame was attached to either trainer, but the inquiry on 21 May formalised the disqualifications and Master Smudge was officially declared the winner of the Gold Cup. Arthur Barrow was always grateful to Fred Rimell for arranging the transfer of the Gold Cup at Warwick a few days after the disqualification and the presentation was made by Dame Ackroyd, a director of the Tote.

Tied Cottage's victory in the Irish National, only weeks after the Gold Cup, was a particularly poignant one. He had been amateur ridden by none other than his owner, Anthony Robinson, who had already been diagnosed with cancer. Sadly, within months of the race, both he and Tied Cottage's trainer, Dan Moore, were dead – a tragic loss to racing.

MASTER SMUDGE (1980)

ch.g. 1972 (Master Stephen – Lily Pond II)
Owned and trained by Mr A. Barrow and ridden by R. Hoare

✢ 1981 ✢

Smudge to master the treble?

If you were to ask a cross-section of jumping enthusiasts which horses could have joined that illustrious trio, Golden Miller, Cottage Rake and Arkle, as the only other horses to win at least three Gold Cups, you would probably get at least half a dozen suggestions. Easter Hero, Pas Seul, Linwell, Dawn Run, The Fellow, Forgive 'N Forget or even Desert Orchid would possibly get most votes. However, if you had posed that question back in early 1981 to a 'cyclisist' – or whatever it is you call people who believe in all things being cyclical – you would probably have been told Master Smudge. It seems that from 1932, Golden Miller's first triumph, a great champion has recorded the first of his three wins every sixteen years, namely Cottage Rake in 1948 and Arkle in 1964. Why not Master Smudge to follow up in 1981 and 1982? After all, it would surely have been stretching the imagination, assuming Tied Cottage had been allowed to keep the race, to believe that Tied Cottage would be able to maintain such a remarkable sequence, especially at his advanced age. In fact, he did compete in the next two Gold Cups, but without success.

Master Smudge had youth on his side and there was no doubting his ability, given his favoured ground. Arthur Barrow always had faith in him and believed that Master Smudge's early blunder in the 1980 Gold Cup cost him at least 20 lengths – far more than he was actually beaten. Barrow, now a public trainer, was confident that Master Smudge could prove himself to be the best again and secure that lost opportunity to meet the Queen Mother to receive the Gold Cup. In early January, Master Smudge won the Mandarin Chase to record Barrow's first win as a public trainer, yet the Cheltenham specialist was still quoted a long-looking 33–1 for the Gold Cup. Barrow recalled, 'Master Smudge was in great shape for the race, better than I had ever had him before. Unfortunately, we think he must have somehow banged himself, because we found him on Gold Cup morning with a massive haematoma on his leg. We had no option but to take him out of the race.'

There were high hopes that rising star Bright Highway, trained in County Kildare by Michael O'Brien and the impressive winner of both the Mackeson and Hennessy Gold Cups, could make his presence felt at Cheltenham. In Irish eyes, this would have gone some way towards redressing the balance over Tied Cottage's disqualification. However, the well-supported ante-post favourite picked up an injury in January which forced him out of the reckoning altogether. Nevertheless, there was still a significant Irish challenge from Tied Cottage, Jack Of Trumps and Royal Bond.

Silver Buck, having won back-to-back King Georges on Boxing Day, went off a well-backed 7–2 favourite, having been as long as 6–1 in February following his bloodless victory in the Jim Ford at Wincanton. The Dickinson representative undoubtedly had the best form leading up to the race, but the prevailing ground was never going to make this be to his advantage. At this stage of his career, if there was a chink in his armour it was definitely soft or heavy ground. Among a competitive-looking field of 15, Jack Of Trumps was back again to try and redeem himself after his fall in the race last year. Peter Easterby, fresh from Sea Pigeon's fantastic win in the Champion Hurdle two days earlier, bolstered a strong northern challenge, a feature of the race in coming years, with the two joint-second favourites, Night Nurse and Little Owl. The former, one of the most popular chasers in training, had returned from a leg injury to try once more to become the first horse to win both the Champion Hurdle and the Gold Cup. His younger stable-companion, the seven-year-old Little Owl, in his second season over fences, had been carrying all before him, notching up seven wins from his eight races over the larger obstacles, his only defeat coming in the Sun Alliance Chase, falling after being hampered when looking the likely winner.

Bred in Ireland, Little Owl had been purchased by Peter Easterby as an unbroken three-year-old at Doncaster Sales for only two thousand two hundred guineas. His original owner, Bobby Gundry, died only days after last year's Festival and left the horse to her nephews, the Wilson brothers – Jim, the leading top amateur of his time and Robin, a Derbyshire farmer, in whose colours Little Owl would run. For a young horse, he certainly had plenty of Festival experience, having finished second to Jim Wilson riding Willie Wumpkins to the first of his three consecutive Coral Golden Hurdle Final wins back in 1979. However, his new owners still regarded him very much as a novice; it was Peter Easterby's advice to go for gold while the horse was fit and well that swayed them to let him take his place.

It turned out to be a race dominated up the hill by the Easterby duo after Tied Cottage fell early in the race, at the sixth fence. From the third last, there were only three horses in with a serious chance: Silver Buck, Little Owl and Night Nurse. Alan Brown, substituting for the sidelined Jonjo O'Neill on Night Nurse, must have been happy with the way Night Nurse had been travelling as he jumped into the lead at that fence and turned into the straight in front, seemingly going best. However, Wilson and Carmody had other ideas and came to press the leader on his outside. Brown took a peep across at the two challengers and probably couldn't believe what he saw as the two passed him in a matter of strides.

As they approached the second last, Wilson asked his partner to quicken up and the response was instant. Little Owl jumped it in front in fine style and getting quickly into his stride began to pile on the pressure ahead of Silver Buck, who had blundered in behind him and lost all momentum with a bad mistake. Night Nurse, who had been caught slightly flat-footed by the two ahead of him, began to stay on and was challenging Silver Buck for second place as they approached the last a few lengths behind the leader. Wilson again asked for a big one, and got a fantastic response from the brave Little Owl, extending their lead as they set off up the hill. In behind, Night Nurse passed Silver Buck jumping the last and switched to the stands side. He began to make inroads on his stable-companion who was some four lengths clear and not looking like stopping. Try as he might under a determined drive from Brown, Night Nurse couldn't quite make up the leeway and was still a length and a half down at the finish.

Wilson had become the first amateur since 1947 to win the Gold Cup and fully deserved the plaudits he received for keeping his cool. One slap down the shoulder and pushing out with hands and heels had got Little Owl home, without having to resort to the whip once.

Like Pat Taaffe, his riding style might not have been pretty but it was certainly effective. He was a fine horseman and as good in a race as practically any professional riding at that time. Like so many Gold Cup winners, the great hopes for the young Little Owl never came to fruition. He never recaptured his brilliance and raced only intermittently due to viral and injury problems that plagued him in later years before he was eventually retired in 1985.

LITTLE OWL (1981)

b.g. 1974 (Cantab – Black Spangle)
Owned by Mr R.J. Wilson, trained by M.H. Easterby and ridden by Mr A.J. Wilson

The reluctant hero, turning on the Dickinson style

Whether there ever has been, or ever will be, a top-class performer sold as frequently as Silver Buck in his formative years is debatable. The auctioneers at Ballsbridge must have known the breeding of the fractious, almost neurotic, bay off by heart, so regularly did he appear in their catalogue. Twice Jack Doyle, bloodstock agent extraordinaire, bought him, initially for one thousand guineas as a two-year-old and then for double that amount a year later.

The future Gold Cup winner had been entered at Goffs in November 1975 by Brian Bamber. He had bought the horse privately from County Antrim breeder, Edith Booth. However, it was a case of once bitten, twice shy for Doyle's clients. The first, the O'Connors from Cashel, wanted a suitable horse for their son to break in and ride but found Silver Buck totally unmanageable. The second, apparently an English trainer, simply ducked out of the deal. With his future in doubt, Silver Buck returned to Doyle's base at Shankill and attempts were made to quell his idiosyncratic tendencies, with some success. He was shown to several prospective buyers as a potential show jumper, as he had shown great aptitude over poles and out hunting. After showing breathtaking speed on the gallops, it wasn't long before Silver Buck joined Jack's son Paul, who was training on the Curragh, and he began to make an impression in point-to-points, winning two before his first outing under rules at Clonmel in a bumper race. After displaying all of his usual antics before the start at Clonmel, Silver Buck duly ran the opposition into the ground.

In stepped legendary Irish punter Barney Curley with an offer of seven thousand pounds that Doyle couldn't refuse and the horse was swiftly on his way to Tony Dickinson at Gisburn. One condition of the sale set by the ever shrewd Curley was that the Dickinsons would let him know when the horse was fancied to win his first race. After an 'educational' outing over an insufficient two miles at Carlisle ridden by Michael Dickinson, the plan in December 1977 was to try Silver Buck over a more suitable three miles, hopefully avoiding soft ground, which clearly wouldn't suit such a good mover. A race for amateurs at Catterick was chosen, with Michael's brother-in-law Tom Tate in the saddle. Curley got the phone call he was hoping for and the gamble was landed from 12–1 to 5–1, with Curley helping himself at the expense of some unsuspecting bookmakers, particularly at home in his native Ireland.

Silver Buck won four novice hurdles in that first season. At this point, his owner Jack Mewles, a Skipton-based solicitor, decided to sell him and the Dickinsons sounded out another of their owners, Mrs Christine Feather, about the possibility of buying Silver Buck. She looked the reclusive Silver Buck over but actually preferred another Dickinson inmate, Cavity Hunter. However, Mrs Feather discovered that the latter was already lined up for another owner. Despite this disappointment, Mrs Feather agreed to buy Silver Buck and he ran in her colours for the first time at the Festival in 1978, finishing a creditable fourth to the odds-on Irish favourite Mr Kildare, despite not being fully wound up. When he reappeared the following season, Silver Buck had a new partner in the crack Irish jockey Tommy Carmody – Michael Dickinson had suffered a career-ending fall at Cartmel, on the inappropriately named Buck Me Off.

A successful first season in his new sphere of novice chasing reaped four wins from seven runs, including a superb defeat of Alverton. However, one of the highlights of the season was undoubtedly the Embassy Premier Chase Final, run over two and a half miles at Haydock in March. This turned out to be a titanic clash between Silver Buck and Night Nurse, the dual champion hurdler, who had taken equally well to the bigger obstacles. Nip and tuck throughout the final circuit, the two youngsters were still locked together coming over the last, Silver Buck getting his head in front only in the final fifty yards of the race. Strangely, both protagonists, renowned for their fighting spirit throughout their careers, also displayed similar behavioural traits off the track. Neither appreciated visitors in their boxes and would shy, spook and duck about amongst other horses on the gallops. But just how much had that epic battle taken out of the novice?

Silver Buck turned out only 11 days later as hot favourite to land the Sun Alliance Chase – a race which the Dickinsons probably wished they had bypassed. Michael Dickinson reflected after the race, 'The ground had turned heavy from good after incessant rain for most of the Sunday and Monday and Silver Buck couldn't handle the heavy ground, although he had jumped the Cheltenham fences really well. It could be that the race had come too soon for him after his tussle with Night Nurse.' Significantly, Night Nurse finished a tailed-off seventh in the Gold Cup, the proverbial street behind stable-companion Alverton. Next season, the reluctant hero, who never wanted to be in front for too long, proved a tough nut to crack, winning the 1979 King George from the Edward O'Grady-trained Jack Of Trumps and was subsequent second favourite for the Gold Cup in March.

Come Festival time, Silver Buck had been distinctly unimpressive in an egg-and-spoon race at Hereford and subsequently his blood count was slightly low. He had failed to sparkle in his home work, and with the Festival ground turning once more against Silver Buck, the Dickinsons took the view that he should miss the 1980 Gold Cup, withdrawing him on the day of the race. This late decision apparently did not go down at all well with Silver Buck's owner or rider but, in the circumstances, it was the right one and certainly a blessing in disguise in terms of the horse's future progression to the top of the chasing tree.

The following season saw Michael officially take over the reins from his father at their new stable at Harewood. Since their move across Yorkshire, Tony had enjoyed continuing success, ending his training career as top trainer numerically, with 94 winners compared to Fred Winter's 86. Silver Buck contributed seven of those wins in his unbeaten run. Silver Buck opened his campaign in the 1980-81 season with three quick wins in November and he began to really blossom into something like the finished article. He was set an almost impossible task a month later, just failing, by a length, to give some thirty-four pounds to another useful northern prospect, Sunset Cristo, in the Hector Christie Memorial race at Catterick. Silver Buck completed back-to-back King Georges, beating seven opponents, including old rival Night Nurse, who fell dramatically at the last and in close contention at the time. But Carmody, after the race, was adamant that the result was never in doubt. 'We had the race won some way out – it may have looked as though Night Nurse was in with a chance until his fall at the last, but my fella had it sewn up.'

With a facile win in the Jim Ford at Wincanton three weeks before the 1981 Festival, everything looked to be falling into place and Silver Buck took over at the head of the Gold Cup market. He ran well enough, but still had to convince his detractors that he could stay the Gold Cup distance in soft ground. A number of Dickinson runners had failed to fire around this time, so with the distinct possibility of Silver Buck being slightly below par, third place in his first Gold Cup, beaten under 12 lengths was by no means an unqualified disaster.

With Carmody deciding to return to Ireland, he now had a new pilot in Robert Earnshaw, a brilliant horseman whose quiet, effective style of riding suited Silver Buck admirably. Earnshaw had ridden horses from an early age and had been with the Dickinsons some three years when 'Bucket', as the horse became known at home, arrived in the yard. The quietly spoken local lad had been given the unenviable task of looking after the new recruit, who bucked and kicked in all directions, both in and out of his box. Patience won the day and he eventually managed to calm him down, but not before one particularly memorable occasion when Carmody first attempted to school the unruly gelding. Silver Buck decided to apply the brakes, quite unexpectedly, approaching a fence and put Carmody through the wing, who only narrowly escaped serious injury. From that day, Earnshaw always schooled Silver Buck. Now came his opportunity to try out the partnership on the racecourse.

The new combination clicked immediately at Wincanton – no great shock considering his 1–6 price in the race against inferior opposition. The real shock came next time out at Chepstow in the Rehearsal Chase – a race renowned for throwing up strange results. Starting at odds of 1–3, Silver Buck was never going well at any stage of the race and crumpled on landing four out, due to sheer exhaustion. Three weeks later he was out to restore his lofty reputation in the Edward Hanmer Memorial Chase at Haydock, with John Francome coming in for the ride. Silver Buck was back to his best and a first Harewood ride for Francome turned out to be a winning one. Next stop a third King George? Unfortunately, it wasn't to be. A white-out prevented any racing from taking place that Christmas, which for Silver Buck's connections was just as well – he wouldn't have made it to Kempton anyway. He was hopping lame, due to a rogue nail that had driven deep into the sole of his off-hind foot. Constant attention was the only cure for the patient, who, for quite some time, couldn't put any weight on his extremely sore foot.

His recovery complete and less than a fortnight to the Festival, it was time to blow the cobwebs away at lowly Market Rasen. Kevin Whyte, one of Dickinson's young guns, took the ride, while Robert Earnshaw partnered Bregawn, another of Dickinson's talented Gold Cup entries over at Haydock. Silver Buck came through his final prep race with flying colours in facile manner. The wraps were off again and he began to work well at home.

In the most open Gold Cup for years, a record field of 22 runners stood their ground. Dickinson had already enjoyed two winners at the Festival, including the Queen Mother Champion Chase with Rathgorman. Earnshaw was pleasantly surprised that he had been reunited with Silver Buck in preference to Bregawn, with Graham Bradley in the plate for the less fancied of the two Dickinson contenders. Night Nurse, runner-up in the race 12 months ago and one of Silver Buck's oldest adversaries, had enjoyed another good season and had captured the public's imagination, trying to giving lumps of weight away to the likes of the up-and-coming Bregawn. Even at 11 years of age, the popular dual-champion hurdler was still regarded by many as a worthy favourite, starting a well-backed 11–4 market leader on the day. Peter Easterby's other intended runner, last year's Gold Cup hero Little Owl, had originally vied for ante-post favouritism with his stable-companion, but his season, by heady Easterby standards, had been a total disaster and he was taken out of the race. Arthur Moore-trained Royal Bond, the hope of Ireland, started at 4–1. He had beaten the best of the Irish at Leopardstown in February, which followed a successful fact-finding mission at Cheltenham in January. With Tommy Carberry riding in his last Gold Cup, he must have hoped he could go out on a winner as Royal Bond seemingly had everything going for him.

However, it wouldn't take long for Carberry to realise that this wasn't going to be a champagne day. Royal Bond trailed the field from the off and never looked like getting in a blow. The frenetic pace set in the heavy ground by Royal Bond's stable-companion, the veteran Tied Cottage, caught out a number of others too, including the well-backed Venture To Cognac. Fred Winter's representative was another who simply couldn't go the pace, running no sort of race in conditions that were expected to suit. Still as brave as a lion, Tied Cottage, making his final Gold Cup appearance at the age of 14, began to feel the pinch after the fourth last and was swallowed up by a trio of northern challengers. From this point, Silver Buck, Bregawn and Sunset Cristo vied for the lead, with Diamond Edge hunting them up for good measure.

Meanwhile, Night Nurse was running a stinker of a race and Jonjo O'Neill wisely pulled up. After the race, O'Neill opined, 'Peter Easterby believed we would be better off sticking to the inner to try and make use of the fresh strip of ground by the rails – unfortunately he didn't enjoy being squeezed up by other horses and sulked. With hindsight, I should have allowed him more daylight. It was very disappointing because I knew exactly what he was capable of.' Among the leaders, there was only one horse travelling like a winner. Jumping the third last, Earnshaw saw a stride and let Silver Buck move into overdrive, and the race was effectively over there and then, bar a fall. Bradley tried manfully to galvanise Bregawn up the final hill in an effort to bridge the gap, but Earnshaw just kept the leader him up to his work, fending off his nearest pursuer to win by a comfortable two lengths. Sunset Cristo, a grand stamp of a horse and trained by the genial Stockton-based permit holder Ray Hawkey, finished a gallant but distant third. For the second consecutive year, the north had enjoyed a clean sweep and Silver Buck had silenced once and for all the sceptics who presumed he wouldn't see out the Gold Cup trip, especially on rain-softened ground.

Silver Buck's love affair with the Tote Cheltenham Gold Cup certainly didn't end there. His final Gold Cup appearance the following year would be equally memorable, despite finishing only fourth – for very different reasons. The famous 'Dickinson Five' became a part of Cheltenham folklore. For the majority of the crowd (except those financially involved!) the finishing order didn't particularly matter. It was enough to just be there and see the Dickinson army swarm up the hill, the first four a country mile clear of the others, with Ashley House completing the rout, running on into a remote fifth place. Silver Buck won no less than nine more races in his final two seasons and as a twelve-year-old won in his usual brave style at Wetherby in April 1984, appropriately on St George's Day – which turned out to be his final race.

Sadly, there was no graceful retirement for the Harewood hero. Five months later, his skittish, nervous nature was finally his undoing. On a dreary September day, he spooked as Graham Bradley tried to clamber on board to take him out to exercise. Silver Buck suddenly took off and careered straight into a yard wall. There was nothing that could be done to save him and in a short time he had died from internal bleeding – a tragic end to a wonderful horse who brought so much pleasure to so many people.

SILVER BUCK (1982)

br.g. 1972 (Silver Cloud – Choice Archlesse)
Owned by Mrs C. Feather, trained by M. Dickinson and ridden by R. Earnshaw

✢ 1983 ✢

Five go to Cheltenham

The last Gold Cup to fall on St Patrick's Day, in 1977, had been a red-letter day for the Irish with Davy Lad. However, there would be no Irish challengers among the 11 runners this time, there would be no shamrocks. This Gold Cup was Yorkshire's finest day. There had been a few fine days for Yorkshire in recent years, but this one would top the lot. It was as if the northern express with the Dickinson engine pulling it had never left Cheltenham sidings since the previous March. This time, there were five carriages attached to the Harewood engine. In total charge at the helm was a thin controller, who had been walking his signal-box since Christmas. Dickinson admitted after the race that he had actually dreamt this result. For once, his dreams became reality, against all the odds.

Indeed, the whole Festival turned out to be very special indeed. A unique finish to the Gold Cup was preceded by an emotional Champion Hurdle victory for Mercy Rimell with Gaye Brief, the last horse that Fred Rimell had purchased before his untimely death some two years earlier. On the Wednesday, two future Gold Cup winners were on view for the first time at the Festival, plying their trade at that time as hurdlers. Dawn Run graced Cheltenham with her presence in the Sun Alliance, although on this occasion found Sabin Du Loir, yet another Dickinson star, simply too good on the day. This was followed by Forgive 'N Forget's annihilation of a quality field in the Coral Golden Hurdle Final, landing a monster gamble in the process. The stage was set for the Dickinson experience on the Thursday.

The season had not been without its usual problems for Harewood. Bregawn had been at his brilliant but quirky best, cocking his jaw at the last but still catching Captain John on the Newbury run-in to secure the Hennessy in November under a welter burden of eleven stone ten pounds. He had pulled a muscle in defeat at Haydock in December, which forced him to miss the King George at Kempton, which his able deputy Wayward Lad won, keeping up the remarkable Dickinson family record in that race. In fact, training Bregawn had never been a bed of roses. Bred in Ireland by Mr J. Fitzgerald, Bregawn had been led out of the sales ring at Ballsbridge unsold, before Joseph Crowley bought him for one thousand pounds, before selling him on to his owner for sixteen thousand pounds. Originally an appalling jumper, the flashy chestnut was sent to Tony Dickinson to 'learn the ropes', something which took this headstrong individual some time to do. But when he did complete his races, he was consistency personified. His final prep race before this Gold Cup came at Wincanton, where in desperate need of the race he was beaten half a length by the talented Combs Ditch, trained by David Elsworth. Combs Ditch was promoted to second favourite on the back of his win, which was possibly a slightly false result in the circumstances. But at least Bregawn had blown any cobwebs away and was ready to run for his life at Cheltenham.

The wonderfully-named Whiggie Geo, a 500–1 outsider, made the running for the first three-quarters of a mile before dropping away. Young Bradley, still only 22 years old, had to make his mind up quickly about what his tactics would be. Taking the bull by the horns, he quickened up the pace and immediately got one or two of the southern challengers off the bridle. Neither of the Winter pair of Fifty Dollars More and Brown Chamberlain got into the race, the former falling second time round and the latter not getting very far at all before being pulled up. Combs Ditch never looked likely to get in the race either and it was left to the Dickinson quartet of Bregawn, Captain John, Wayward Lad and Silver Buck to power away from the rest of the field with four fences to go. The chasing trio caught Bregawn by the time they reached the second last, but, brave as a lion, he refused to give in. Although Captain John, ridden by 'Gypsy' Dave Goulding, might have headed him fractionally over the last, there was only going to be one winner on the climb to the line. Ashley House, ridden by the since-disgraced Dermot Browne, seemed to take an eternity to reach that much-awaited fifth placing.

In typically modest Dickinson fashion, the master of Harewood summed up his own feelings about the task of getting all five horses to post fit and well (a major achievement in itself), explaining, 'We've had quite a few problems, as one always does training steeplechasers. I wish people realised what a hell of an achievement it is for anyone to get a horse to Cheltenham fit enough to run well in the Gold Cup. To get horses here, let alone win the race, is almost impossible.'

This Gold Cup triumph had crowned a wonderful week for Dickinson. He had saddled the speedy Badsworth Boy to win the Queen Mother Champion Chase by a distance, the first of his three wins in the race. Dickinson, only 33 years old, had nothing more to prove. He owed everything to his parents, Tony and Monica, who had been involved with hunting and point-to-pointing most of their lives. Tony took out a permit licence in the late '60s so that Michael could ride their horses and went public with great success. Many people forget that Michael became champion amateur in 1970, having already tasted Festival success in the National Hunt Chase riding Fascinating Forties. He turned professional in the same year and although his six-foot frame meant a constant struggle with weight, he continued to enjoy considerable success, particularly with chasers, the highlight being Gay Spartan winning the 1977 Sun Alliance Chase. He always had a strong desire to train and spent his summers learning from the master of Ballydoyle, Vincent O'Brien. In the spring of 1978, a serious accident in the saddle meant a premature end to Dickinson's riding career, although it was always the plan that he would take over from his father and this factor simply accelerated matters.

By November, and with a record-breaking 120 winners in his third season training, he received an offer he couldn't refuse from flat racing's leading owner Robert Sangster. Dickinson became Sangster's private flat trainer, based at Manton in Wiltshire. From the outset, the innovative Dickinson set about bringing much-needed physical additions and improvements to Manton House Yard complex. Time was against him and a lack of results with the dire offspring of Derby-winning Golden Fleece meant Sangster ran out of patience and sacked Dickinson. Whatever the exact reasons for the split, at least Dickinson was able to look back on the platform for success that he provided at Manton for Sangster's Derby-winning son-in-law, Peter Chapple-Hyam – who has since been sacked too!

Dickinson chose to start a new racing life with new goals in the States. He has enjoyed considerable and consistent success ever since, the undoubted highlight being Da Hoss's two Breeders' Cup Mile victories of 1996 and 1998. It was my pleasure to persuade him to return to England for the 75 years celebrations that took place at Cheltenham, his first return visit to Cheltenham in over ten years – and it gave him an excuse to come home and visit his mother!

Although Dickinson was lost to the jumping scene shortly after this Gold Cup, his young jockey Graham Bradley, so stylish and a supreme judge of pace, would be around for a long time yet, almost until the millennium. Bradley always attributed his longevity in the saddle to his mentor Michael Dickinson. Dickinson advised Brad in the early stages of his career to 'be selective in what you ride and avoid the bad horses – that way you will lose neither your confidence nor your bottle'. Bradley went on to ride in more Gold Cups than any other jockey – an incredible 14. Even his great friend A.P. McCoy might struggle to match that one!

The achievement of the Dickinson 'boys' in the 1983 Gold Cup was almost too much to comprehend at the time. The enormity of the achievement made front-page headlines the next day, right across the media spectrum. One of the best aspects of the race for me was to hear Bradley speaking on his retirement, reminiscing about the party back at Harewood and the fact that the stable lads had landed some hefty bets after the Dickinson clean sweep at rewarding odds. According to Bradley, Bregawn was never the same horse after winning the 1983 Gold Cup; although he ran in the next two Gold Cups he ran without distinction. The increasingly reluctant Bregawn, trained in Ireland in the latter stages of his career by Paddy Mullins, did grab hold of the bit one day when he won a two-mile bumper ridden by the eldest son Willie Mullins, former Irish amateur champion and now a top-flight trainer. Bregawn, now 26 years old, still lives in happy retirement at his owner's Mylerstown Stud.

It is inconceivable that Dickinson's Herculean effort in saddling the first five home in a Gold Cup will ever be matched, certainly in a championship race. You have to add the final proviso because of a certain trainer lurking in deepest Somerset who will do his level best to top most records! But not this one, surely.

BREGAWN (1983)

ch.g. 1974 (Saint Denys – Miss Society)
Owned by Mr M. Kennelly, trained by M. Dickinson and ridden by G. Bradley

✠ 1984 ✠

Tuck in to a young Green Monkey?

It's one place that could never be described as dull. The late Jeffrey Bernard encapsulated the world of Lambourn in his own inimitable way, from the confines of . . . yep, you've guessed it!

'I have stood in a bar in Lambourn and been offered, in the space of five minutes, a poached salmon, a leg of a horse, a free trip to Chantilly, marriage, a large unsolicited loan, ten tips for a ten-horse race, two second-hand cars, a fight, and the copyright to a dying jockey's life story.' Many would cast doubt upon the legitimacy of his claim, simply because Bernard would have been unlikely to have been in a fit state to stand for five minutes anywhere, let alone his favourite watering hole! It's a wonder that the local Trainers' Association didn't use this particular gem to advertise the joys of Lambourn to prospective owners – well, at least the more appealing parts of Bernard's tale.

On reflection, in early 1984 there was one offer that Bernard would certainly not have declined – an ante-post Gold Cup voucher on Burrough Hill Lad at juicy odds. Despite all the injury problems that Jenny Pitman's Gold Cup hope had endured over the years, it was strange that, at least from the public's viewpoint and perhaps naïvely so, there seemed to be a certain inevitability about the destination of this particular Gold Cup. Perhaps it had a lot to do with the fact that the Pitman stable had been on a high since the Corbiere success at Aintree the previous spring. This, coupled with Burrough Hill Lad's impressive progress throughout the season, made this result one of those where the season's top performer came through the ultimate test with flying colours. At the risk of generalising, this only seems to happen in the Cheltenham Gold Cup around once a decade, the most recent example of a trainer and horse 'on fire' being Kim Bailey and his mud-loving Master Oats.

It is presumably quite rare for any prospective Gold Cup runner, or indeed any Festival runner, to go through the season without any semblance of a hitch and, to be fair to the majority of current trainers, they do endeavour to keep the public well informed of the wellbeing of their runners. Sometimes, however, for whatever reason, this information is withheld and problems that trainers have faced are not communicated. They only come out in the wash after the event, sometimes happily in the aftermath of victory, often trying to make defeat slightly more palatable. This brings to mind the case of Ask Tom. A couple of years ago, trainer Tom Tate, Michael Dickinson's brother-in-law, appeared to incur the wrath of the majority of the racing press and Festival punters alike following the demise of his star chaser in the 1997 Queen Mother Champion Chase. Tate was deemed by certain members of the press to be guilty of not informing the public of the severity of Ask Tom's problems in the weeks leading up to the Festival. Post-race these problems were offered as possible reasons for the horse's below-par run; he had been well backed into favouritism on the back of superb past performances. To be fair to Tate, it is owners who pay the bills and a trainer's responsibilities are to the owners, not to anyone else. After all, problems are always discussed with the owner first and most trainers would tell you that it is the owner's prerogative to decide how much detail should be released, if any. Woe betide any trainer who would break any such agreement. This was a particularly thorny case because of the high profile of the race involved.

In contrast to Ask Tom, Burrough Hill Lad's problems were often very public, like the time in early 1980 when the green tarpaulin was readied, waiting for the Kempton vet to put the stricken hurdler out of his misery. Ironically, he had been in the process of handing out a beating at Kempton in the January to none other than Corbiere, his future stable-companion, when he dramatically capsized at the last. Fortunately, after what must have seemed an eternity, particularly for connections, the Jimmy Harris-trained four-year-old eventually scrambled to his feet, although not looking too good. In a desperate state for ten days, he was sent to equine osteopath Ronnie Longford. Burrough Hill Lad had suffered displaced vertebrae in his neck and back, which were promptly sorted out. Unfashionably bred by his owner Stan Riley, Burrough Hill Lad was a strapping black powerhouse of a horse with a long raking stride. Sired by Richboy, who was exported to Japan after only four seasons at stud in England, his dam was Green Monkey, a half-sister to useful sprinter Monkey Palm and purchased by Riley at the Leicester sales for a mere six hundred and fifty guineas. Green Monkey may have been cheap, but Riley knew all about her record of producing winners, albeit sprinters thus far, and hoped that her latest produce would prove to be good enough to run on the flat. Burrough Hill Lad was a well-travelled horse by the time he arrived at Weathercock House, having already experienced life at two different stables, and a similar number of bouts of leg trouble. He had won four hurdles as a four-year-old, two in the space of four days for Jimmy Harris and subsequently two for Harry Wharton the following season.

Mrs Pitman spent a frustrating amount of time on the Mandown gallops at Lambourn, trying to educate the long-striding Burrough Hill Lad to shorten up at the practice fences rather than ploughing straight through them. Although he was never going to be a natural like Corbiere, slowly but surely, the penny dropped. Despite some subsequently horrendous blunders, similar to the one that catapulted his jockey Colin Brown from the saddle in the Sun Alliance Chase at the 1982 Festival, the potential was there for all to see. He proved himself to be a classy performer when winning impressively over three miles in the valuable novice chase at the Aintree meeting. After two further successes to open his autumn campaign, Jenny decided it was time to pitch the gelding in with the big boys at Haydock in November. Many observers questioned the decision by his trainer to take on Gold Cup-winning Silver Buck at the peak of his powers in the Edward Hanmer Memorial. But, in typical fashion, she shrugged aside such talk, reflecting, 'For the past twelve months I've said I would not build mountains for this horse to climb. Now he is ready for the peak. I gather Silver Buck's trainer is not worried about my horse but is more frightened of the trainer.' Weren't we all!

In the event, Burrough Hill Lad was only beaten two and a half lengths – no mean feat, even in receipt of twenty-one pounds, at that stage of his chasing career. But unfortunately he strained a check ligament during the race and not taking any chances, he was put away for the rest of the season – to emerge better than ever. After more than a year off, a Coral Golden Hurdle qualifier over hurdles at Nottingham was chosen as the stepping stone to greater things. After finishing a creditable third, beaten only two lengths, it was time for the champion jockey John Francome to enjoy the first of many famous wins on the great horse. A massive ante-post plunge on the Coral Welsh National saw the extremely well-handicapped Burrough Hill Lad drop like a stone from 20-1 down to 10-3 favourite on the day. The win was achieved in some style as Francome, even carrying three pounds overweight, coasted to victory. It could have been a stone overweight and that wouldn't have affected the result.

The rapid climb up the steeplechase ladder, through further facile victories at Sandown and Wincanton, mirrored Burrough Hill Lad's rapid rise to the top of the ante-post market for the Gold Cup itself. By the time March arrived, Lambourn was buzzing with excitement, with not only a Weathercock House challenger vying for favouritism, but also Fred Winter's classy duo of Brown Chamberlain and Observe well fancied in their own right. However, the fact that Francome had struck up such a rapport with Burrough Hill Lad counted for nothing when it came down to riding arrangements for the Gold Cup itself. The champion had ridden Brown Chamberlain to all his important chasing wins to date, including the season's Hennessy Gold Cup and a more recent impressive win in a match against Wayward Lad, again at Newbury. Loyalty to Uplands meant a lot to Francome; he couldn't, more importantly wouldn't, desert the high-class Brown Chamberlain, despite believing that it would take quite something to prevent the Pitman horse from winning on the day – whether he was in the saddle or not.

Phil Tuck was recalled into the breech on his old partner and, despite having badly broken his nose in a fall the week before Cheltenham, he assured connections that he would be fit and ready to do the business, even though he looked like he had run headlong into an oak door. Phil Tuck has been regarded as one of the best jockeys never to have been champion and his incredible sense of timing would be shown to great effect on this, his first Gold Cup ride. He spent many fruitful years attached to the powerful Greystoke stable of the late Gordon Richards. He now works for the Jockey Club as a Stewards' Secretary.

At this late stage, the Lambourn rumour machine was extremely active, not altogether surprising considering Burrough Hill Lad's past record of problems. The negative vibes this time, though, were about him apparently breaking blood vessels. The rumours, though totally unfounded, soon reached the bookmakers and they couldn't push his price out quickly enough from 7–4 out to double those odds, despite Mrs Pitman's vociferous assertion that everything was hunky-dory. Wayward Lad, as he had been before Christmas after winning his second King George, was back in pole position at the head of a topsy-turvy market. Fully expecting Brown Chamberlain to be their main danger, despite his tendency of jumping right-handed at his obstacles, trainer and jockey got their heads together and planned a late thrust up the unforgiving hill, knowing that their fellow's burst of speed at the end of a stamina-sapping race that was likely to be run at breakneck speed could prove vital to their cause.

Twelve runners lined up on good ground and Francome immediately took Brown Chamberlain into the lead over the first and set a strong gallop which had a number of the field in trouble by halfway. Uncharacteristically, Wayward Lad wasn't jumping with his usual fluency and Robert Earnshaw did well to keep the partnership intact on a number of occasions. In contrast, Brown Chamberlain's jumping seemed to get better as Francome kept asking him for more, increasing the pace as he headed down the far side for the final time. Tuck had Burrough Hill Lad tucked in behind the leader coming down the hill, with only Drumlargan close enough to be in with a serious chance. Over the third last and barring accidents, it was looking like a two-horse race as the Irish challenger Drumlargan struggled to keep tabs on the leaders. Rounding the final bend, Brown Chamberlain began to drift towards the middle of the track and by the time he had jumped the second last, he was heading towards the hurdles course. Francome, using his whip in his right hand, did all he could to straighten up Brown Chamberlain, but as he approached the final fence he was on the drift yet again, losing lengths in the process. Tuck stayed glued to the far side and Burrough Hill Lad jumped the last in fine style, just a half-length ahead but moving like a Rolls-Royce. Powering up the hill, Burrough Hill Lad always had the edge on his rival and Tuck kept him going under a strong drive to win by a hard-fought three lengths.

A well-prepared Tuck had known exactly what was expected of him and carried it out to the letter in almost ruthless fashion, beating an extremely game Brown Chamberlain. Francome explained after the race, 'My horse never put a foot wrong, but Cheltenham was always going to be the wrong way round for him. He lost a lot of ground going right-handed, but you are better off letting them go that way'. Fred Winter agreed that his charge, sometimes accused of not being altogether in love with racing, couldn't have given more than he did and graciously declared that 'they had been beaten by a better horse on the day'.

The Dickinson domination of the past two Gold Cups had been well and truly smashed, with the unaccountably poor showing of the hot favourite Wayward Lad, who was eventually pulled up, and the antics of the increasingly mulish Bregawn. It was ladies day in more ways than one, as Welsh lass Linda Sheedy created history by becoming the first and only female rider to date to take part in the Gold Cup. However, it wasn't the biggest shock when she failed to complete the course on Foxbury, the 500–1 outsider. Burrough Hill Lad went on to add a Hennessy Gold Cup and a King George for his owner, but would sadly never compete in another Gold Cup – a catalogue of injuries would see to that. Seven years later, Jenny Pitman would win a second Gold Cup, with a locally owned horse, taking a similar route up the hill to a heart-stopping victory.

BURROUGH HILL LAD (1984)

br.g. 1976 (Richboy – Green Monkey)
Owned by R.S. Riley, trained by Mrs. J. Pitman and ridden by P. Tuck

Never forget Forgive 'N Forget

Jimmy Fitzgerald would definitely not have agreed at the time, but every cloud has a silver lining, the cloud in this case being the supposed less-than-vintage John Francome ride given to Forgive 'N Forget in the 1984 Sun Alliance Chase. The silver lining? The stable star's 33–1 ante-post price for the following year's Gold Cup, snapped up post-Cheltenham by the trainer.

Some 15 years on, Fitzgerald stands firm in his belief that the seven-times champion jockey, for whatever reason, never gave Forgive 'N Forget a cat in hell's chance of winning, coming from another parish to finish runner-up to A Kinsman. Francome, in his defence, recalls speaking to the injured Mark Dwyer before the race, explaining, 'I hadn't ridden the horse before, although I obviously knew a bit about him. Mark advised me to hold him up for a late run, which I did. I know Jimmy was furious afterwards and wouldn't talk to me for about ten years. From my experience, I thought the horse was a bit of a monkey and had two ways of running.' Monkey or no monkey, Fitzgerald always believed he had a serious horse, even after the bright chestnut ran an even more disappointing race at Aintree when reunited with stable jockey Dwyer some three weeks later. The common denominator in the two defeats seemed to be fast ground and checking the form book lends credence to this argument. Forgive 'N Forget's best performances had been on soft or even heavy ground, and when held up for a late run . . .

In the run-up to the Gold Cup, Forgive 'N Forget had been admirably consistent, winning three times in six races. Interestingly, two of those defeats were on fast ground. His final prep race was his most impressive, taking the Timeform Chase at Haydock only 12 days before the Gold Cup, comfortably beating the talented Harewood runner, the ill-fated By The Way, in a very fast time. Meanwhile, Burrough Hill Lad was yet again carrying all before him. His tremendous victory in the Hennessy Gold Cup, backed up by a win in the King George, were the undoubted highlights of his five wins. It takes some horse to carry twelve stone around Newbury in such a competitive race, but he managed it with ease, oozing class. Add to that a workmanlike performance at Kempton, enough to see off top-notch performers like Combs Ditch and Wayward Lad, and he looked set fair for a Gold Cup encore. Unfortunately, days before the race, the news emerged from Weathercock House that Burrough Hill Lad was now a doubtful starter, having cut the back of his knee quite badly with his own teeth, the result of a habit he had of hanging his head very low as he galloped at exercise! Time was to run out for the red-hot ante-post favourite and any dreams of back-to-back wins were over. He would return by the end of the year, but further injuries would mean that Burrough Hill Lad would never again line up at Cheltenham.

Fifteen runners eventually faced the starter on a thoroughly dank afternoon, including the quirky but talented Combs Ditch, now at the head of the market, with the genial Colin Brown in the saddle. The hope of Hawick, former hunter chaser Earls Brig, was fancied to run a big race for his owner/trainer/breeder Billy Hamilton. Another thought to have a chance was the headstrong Drumadowney, a first Gold Cup runner for Lord Vestey and the late and lamented Tim Forster. The ultimate in pessimists, he would have written off his front-runner's chances beforehand as being 'extremely minimal', in true Forsteresque fashion. Wayward Lad would be making his third Gold Cup appearance and represented Monica Dickinson, along with one of the young pretenders to the Harewood throne, Righthand Man. And, of course, Forgive 'N Forget, but not until after a last-minute scare: he developed a corn, which necessitated the use of an exercise shoe to lend extra support to the foot in question.

In thoroughly miserable afternoon weather, which seemed to worsen as the afternoon progressed, the Gold Cup got under way, with Drumadowney allowed to pursue his preferred tactics. At the top of the hill second time round, Hywel Davies still had the novice in pole position leading them all a merry dance, with Earls Brig in close attendance. However, a mistake at the last ditch gave Earls Brig a mountain to climb as he dropped back, just as dual Mackeson winner Half Free began to make his presence felt, tracked by a host of challengers including Ireland's best hope, the outsider Boreen Prince, along with Combs Ditch, Righthand Man and Forgive 'N Forget.

Drumadowney made his first real mistake at the third last, but was still in with every chance coming down the hill as Richard Linley began to get serious on Half Free. Sticking like a limpet to the far rail, Mark Dwyer must have known that with only the doubtful stayer Half Free in his sights as they approached the last it was only a matter of when to press the power button. Dwyer saw a perfect stride at the last and Forgive 'N Forget came up for him in grand style, gaining lengths on his rivals as they soared elegantly through the air to land running. In a matter of strides, the race was effectively over as the Malton duo powered up the hill impressively, leaving the chasing pack to play for places. As they reached the post, they finished a comfortable length and a half clear of Righthand Man, who had responded well to Graham Bradley's urgings, staging a late rally to pass the tiring Half Free on the run-in. Earls Brig and Drumadowney had plugged on admirably to finish in the frame, ahead of Half Free.

Forgive 'N Forget had been bought by Fitzgerald, the former national hunt jockey from Tipperary (now a successful dual-purpose trainer based near Malton) for Manchester-based owner Tim Kilroe, originally from County Roscommon. Kilroe had lost two potentially top-class young chasers, Fairy King and Brave Fellow, the former having broken his back at Kempton and the latter having suffered a heart attack on the gallops. Knowing this to be the case, Barney Curley had contacted Fitzgerald with a view to selling the lively chestnut with, in his opinion, the potential to go all the way. For the second time in three years, Curley would be a major link in the chain of events that led to the making of two Gold Cup winners. It's no wonder that bookmakers run shy of taking on 'yer man'.

FORGIVE 'N FORGET (1985)

ch.g. 1977 (Precipice Wood – Tackienne)
Owned by T. Kilroe and Sons Ltd, trained by J. Fitzgerald and ridden by M. Dwyer

✣ 1986 ✣

The Doninga mare the dawn of girl power?

You often see Dawn Run described as the Queen of Cheltenham, but that is a bit of a contradiction in terms. Her trainer Paddy Mullins knew her better than anyone and if he tells you she possessed many masculine traits, you sit up and take notice. Certainly she appeared, at times, to be a bit of a freak of nature. There is something wholly appropriate about her success in a predominantly male world – the world of Champion Hurdles and Gold Cups where females, even if good enough, tend to be kept well clear in the hope of producing winners of such races. Very few compete like Dawn Run did.

The five-pound weight allowance granted to mares for the first time in 1984, the year of Dawn Run's Champion Hurdle win, was almost an insult to her. If she could have refused it herself she probably would have done, although the owners of Wayward Lad will always maintain that without the allowance it would have been them clutching the Gold Cup and not Charmian Hill, the diminutive grandmother who rode Dawn Run to her first win in a bumper at Tralee. Whatever the rights and wrongs of that particular hot potato, the irresistible combination of Jonjo O'Neill and Dawn Run around Cheltenham far outweigh any talk of allowances.

On another issue, O'Neill's two from two record on the mare at Cheltenham in both championship races lends some support to Mrs Hill's decision to go for experience and choose O'Neill – both Ron Barry and Tony Mullins rode her at Cheltenham and failed. O'Neill knew just how far he could go with the mare, how much coercion she would need, but he also knew how tough it was on Mullins to have the more than capable Tony replaced, especially after he had done all the hard work on the mare. To cap this, Paddy Mullins had grown to accept that if Mrs Hill wanted to do something, she usually had her reasons. 'She had the final say and she knew it. As an owner, I had no complaints about her, but I did hear that the mare's trip to France had become a necessity, from a financial viewpoint.' He added, 'You feel very vulnerable as a trainer – I wasn't always fully in control with Dawn Run, but there was nothing I could do about it if I wanted to continue training the mare.' He's a shrewd man, Paddy Mullins. The mare had been bought by Mrs Hill for five thousand eight hundred guineas at Ballsbridge Sales in November 1981; she fell in love with the big, unfurnished and unbroken filly from the moment she saw her.

Ridden extensively by Mrs Hill, who was in her early sixties, Dawn Run was transferred to Doninga, the Mullins' family home and stable in the spring of 1982 and was ridden by her intrepid owner to a famous win on her last ride, in that Tralee bumper in June 1982. After this the Irish Turf Club had refused to renew Mrs Hill's licence and she was forced to give up any thoughts of riding in public again. According to Tom Mullins, another of Paddy's four sons and now his assistant, Mrs Hill never liked the fact that young Tony became a professional at around the same time that she had her licence taken away. Tom confirmed, 'After that, she seemed to take a dislike to Tony and often wouldn't even acknowledge his existence in the yard. It was no surprise to us that she kept "jocking" Tony off, but he really didn't deserve that sort of treatment.' In fact, Tony Mullins rode the mare to 13 of her 21 wins, but always missed out on riding her at a Cheltenham Festival. The mare went from strength to strength as a hurdler and in March 1984 became the first mare to win the Champion Hurdle since African Sister in the last pre-war Festival of 1939 before going on to win the French equivalent in June of that year. Dawn Run then went novice chasing in November and had the one run, winning at two miles at Navan, before having more than a year off with a pastern injury.

It was at this point that Mrs Hill decided she had big plans for the mare. As Mullins reflected, 'Mrs Hill's plan was for the mare to be schooled for the Gold Cup, which at the time would look a very tall order after just one novice win – but the mare was capable of it.' After two facile wins in December at Punchestown and Leopardstown, the mare went to Cheltenham in January to have a practice at the Cheltenham fences. Mullins explains, 'We came to win if we could but the mare made a mistake and flipped Tony (Mullins) out of the saddle. He managed to grab hold of her, remounted and finished fourth. She had her school, but the thanks for it was being jocked off for the Gold Cup.'

Gold Cup day arrived and the whole of Ireland seemed to want to back the mare. Backed down to 15–8 favourite, she had ten rivals, all of whom had a considerable advantage in experience. Forgive 'N Forget had experienced an up and down season of mishaps and disappointments, but he was back at his favourite hunting ground and had won the race last season. You could never write him off. Wayward Lad had gained his third win in the King George VI Chase, a record at the time, but Kempton was made for him and he always seemed to struggle with the Cheltenham hill. With the ground officially good, following a cold snap that had prevented racing for a month, Dawn Run wasn't going to be hanging around. She led the field with Run And Skip, the Welsh National winner, for company. Then O'Neill's plan to give her a breather before the final push went out of the window. Dawn Run dragged her hind legs through the water and a blunder at the fifth last meant her canny partner had to sit tight to survive and then get after her to retrieve the lost ground and try to regain the favoured rail position that Steve Smith Eccles had gained on Run And Skip.

Having jumped the third last brilliantly on Run And Skip's inner, O'Neill used the mare's giant stride to gain ground up the inner and regain the rail as they turned for home. With Wayward Lad and Forgive 'N Forget closing in on the two leaders as they approached the second last, O'Neill knew he had no option but to go for broke. He kicked the mare into the fence and she picked up once more in tremendous style and gained a length in the air over the diminutive Run And Skip. However, the two northern raiders had arrived on the outside to swallow them up and it looked to be between Wayward Lad and Forgive 'N Forget as, side by side, they jumped the last. Monica Dickinson must have thought she was going to follow in her son Michael's footsteps and train a Gold Cup winner. Wayward Lad sailed over in front, with Graham Bradley hoping to have conserved enough on the eleven-year-old to keep their advantage up the hill and secure a belated Gold Cup victory for the evergreen Lad. To his right, Mark Dwyer had jumped the last adequately, but lost the vital momentum that he needed to sustain his challenge up the gruelling hill. Behind the front two, Dawn Run looked to the majority of the crowd to be booked for third. It didn't seem possible that in the last one hundred and fifty yards the mare could make up the three lengths needed to get past Wayward Lad. Somehow, with the irresistible combination of O'Neill, refusing to give up, and the brave mare's incredible will to win, the impossible happened. While Wayward Lad drifted violently left-handed, almost diagonally up the run-in, O'Neill and Dawn Run, working in total unison, began a surge of raw power that devoured the ground ahead of them. As the line approached, victory was theirs for the taking in the dying strides, as Wayward Lad, continuing to drift across the course, began to tread water. As the mare drew upsides with less than 20 yards to the line, you just knew that she was going to do it and so did Jonjo O'Neill. He punched the air as he crossed the line and the crowd erupted. Even with the benefit of video replay 14 years on, the result beggars belief. It took a course record to achieve the impossible that day and even Dawn Run's belligerent appearance after the race takes some believing.

Paddy Mullins told me that after the race he felt numb at a time when he should have been overcome with joy, following the greatest triumph of his forty-year training career. All he could think about was his son Tony who had missed out once more. He believed that Tony got the best tune out of the mare and that Mrs Hill had been wrong to axe him. It would be wonderful to say that Dawn Run returned to defend her crown in 1987. Sadly on 27 June 1986, almost four years since Charmian Hill had ridden the mare to her first win, Dawn Run broke her neck attempting her second French Champion Hurdle – a crushing blow to national hunt racing. John Clarke, who had always looked after the mare, couldn't bear the thought of life at the Mullins yard without her and left the yard to cross the divide to work in a credit betting office.

Paddy Mullins, with no thoughts of retirement from the sport he loves after nearly fifty years, has won over fifteen hundred races on the flat and over jumps. He has trained many good horses under both codes, including his Irish Grand National winners Vulpine and Herring Gull, as well as Hurry Harriet, who took the Champion Stakes at Newmarket back in 1973. However, don't expect too many Mullins runners at Newmarket over the next few years – he is immensely proud of his 100 per cent record at Newmarket and wants to make sure he maintains it. He knows a good horse when he sees one and spends many hours at home checking out pedigrees, going back many generations to try and establish bloodlines. Mullins comes alive discussing pedigrees and it sounded as if he was suitably impressed with that of Dawn Run. He enthused, 'Dawn Run's dam was an Arctic Slave brood mare and there is no doubt they were brilliant brood mares and Deep Run was a great sire. His legs were twisted and for a national hunt sire he was small too, but that didn't stop him. In my opinion, a good national hunt family can be ruined in a couple of generations by mating with staying stallions – you need class and speed.' He added, 'Glacial Storm is my idea of a new national hunt sire that could become a great one.'

Mullins would have loved dearly to have had a chance to train Dawn Run's offspring – they too would have spun around that miniscule all-weather oval to the side of the yard, just yards from the Mullins's house. If you see where Dawn Run did the majority of her work each day, you begin to understand why this big, strong mare, nearly seventeen hands high, was so nimble and able to nip up Run

And Skip's inner on the final turn like a greyhound railing at the first corner. How good was she? Better than Desert Orchid? Paddy Mullins diplomatically sidestepped that one, but did point out fellow trainer and pundit Ted Walsh's comment that 'the mare would have kicked him out of the way!'.

Before racing on the opening day of the 1987 Festival, Princess Anne unveiled a half-size bronze of Dawn Run with O'Neill in the saddle which depicted their Gold Cup victory. Not surprisingly, O'Neill has a special regard for Cheltenham and all it stands for, with so many memories of his incredible triumphs there. He is immensely proud of the statue and reflected at the unveiling, 'It is a wonderful feeling to think that I am there for all time now, looking across at the statue of Arkle as he surveys the unsaddling enclosure.' This emotional view came from O'Neill at a difficult time for him, having spent the past six months bravely fighting lymphatic cancer, just at a time when he needed to be active, having just set up as a trainer. Two years ago, he opened his heart about that time and how he had been forced to write to all the owners of the 18 horses in his yard, telling them that he was having to temporarily quit. He recalls, 'Every one of those owners promised that as soon as I was diagnosed healthy again, I would have their horses back. After the doctors gave me the all-clear, I got two back. Situations like that teach you a lot about life.' O'Neill knew that he would have to fight prejudice to get the show on the road again. 'If you have cancer, you're a dead man as far as most people are concerned. My whole career, everything I did as a jockey, meant nothing. I felt I had to go out and prove myself all over again.'

O'Neill's sense of occasion hasn't deserted him over the years. He married his attractive girlfriend Jacqui Bellamy at Cheltenham racecourse in January 1997. It is great to think that soon O'Neill will be back again on Gold Cup day, in the winners' enclosure greeting his own Gold Cup winner from his Cumbrian yard. He has the right quality of horse now and couldn't be happier with life. It would be the final and deserved piece in the jigsaw of life for the genial O'Neill, who has emerged from the shadow that Dawn Run's tragic death seemed to cast over him personally and, for a time, the whole jumping world.

Willie Mullins has a slightly offbeat memory of the mare. 'After falling at the first in the race at Aintree after her Gold Cup, she got loose and jumped the Grand National fences – and cleared The Chair for fun!' She was that sort of mare.

DAWN RUN (1986)

b.m. 1978 (Deep Run – Twilight Slave)
Owned by Mrs C.D. Hill, trained by P.W. Mullins and ridden by J.J. O'Neill

✛ 1987 ✛

Rodin's big bloater

There can't be too many trainers around who would risk missing out on the buzz of being on hand to greet their returning Gold Cup hero; dreams like that often come once in a lifetime, if at all, unless your name happens to be O'Brien or Dreaper. Even more so if your last runner to reach the frame in the Gold Cup was 25 years ago – 50–1 outsider Cocky Consort, scampering up the hill to finish a fine third to wise old Mandarin. But then Arthur Stephenson, or 'W.A.' as he was generally known, wasn't just any trainer. He was the original legend in his own lifetime: hundreds of winners, year in, year out, buying and selling, the north country forerunner of the Martin Pipe phenomenon. 'Little fish are sweet,' he would declare as the racing press cocked a collective ear to scribble down the gems of knowledge offered, usually in the winners' enclosure.

Anyway, he had seven little fish to cook at Hexham this Gold Cup day, and it was probably market day too! He had been winning races at his local course since just after the war. Not surprisingly, his first winner came here – owned, trained and even ridden by the then permit-training farmer. More than forty years down the road, a clean sweep through the card at Hexham by local trainers would have pleased him enormously, especially his own contribution, the least one could expect on such a day, the appropriately named Succeeded.

Meanwhile, his assistant and nephew, Peter Cheesborough, was fighting the elements down at Cheltenham, enduring desperate conditions that would suit their relentless galloper through and through. The question on frozen lips was how could the big race go ahead in the teeth of a snowstorm? It had arrived quite unexpectedly during the Foxhunters', the race run prior to the Gold Cup. An inch of snow fell in under an hour and no sooner had the 12 runners got to the start, than they were recalled to the paddock area following the sensible decision that the conditions had become simply too dangerous. It began to look as though abandonment was an odds-on certainty as the snow continued to cover the entire course. It was around this time that a mystery caller to Major Arkwright informed him that the sun was now shining where he was at Upton-on-Severn, to the west of Cheltenham, and not to give up hope just yet as he was certain it would clear shortly. He was right. Eleven years on, while organising a competition which involved *Sporting Life* readers detailing their favourite Gold Cup moments, I received a call from Edward Gillespie's predecessor who claimed that he had been the caller that day. In his view, he was directly responsible for three Gold Cups going ahead in the past, including this one, and that these were his favourite Gold Cup moments! I got the distinct impression that Edward Gillespie, as one of the competition judges, wasn't too impressed with this particular entry and, needless to say, our weatherwise friend didn't get to go to the ball. The snowstorm came to a halt as abruptly as it had started and a rapid thaw meant that at least some of the snow began to melt away. Major Arkwright was adamant that conditions were safe enough to race and although some of the jockeys didn't particularly agree with the official assessment, the Gold Cup went ahead some eighty minutes late. Forgive 'N Forget went off the 5–4 favourite to regain his crown, having won impressively in Ireland in February, and The Thinker was the subject of a late gamble as punters latched on to the idea that conditions would now suit horses that were stamina-laden. The Thinker, winner of the 1986 Midlands Grand National in similar conditions, had never been in better form and stayed all day. Needless to say, stable jockey Ridley Lamb wasn't one of those who wanted to retreat to the comfort of the weighing room!

The dashing Cybrandian, with Chris Grant a late replacement for the injured Lorcan Wyer, made the running ahead of a tight pack that included Charter Party, who would fall as early as the fifth fence. Although the favourite was in touch at this stage behind the pack, he wasn't going with his usual fluency. Old Wayward Lad was making a mockery of his twelve years, in his fifth and final attempt to capture the Gold Cup, going as well as anything with three to go. At the third last, The Thinker went through the top of the fence and was lucky to get away with it, although losing many lengths in the process. Cybrandian, in front as he had been from the off, was still in pole position as Grant piled on the pressure coming down the hill. Over the last, Wayward Lad, challenged on the far side and not for the first time, seemed to be in the perfect position to strike gold. No sooner had Graham Bradley got Wayward Lad's head in front, then he began his customary left-hand drift under pressure as the hill sapped his stamina reserves. In contrast, Cybrandian began to drift right-handed as he was strongly challenged by The Thinker, whose limitless stamina was beginning to come into play. Lamb powered past the flailing Grant to record a well-deserved length and a half victory in the toughest of conditions.

To his eternal credit, Cybrandian hung on bravely to second place, ahead of Door Latch and West Tip, both storming up the hill, coming from a long way off the pace. Forgive 'N Forget trailed in a well-beaten seventh, a performance his trainer put down to having boiled over in the extended preliminaries, a view backed up by Mark Dwyer who knew from the time the tapes went up that he was fighting a losing battle.

The chestnut with the white blaze, picked out by Stephenson at one of his many visits to his old friend Tom Costello, would return from a lengthy absence through injury with Aintree as his long-term goal. He almost pulled it off, too, finishing a highly creditable third to the impressive Little Polveir, under the welter burden of eleven stone ten pounds. Preparing for a remarkable return to Aintree as a thirteen-year-old in 1991, The Thinker had to be put down after breaking a leg – a sad end to a wonderfully brave and resolute galloper who was handled with great skill by the late Arthur Stephenson, an acknowledged master of his craft.

THE THINKER (1987)

ch.g. 1978 (Cantab – Maine Pet)
Owned by T.P. McDonagh Ltd, trained by W.A. Stephenson and ridden by R. Lamb

✣ 1988 ✣

The Duke of Hazards

The Duke's day had finally arrived at Cheltenham two years earlier, after what must have seemed a lifetime of waiting for that elusive first Festival winner. Unfancied Daily Express Triumph Hurdle outsider Solar Cloud had broken the ice at the remarkable price of 40–1, only for the floodgates to open later in the afternoon with Charter Party winning the Ritz Club National Hunt Handicap Chase. Ironically, the fortunes of the two winners would be contrasting over the next few years.

As delighted as he was that famous day, I don't think even the Duke would have dared to suggest that here was a Gold Cup horse in the making. He did say that he had always believed there was a decent race in the unfashionably bred son of the obscure Document, particularly if he could learn to jump. Charter Party was as tough as teak and he had to be considering the mistakes he would make almost every time he raced, a prime example of this being the 1985 Hennessy Cognac Gold Cup where he forfeited any chance of winning with yet another of his trademark falls. Charter Party had been bought as a four-year-old for first-time owners Raymond Mould and his wife Jenny at Doncaster Sales for eight thousand guineas in May 1982. His owners subsequently sold a half share in the bay gelding to their friends Colin and Claire Smith, alternating their colours race by race. Although he never set the world alight over hurdles, at times he would show distinct promise, but the errors that plagued his jumping would prevent him from doing himself justice. Although the same could be said about his early novice chasing days, he began to improve gradually with experience, managing a total of three wins in each of his first two seasons over the bigger obstacles, including his win in the Ritz Club. Following a soft palate operation and having been hobdayed, the wheels rather came off Charter Party, as he failed to add to his tally over fences the following season. But he was still held in high regard at Condicote and ran in the Gold Cup – only to tip up at the fifth.

Intermittent lameness, the scourge of many a trainer, restricted Charter Party to only three runs prior to this Gold Cup. His final appearance in February had been an impressive one, beating Rhyme 'N Reason and Desert Orchid by some eight lengths, albeit receiving a stone from the flying grey. How Charter Party would cope with Dessie on level weights didn't become a factor as the flying grey was switched at the eleventh hour to the Queen Mother Champion Chase, David Elsworth blaming the worsening ground conditions for the decision to revert to the minimum trip. However, there were plenty of others to consider, including Kildimo, the classy but slightly unpredictable Sun Alliance winner, the impressive King George winner Nupsala, trained in France by François Doumen, and the favourite Playschool.

Playschool, a tough New Zealand import trained by David Barons, had slammed Forgive 'N Forget at level weights by eight lengths in the Vincent O'Brien Gold Cup at Leopardstown on heavy ground. He was fully entitled to go off as favourite on the day, but was never at the races, pulled up three fences from home. Many, including the trainer, believed that to run that badly Playschool must have been got at in some way, but no evidence from the dope test ever supported that view. It is worth noting he was never the same horse again after this race. Beau Ranger, from the all-conquering Somerset yard of Martin Pipe, made the running, with Golden Friend taking over briefly on the second circuit. As they reached the fateful fourth last, the Elsworth-trained Cavvies Clown skipped clear of the field with Charter Party and Forgive 'N Forget in close attendance. Following Forgive 'N Forget's demise and Rhyme 'N Reason's fall at the last ditch, it was left to the two leaders to scrap it out over the final three fences. Richard Dunwoody against Simon Sherwood, both looking to secure their first Gold Cup. A blunder worthy of his rival sealed Cavvies Clown's fate at the second last, just as the diminutive bay appeared to be getting the better of a battle royal between the two brave horses. Sherwood did well to keep the partnership intact, but as a contest it effectively ended there and then. Safely negotiating the final fence, Dunwoody merely pushed out Charter Party to secure a memorable win by six lengths – not bad for a horse once described by his breeder, Mrs Avia Riddell Martin, as 'the biggest ugliest camel you have ever seen!'.

After the race, beaten parties were left pondering what might have been. Brendan Powell's run of Festival bad luck continued unabated and he felt that it was a race he could, and perhaps should, have won. He explained, 'I don't think it is any secret that Rhyme 'N Reason was very unlucky. We were going as well as anything, but after jumping the downhill fence we slipped on landing and that was that. However, knowing the way that the horse finished his races, I have no doubts he would have beaten Charter Party. He went on to prove himself in the Grand National, but it was certainly an opportunity missed.'

Whether he would have beaten that ill-fated hardy perennial Forgive 'N Forget, who tragically suffered a more permanent fate at the very same fence, is debatable. Jimmy Fitzgerald believes that if his stable star, a veteran of six consecutive Festivals, had been able to complete the race, there would have been only one winner. 'He'd never been better at home and was only cantering at the time.' Sadly, it proved to be Forgive 'N Forget's last race, but not in the way connections, who had planned to retire him that day, could ever have envisaged. As he jumped that final ditch on the hill, his hind leg had already shattered under him and any hopes of a second Gold Cup vanished in that instant. Minutes later, Forgive 'N Forget's exuberant hold on life was over and realisation of the tragedy that had just occurred on the hill cast a huge shadow over any post-race celebrations, which were muted and kept to a bare minimum by the respectful winning connections.

After the race, The Duke spoke from the heart when he reflected, 'The death of Forgive 'N Forget ruined the race for me. I was very sad.' Forgive 'N Forget had been such a vital contributor to the magic of Cheltenham for so many years that it is only fitting that he is there, at least in spirit. His ashes, together with the race cards of the four consecutive Gold Cups he contested, lie behind an enscribed plaque on a wall near the Royal Box. Charter Party was X-rayed after the Gold Cup and found to be suffering from navicular disease, a painful inflammatory condition of the navicular bone, brought on by thrombosis in the feet. This could well have explained some of the horse's fencing problems, due to the pain that must have plagued him for years. The Duke had been fearful of a foot problem, but was loath to have the horse x-rayed before the Gold Cup in case the diagnosis ended the dream there and then. The condition must make the gelding's achievements, in retrospect, all the more laudable.

This particular renewal may not go down in the annals of Festival history as one of the great Gold Cups in terms of quality, but it certainly was one of the most memorable and incident-packed, though sadly not for all the right reasons.

CHARTER PARTY (1988)

b.g. 1978 (Document – Ahoy There)
Owned by Mrs C. Smith and Mrs J. Mould, trained by D. Nicholson and ridden by R. Dunwoody

✢ 1989 ✢

On a grey wing and a prayer

If there was ever a horse, in the modern era of national hunt racing, that didn't need to win a Cheltenham Gold Cup in order to enhance his reputation, it was Desert Orchid. It hadn't mattered to his adoring public that 'Dessie', as the flying grey had become universally known, had been to every Festival since 1984 and come away, along with many hundreds of other horses, empty-handed. However, this horse was different, a horse brimming with style, panache and charisma – the ultimate Steed of the '80s, with enough presence to make adrenaline pump through the most wooden of hearts.

No distance seemed to be a problem as his versatility in that sphere was quite remarkable. Now, on the eve of the Gold Cup, Dessie's sixth attempt to break his Cheltenham hoodoo was being scrutinised *ad nauseam* by the media and talk of Dessie and his Gold Cup chances echoed around the hotels and pubs within range of Cheltenham long into the night. It would be new territory even for him at Cheltenham – he had only ever tried the minimum trip of two miles at the Festival, over both hurdles and fences, and had failed each time. Nevertheless, on the plus side, Dessie had proved himself to be the best staying chaser in Britain and was, undeniably, at the peak of his powers. His unblemished record in a season of competing over a range of distances from two to three miles had shown him to be the personification of versatility. He always battled his heart out and had secured his second King George VI Chase, at the expense of a small but select field.

However, the odds of the ten-year-old continuing the winning run were heavily stacked against him. His Festival record couldn't have been much worse: two Champion Hurdles, an Arkle Chase and, most recently, two Queen Mother Champion Chases had all resulted in defeat. It was hardly surprising considering his particular bias for right-hand courses. Dessie only ever encountered Cheltenham's left-hand turns in March and against the cream of Britain and Ireland.

Kempton, Sandown, Ascot, Wincanton, and Devon and Exeter – the form books were full of Dessie's successes, 26 of them to date from 54 races, including 19 wins over fences. The record going left-handed didn't have quite the same ring to it: nine runs, with one solitary win at Aintree. The 100 per cent failure record at Cheltenham was a pretty damning statistic for any self-respecting superstar to overcome.

One of Henry Cecil's senior head lads once told me a gem of information, which had been passed on to him from the usually pursed lips of none other than Lester Piggott. Lester had told him that he firmly believed that at least eight out of every ten horses in training had a pronounced preference for going either right-handed or left-handed. He felt that this was the most significant factor when selecting future rides, often other jockeys' rides which would soon be his and inevitably soon be winners.

So that explains what the greatest flat jockey did when he wasn't riding: in the sauna, a cigar in one hand and a form book in the other, checking out the tools of his trade for their individual biases and getting on the phone to make sure he was riding them. If only the mystique surrounding Lester Piggott's genius was that simple.

Dessie was bred by James Burridge, who had won a point-to-point with Desert Orchid's granddam Grey Orchid. Grey Orchid was subsequently mated with the obscure stallion Brother, producing Flower Child, a spectacular jumper with a tremendous zest for racing, but not a horse you could describe as a quality performer. Fortunately, it appeared that the best of her qualities were passed on in abundance to her grey son, the product of her mating with top-class miler Grey Mirage. Put into training with Hampshire-based dual-purpose handler David Elsworth, the headstrong young Dessie almost didn't make it beyond his first visit to the racecourse in January 1983 at Kempton, crashing to the ground at the final flight of hurdles before eventually clambering to his feet, having been badly winded.

Just over a year later, and unbeaten as a novice hurdler in six races over the minimum trip, Dessie ran in the Champion Hurdle but found Dawn Run and others to be just too good. Although he became a top-class hurdler over the next two seasons, winning six times for his regular partner Colin Brown, it was all a prelude to what was to come over fences, when all that natural fencing ability would come to the fore. He won four novice chases on the trot in the 1985–86 season before finishing third in the Arkle at the Cheltenham Festival.

In December 1986, and partnered for the first time by former amateur champion Simon Sherwood, Dessie ran a classy King George field ragged – the first of a record four wins in the race and the start of an high-octane adventure for Sherwood that would eventually peak with glory at Cheltenham. Two seasons later, and Dessie having made the frame in two Queen Mother Champion Chases, Sherwood took over as his regular pilot and matched his King George win some eighteen months later with an exhilarating Whitbread Gold Cup win at Sandown. This victory set the seal on a memorable season, with increased hopes that there was still more to come from the grey wonder.

Unbeaten in four runs, including his annual Boxing Day outing to Kempton to record a third King George win, Dessie headed for the first of three attempts at the Gold Cup. Gold Cup day arrived and so did the fire engines at Cheltenham, pumping water off the course as a mixture of rain and snow transformed Prestbury Park into a veritable bog and, for a considerable time, put the whole day in jeopardy.

Even if the Gold Cup were to go ahead, the conditions would be very much against Dessie. His connections, Elsworth apart, were not over keen to press ahead with the Gold Cup plan on what seemed such an uneven playing field. Elsworth, ever the realist, took the view that Dessie wouldn't have to be at his best to beat the opposition on the day, despite the appalling conditions. When the meeting got the go-ahead, the decision was taken by Dessie's camp to go with Elsworth and let the favourite take his chance.

Not surprisingly, Dessie proved to be an uneasy favourite, with any self-respecting bookmaker happy to lay him. Consequently, he drifted a whole point out to 7–2, before solid support arrived from Dessie's faithful army of supporters to push his price back in again just before the off. His effort might have taken at least a quarter of a million out of the ring, but it was by no means a disaster day for the bookies as the first and last races both went to unfancied 66-1 chances.

Dessie eventually lined up at the Cheltenham start, pitting his wits against 12 opponents, many of whom were going to be better suited to the quagmire conditions. Simon Sherwood, attempting to stretch to nine his unbeaten record on Dessie, dictated the pace from the off, closely followed by the useful Ten Plus, unbeaten in his last four races, and last year's winner, Charter Party. Carvill's Hill, the Jim Dreaper-trained novice who was well backed into second favouritism and had been making such an impression in his completed races came a cropper at the tenth. Joined by Cavvies Clown and Ten Plus going out onto the second circuit, Dessie seemed to be travelling well within himself.

Eight fences from home, Kevin Mooney pushed Ten Plus into the lead for the first time and began to step up the pace. He was still in front, and was beginning to get the jockeys in behind niggling along, as he approached the ditch on the hill, closely followed by the chasing pack, which included Dessie, Yahoo, Charter Party and Ballyhane. Disaster struck as Ten Plus, two lengths clear and going possibly best of all, took a heavy fall, which sadly proved to be fatal. In behind, a closing Ballyhane, a 50-1 outsider sporting the famous Jim Joel colours, was brought down by the stricken Ten Plus. Yahoo jumped the second last ahead in front of Dessie, with Charter Party plugging on gamely in third place. Looking all over the winner as they approached the last, Yahoo slowed into it and only cleared it fractionally ahead of Dessie. It became a real war of attrition on the famous climb for home. Although Dessie had looked to be under pressure from two out, he nevertheless dug deep to wear down Yahoo within sight of the post and battled on to gain the day by a length and a half at the line, Sherwood punching the air in victory. Dessie was given a well-deserved hero's welcome on his return to the winners' enclosure, reminiscent of that given to Dawn Run. Dessie had won in very similar fashion to the great Irish mare, albeit in very different conditions.

Whether Dessie would have won had Ten Plus not fallen is highly debatable. Kevin Mooney was certain his horse was going like the winner at the time and, according to Tom Morgan, Yahoo's jockey, it was Ten Plus's fall that changed the whole complexion of the race. Morgan, now assistant trainer to Graham McCourt, felt he had only one horse to beat as they approached the downhill fence for the final time – and it wasn't Dessie. 'Ten Plus definitely had Dessie on the stretch at that time. He was struggling to keep up and I remember thinking Ten Plus is the one I was going to have to beat.' He added, 'I had just started putting my fellow into the race, and was only a couple of lengths in arrears, when Ten Plus fell. Suddenly, we found ourselves getting there too soon and although Yahoo battled on really well up the hill, towards the end Dessie started hanging right-handed away from us, which actually didn't help us. Although I felt gutted about the result afterwards, we would have been happy, before the race, to settle for a place.'

An emotional Simon Sherwood, speaking after the race, confirmed that Dessie had hated the ground, but that the horse's sheer guts and determination had seen him through. If only Channel 4 had enjoyed the rights to screen the Festival on Dessie's day. It would have been extremely satisfying to watch John McCririck, who had positively foamed at the mouth with damning negativity concerning the statistically negligible chance of a grey winning the Gold Cup, waddle disconsolately through a sea of passionate arm-wavers to report back on the 'grey day'.

Two more King George VI Chases and, just for good measure, an Irish Grand National were added to the already remarkable record. However, in December 1991, following an abortive attempt at an unprecedented fifth win in the King George VI Chase at Kempton, owner Richard Burridge made the decision to retire Dessie. He delayed his announcement until the following day, so as not to impinge on the plaudits rightly accorded to the course record-breaking performance of the winner, The Fellow. In a strange quirk of fate, Kempton's Boxing Day feature links two Gold Cup heroes, Arkle and Desert Orchid. Exactly 25 years after Arkle's final appearance on a racecourse at Kempton in 1966, the much-loved Dessie would also run his last race, eventually falling at the third last, but already well beaten, in the King George VI Chase.

Dessie's amazing popularity had virtually nothing to do with his volume of success, it was more his style of racing that ignited such adulation. He was fearless, knuckling down to the job at hand in his unique way, which involved launching himself, often from beyond the wings of a fence, to land running at pace. Dessie did everything at pace.

He enjoys a happy retirement, which includes ambassadorial duties, appearing at a number of racecourses to lead parades for important races. Even now, at 21 years young, he is still poetry in motion and has a certain aura about him. The buzz he creates among the crowd, eager to catch a glimpse of racing history, is tangible. The latent power on display when he gallops in front of the stands, showing off his paces, evokes memories of past glories. His regular partner for these jaunts, the retired jump jockey Colin Brown, rode him more than anyone else and helped mould Dessie into the finished article, particularly in those hair-raising early days. He has got used by now to having his arms virtually pulled out of their sockets by his eager grey friend with the marbled coat.

In January 2000, in typically forthright style, David Elsworth, former jockey and national hunt champion trainer, announced that he had 'lost his appetite' for preparing horses for the winter game. 'I am not enjoying it any more, it is a change of attitude on my part and what is the point in doing something you don't enjoy? It is a great sport but I have lost my appetite for the training because of the physical welfare aspect.' Reflecting on Dessie's phenomenal success, he added, 'He achieved the most and don't forget he was a top-class hurdler and a very good two-mile chaser too. He set the record for prize money earned, which still stands [£542,629 in first-prize money], and he has been retired for nearly ten years!' The grey legend lives on.

DESERT ORCHID (1989)

gr.g. 1979 (Grey Mirage – Flower Child)
Owned by Mr R. Burridge, trained by D. Elsworth and ridden by S. Sherwood

✢ 1990 ✢

Dessie's roars, silenced by a powerful Norton

Up until the previous season, the aftermath of being connected with a Gold Cup winner in a 'normal' year was both tolerable and enjoyable. Nothing too taxing – interviews, requests for photographs, a few award dinners and perhaps opening a local supermarket or bookmakers. Unless you were already high profile, with flat racing in full swing it would soon be back to normality, if not relative obscurity in some cases. Somehow, in 1990, it was not going to be like that post-Orchid, not if you had beaten the flying grey, at fairytale odds of 100–1.

The year of the Orchid had also been a watershed in terms of the perennial Festival squeeze. 'We're not looking to get more people racing here during the Festival. In 1989, we had sixty-three thousand on Gold Cup day, and that was too many.' That was Edward Gillespie's verdict on the gigantic sardine tin that Prestbury Park became on the big day last year. This renewal would be no different, everyone wanting to see the flying grey who was now approaching veteran status. It's a tough decision to restrict numbers, but safety must come first. Eventually, come Gold Cup day in 1998, the tin was fitted with a cap – fifty thousand and no more.

The stampede to see Desert Orchid thundered on unabated in the early months of the season. Richard Dunwoody was now in the saddle, following the retirement of Simon Sherwood. This change of jockey had surprising repercussions for another Gold Cup contender, albeit an unconsidered one, going by the rather odd name of Norton's Coin. Norton's Coin, trained at Rwyth Farm in the small village of Nantgaredig in Dyfed by permit-holder and dairy farmer Sirrell Griffiths, had hit a rich vein of form last spring, finishing a creditable second in the Cathcart an hour after Desert Orchid won his Gold Cup. Dunwoody had won on the eight-year-old prolific point-to-pointer/hunter chaser back at Cheltenham at the April meeting, having also won on him earlier in the season. Griffiths recalled, 'Richard got off and said he was so impressed that he wanted to ride him in the Gold Cup next season. Naturally, come the autumn, Richard had been offered the ride on Desert Orchid and telephoned to let me know the situation. He was very disappointed to let us down, but there was a retainer involved and we understood perfectly.'

It was somewhat ironic then that the two met in December, at Desert Orchid's favourite hunting ground, Kempton. In truth, it wasn't a contest, being Norton's Coin's first run of the year and Desert Orchid's favourite race, resulting in his third King George VI Chase win. Ridden by Graham McCourt, Norton's Coin would have needed the race badly, but wasn't totally disgraced despite one or two fencing errors. It was a return to Cheltenham a month later that would start Griffiths thinking that the Gold Cup was a distinct possibility, finishing a close second to the useful youngster Willsford, giving him ten pounds and beaten only a length. But a disappointing run at Newbury in mid-February, followed by a bout of coughing, meant that the Gold Cup was becoming a bit of a pipe-dream. So Griffiths lowered his sights and looked at some Festival alternatives. He was no longer eligible for the Cathcart, only open to first and second season chasers, and he had missed the entry date for the Mildmay of Flete. The Gold Cup was the only option left open to Griffiths, with the star of his three-horse yard on the easy list, undergoing a course of antibiotics for a sore throat, less than a month before the big day.

It is as unlikely a tale as Norton's Coin's breeding. His dam, Grove Chance, and his sire, Mount Cassino were both on the Griffiths' farm before Grove Chance was sold in foal to a local farmer, while Griffiths stood the obscure stallion himself. He eventually had to go to nearly five thousand pounds to get back their offspring, after Norton's Coin, now a six-year-old, won numerous point-to-points and a hunter chase for his friend Percy Thomas.

When Norton's Coin had responded to the medication, McCourt suggested that he should go and work with Peter Cundell's horses at his Compton base, which he duly did. He proceeded to thrash the very useful Celtic Ryde and two others in a decent 12 furlong gallop.

The firmish ground had scared off the new hope of Ireland, the Jim Dreaper-trained Carvill's Hill, as well as a number of others who would have preferred it hock deep. In view of all this, Desert Orchid was backed down to a shade of odds-on and the mud-loving Bonanza Boy, trained by Martin Pipe, was a rather surprising second favourite, given the ground conditions. Jenny Pitman had Toby Tobias in the field, a first Gold Cup ride for son Mark.

Not over-big, the unconsidered Norton's Coin, on offer at 100–1, had been milling around at the start in among the other runners when he received a hefty kick from Toby Tobias. He was allowed to race, although nine times out of ten when something like that happens it usually results in a below-par run. Griffiths reflected, 'He was as tough as nails and when we had him x-rayed at a later date he was found to have a hairline fracture. For twenty minutes after the race he was hopping lame, too, which makes his run that much more creditable.'

The 12 runners were headed by Ten Of Spades and Desert Orchid at the first as the two leaders went hammer and tongs for the lead for the majority of the race, probably doing each other no favours at all. Pegwell Bay and Yahoo raced in behind, with Cavvies Clown finally making up the lost ground to hunt up the leaders. Toby Tobias, with Pitman sitting very quietly, moved sweetly up the inside to take over in the lead coming down to two out, with Desert Orchid on his outside and Norton's Coin coming with a strong challenge between the two. At the second last, the three jumped almost in unison, but Desert Orchid began to send out the distress signals, struggling to keep tabs on the two leaders just ahead of him as they approached the last. Ten Of Spades had suffered a spectacular fall behind them at the second last and was fortunate to survive. Pitman coaxed a magnificent jump from Toby Tobias at the last and settled down on the far side to battle it out with McCourt, working overtime on the game chestnut on his favourite hunting ground. Slowly but surely, Norton's Coin dug deeper into his stamina reserves and caught Toby Tobias with less than fifty yards to go. Try as he might, Pitman simply couldn't hold off the late challenge of the determined Welsh terrier and went down by three-quarters of a length, with Desert Orchid, keeping on at the one pace, some four lengths further behind in third.

A lightning pace had been set by habitual front-runners, which probably led to the course record time being smashed. The time of just under six minutes thirty-one seconds still stands at the turn of the century. McCourt picked up a three-day ban for using his whip with excessive frequency, but it wouldn't have dampened his spirits too much – it's not every day you win the Gold Cup on a 100–1 no-hoper, not according to the race-card anyway! Griffiths recalled that he had been shocked at the amount of mucus that Norton's Coin had discharged within the hour post-race into his water bucket. It's surprising he even stayed the course of the race, the state he had been in.

So the locally bred gelding, named after a motorbike that powered around the fields at the farm and a Grand National winner, was the toast of Cheltenham. Griffiths had numerous offers to train significantly more horses but turned them all down on geographic grounds. Although he would have loved to have become a public trainer, it simply wasn't feasible.

McCourt is now a dual-purpose trainer and was one of the strongest and probably most underrated riders of his generation. He followed up this unexpected success with another 'classic' two years later, partnering the ill-fated Royal Gait to victory in the Champion Hurdle for James Fanshawe. He rode over nine hundred winners in a career that spanned over twenty years.

Norton's Coin, still enjoying life at 19 years of age, was never the same horse after an operation on his throat, undertaken to sort out his sinus problems, went seriously wrong, something that clearly angers the mild-mannered Griffiths to this day.

NORTON'S COIN (1990)

ch.g. 1981 (Mount Cassino – Grove Chance)
Owned and trained by S.G. Griffiths and ridden by G. McCourt

✢ 1991 ✢

Mark Pitman, Gold Cup hero and
the man who fell to earth

It must have been a record for first-time owners, certainly in the national hunt game. A six thousand pounds outlay for a return of over two hundred thousand on a horse that reminded Jenny Pitman of 'a different-coloured Corbiere'.

Bought as an unbroken three-year-old in the autumn of 1986 at the Derby sale at Ballsbridge in Ireland, the horse returned with the trainer to Weathercock House. As luck would have it, his arrival coincided with a speculative phone call from the Cheltenham-based Autofour Engineering company, whose three directors, all racing fanatics, were looking for their first plunge into ownership.

Showing early promise in a bumper, Garrison Savannah won over hurdles before having a year off the course due to a slight stress fracture to his cannon bone. Having schooled brilliantly, he made his reappearance over fences, where it was always believed he would make his mark. He won unchallenged at Wincanton, equipped with blinkers, by 25 lengths. He was entered for the Sun Alliance Chase along with stable-companion Royal Athlete and came late to win, while Royal Athlete, who would have his turn at the glory game at Aintree in years to come, fell heavily. The following season, following an encouraging second behind former Champion Hurdler Celtic Shot at Haydock in December, Garrison Savannah was found to be lame in his shoulder.

His participation in the Gold Cup was in doubt right up until the day, but he benefited from acupuncture and homeopathic remedies and general kid glove tactics, not even working with another horse, right through from December to Gold Cup day in March. He seemed to be fine physically and mentally, but how would his fitness hold up on the big day? In her intriguing book *Jenny Pitman: The Autobiography*, the trainer explains her attempt at trying to convey positive instructions to her son in the paddock beforehand. 'Ride him like you rode Toby Tobias last year. Only don't get beat this time.' Son Mark was looking to make up for losing out narrowly in the race last year on Toby Tobias and already felt he had a point to prove.

Celtic Shot went off favourite ahead of a now veteran Desert Orchid. There was a Gallic challenge from the The Fellow, precisely half Dessie's age and trained by the now familiar figure of François Doumen, who had proved himself extremely adept at coming over and plundering our top races. On officially good ground, confirmed front-runner and fellow Lambourn raider Arctic Call took the field of 13 along at a brisk pace, before blundering his chance away at the eleventh. Desert Orchid took over at this point, with Nick The Brief in close attendance. Meanwhile, Garrison Savannah had been jumping in fine style and going well within himself.

Celtic Shot led four out, before a blunder put paid to his chances of emulating

Dawn Run. At this point, Pitman took the bull by the horns and committed his horse, putting a few lengths between himself and the rest of the chasing pack. The Fellow, despite a bad mistake at the fifteenth fence, had got back in contention and was still going well and closing the leader down as they approached the last, with the race between them. Just as he had last year on Toby Tobias, Pitman asked for a big effort from his willing partner, and got it. He jumped it like a stag and set off up the hill with The Fellow inexorably closing him down as the line approached. It was impossible to separate them as they crossed the line. The two jockeys shook hands, neither knowing which had won. Before they reached the unsaddling enclosure, the result was called and Garrison Savannah had held on to beat The Fellow by the shortest of short-heads and provide his trainer with her second Gold Cup victory to add to Burrough Hill Lad's fine win in 1984.

Instead of being part of the Weathercock House celebrations back in Lambourn that evening, Mark Pitman ended Gold Cup day in hospital, having suffered a broken pelvis in a bad fall in the closing County Hurdle, with half the field trampling over him. Some way to end the best day of your life as a jockey.

With faint hopes of riding Garrison Savannah in the Grand National, Pitman tested himself on Wonder Man, in the Welsh Champion Hurdle at Chepstow, on April Fool's Day. It turned out to be no joke for Pitman, but he beat the pain and came through to win the race. Even allowing for having proved himself fit to ride in a hurdle, how Pitman could envisage riding over four and a half miles, in one of the toughest steeplechases in the world, is almost beyond belief. And they say Dunwoody was driven? To give the horse the ride he did, only caught in the final yards of the race by a jet-propelled Seagram, says a lot about the character of the man.

Despite being forced to miss much of next season following back problems and spasmodic lameness, Garrison Savannah did go on to contest a total of three Gold Cups, his last in 1994 at the ripe old age of 11, ridden by Graham Bradley, fast approaching veteran status himself at the time. Although a 50–1 outsider, he didn't jump with his usual fluency and couldn't get into the race. Bradley wisely pulled him up. There was still life in the old champion, though, as he proved by winning three more races and still enjoying his racing as a thirteen-year-old. In mid-November 1996, after the Badger Beer Chase at Wincanton, the curtain was finally drawn on his racing career. What a servant he had proved to be for Jenny Pitman, who surprisingly announced her own retirement at the Festival in 1999 in order to hand over the reins to son Mark at Weathercock House.

'Gary' had been successful in nine of his fifty races. On his retirement, his trainer summed up her feelings for him. 'Any words that I say aren't good enough for Garrison Savannah. I don't think he's one of Britain's true treasures, I think he's one of the world's true treasures – and I've been very fortunate and blessed to have him here.' A fitting tribute to a gutsy champion, who might well have emulated Golden Miller's famous double in the same season had the rain not arrived on Grand National morning in that famous Gold Cup year of 1991.

GARRISON SAVANNAH (1991)

b.g. 1983 (Random Shot – Merry Coin)
Owned by Autofour Engineering, trained by Mrs J. Pitman and ridden by M. Pitman

✢ 1992 ✢
Mr Cool and the Behemoth

Every so often, probably too often, a monster is created by the press. In this case a true behemoth, the ultimate Job horse by the name of Carvill's Hill. He seemingly underwent a complete metamorphosis following his move from his native Ireland to the Martin Pipe Academy of Excellence. According to the racing media, all he lacked now was wings. In a way, you couldn't entirely blame them. Pipe had transformed so many problem horses over the years that all the troubles that Jim Dreaper had experienced with the talented but injury- and accident-prone enigma seemed to be a thing of the past.

Demolition followed demolition in his three races for Pipe and his new owner, Jersey-based millionaire Paul Green. The relentless power that Carvill's Hill displayed, winning the Welsh National and the Irish Hennessy Gold Cup, could not fail to leave an impression of invincibility. This did appear to be the horse to secure Pipe his first of many Gold Cups.

Happily blitzing from the front, Carvill's Hill would actually dovetail perfectly into the Pipe system. It had become a way of life to run horses this way down at the Pipe factory and Carvill's Hill was no exception. Plan A stood for annihilation of the opposition. Was there a plan B? In the Gold Cup, things don't always work out quite as expected – you only have to think back to Pendil and Mill House to realise that. There was no way the even-money favourite was ever going to be allowed simply to dash off in front and dictate matters from there – not without facing some sort of challenge, particularly in the early stages of a Gold Cup.

If connections did have any worries at all about their star performer, it would have been that he hadn't been put under any pressure all season, so overwhelmingly superior had he been in all his three races. How would he react here if he was forced to battle? The acid test came right from the off. Peter Scudamore's desire to get to the inside with Carvill's Hill soon became apparent as he bounded down to the first fence on the outside of the Jenny Pitman-trained Golden Freeze. Carvill's Hill did have a tendency to jump left-handed and Scudamore knew that it would be in his interest to secure the inner, to reduce any problems this could cause in the race. Something or someone had to give and, unfortunately for punters, it was the favourite.

Jumping at breakneck speed, Michael Bowlby, riding Golden Freeze, managed to negotiate the first safely enough, but on his outside Carvill's Hill almost fell, crashing right through it. It is highly likely that the favourite might well have injured himself even at this early point of the contest. He ballooned the second behind Golden Freeze and from there didn't jump with any of his usual fluency. Taken on throughout the first circuit by the now fizzed-up Golden Freeze, Carvill's Hill seemed to be totally unnerved by that initial error of judgement and proceeded to make more mistakes as the race progressed, as the two leaders took each other on.

By the time they reached the thirteenth, Golden Freeze had shot his bolt, but by sheer brute strength alone, Carvill's Hill was still in front jumping the third last. In behind, the other jockeys had been biding their time, waiting to see the outcome of the supremacy war that had raged ahead of them and now began to close him down, as he inevitably began to tire. The diminutive Docklands Express seized his chance to take up the running, closely followed by The Fellow and Cool Ground, second and fourth respectively in the race last season.

Cool Ground was partnered by the jockey find of the season, Adrian Maguire. The chestnut was thought to be more of a Grand National type who would need much softer ground than the officially good ground here to be seen to best advantage. But here he was, running out of his skin, and coming to the last with every chance of making Maguire's first Gold Cup ride a winning one.

Leaving Carvill's Hill well behind, the leaders jumped the last almost in unison. All three landed running and Docklands Express got away the quickest on the stands side and looked to be in control halfway up the hill. But he began to drift right-handed and, to his left, The Fellow and Cool Ground were having a ding-dong battle of their own towards the far side. Maguire simply refused to give in and, riding as if his life depended on it, asked his willing partner for one final effort. In the shadow of the winning post, Maguire virtually lifted Cool Ground over the line to beat The Fellow by the minimum distance, with Docklands Express drifting right-handed to finish only a length behind in third.

For the second successive year, The Fellow had done nothing wrong and had been beaten by the minimum distance, while Maguire picked up a holiday for excessive use of the whip in the final furlong. There was never going to be any danger of Adam Kondrat picking up a similar ban, as The Fellow's owner, the Marquesa de Moratalla will not have her horses abused in any way.

Despite the nail-biting finish, most of the post-race discussion revolved around the performance of the disappointing favourite. Surely he should have been able to cope with the close attentions of Golden Freeze. However, had it been his fault? There were suggestions in some quarters that Golden Freeze had been entered by Jenny Pitman purely as a spoiler to unsettle Carvill's Hill. Pitman, incensed by such accusations, contacted the Jockey Club to request an enquiry. She knew in her own mind that she had done nothing wrong and certainly hadn't given Bowlby any instructions to do anything other than, if at all possible, win the race. An enquiry did take place in May, finding Bowlby and Pitman not guilty of any wrongdoing. In fact, Pitman and Bowlby came out of the enquiry positively smelling of roses, which is more than could be said of Scudamore. He had suggested post-race that Bowlby had apologised to him during the race itself for employing spoiling tactics. This had been flatly denied by Bowlby and couldn't be proven either way by the enquiry team, despite studying the tapes of the race for a considerable time, as well as asking Scudamore to indicate at which point the supposed conversation had occurred, which he couldn't.

The surprise package of this controversial Gold Cup had without doubt been the 25–1 winner Cool Ground, trained in deepest Dorset at purpose-built Whitcombe Manor. According to Andrew Sim in his excellent *English Racing Stables*, 'Whitcombe Manor is the most significant new yard to be built in Britain since Sam Darling built Warren Place in the late 1920s.' Built in the late '80s by local businessman and long-time owner Peter Bolton, Whitcombe attracted top trainers like a magnet, hardly surprising considering the level of facilities on offer. As Reg Akehurst was leaving to return to his Epsom roots, Toby Balding arrived, albeit for a relatively short time, while he was having a new yard built on the Hampshire Downs, close to his old Fyfield yard.

One of the country's top dual-purpose trainers, Balding had won the Grand National in 1969 with Highland Wedding and again 20 years later with Little Polveir, as well as the Champion Hurdle twice with Beech Road and Morley Street the previous season. Balding inherited Cool Ground from the departing Akehurst.

It transpired that during the race, the favourite had sustained pulled chest and back muscles, as well as a serious tendon injury. Sadly, Carvill's Hill never recovered sufficiently to race again, while Cool Ground and The Fellow would be back again in 12 months' time on infinitely faster ground and at opposite ends of the betting scale, with The Fellow a heavily backed favourite.

COOL GROUND (1992)

ch.g. 1982 (Over The River – Merry Spring)
Owned by Whitcombe Manor Racing Stables Ltd, trained by G.B. Balding and ridden by A. Maguire

Another bet of the century – at lowly Kelso?

Back in 1990, now that was the bet of the century (if you were in the know, that is). Trouble is, not many of us were. If you weren't from Carmarthen, there was a pretty fair chance that your money was on the grey one that trailed in third. That Norton's Coin must have kept bookmakers, outside of Wales, in cigars and Mercedes cars for years.

The following week, a horse called Jodami did a few more bookies a favour or two by winning division one of the bumper, the second last at Kelso. Not many spectators at northerly Kelso would have bothered to stay to see the two bumper winners, Jodami followed by Forget The Rest. Even the results that Kelso night had that ring about them. Jodami, ridden by Yorkshire-trainer Peter Beaumont's daughter Anthea, went off a 33–1 outsider and couldn't have been more impressive, beating a certain Mudahim by 11 lengths – Jenny Pitman's future Irish Grand National winner!

The next bet of the century came less than a week after the previous one. Peter Beaumont took out a full licence in 1986, following a successful background in point-to-points. Jodami, a rangy five-year-old, had been bought the previous year by Beaumont in a private deal in Ireland and soon showed his Brandsby trainer that he was something out of the ordinary. Jodami ran in two more bumpers before switching to hurdles. He proved more than useful over hurdles, winning no less than five from six with his regular partner, Anthea's then husband, Patrick, in the plate. It didn't take a genius to see that the powerful bay had a serious future over fences and his canny trainer returned to Kelso to introduce Jodami to the bigger obstacles, winning comfortably, but not impressively. That novice season was very much a learning curve for Jodami and the fact that Timeform's *Chasers & Hurdlers* devoted over a page to him spoke volumes for the high regard in which he was held by the sagacious Halifax boys.

Back at Foulrice Farm, the decision was taken to employ Mark Dwyer for the coming season and Jodami never looked back. The winning run started in the Mandarin Chase and he reversed an earlier defeat by the useful Run For Free in the Peter Marsh Chase at Haydock. Beaumont chose to go to Ireland for his final Gold Cup warm-up to contest the Hennessy Cognac Gold Cup at Leopardstown, a race he would make his own, winning it for the next three years. Yet another Pipe chaser provided stiff opposition, but Dwyer had to pull out all the stops to beat the year older and more experienced Chatam to win by a head. Jodami was promoted to second favourite behind The Fellow, with a host of Pipe runners and the ultra-consistent Docklands Express, trained by Kim Bailey at Lambourn, expected to go close.

Jodami, despite looking trained to the minute, drifted from an opening 4–1 to double that price before the off, the prevailing fast ground not thought to be ideal for the northern challenger. The Fellow, winner of the King George VI Chase at

Kempton, hadn't been seen in public since, but appeared fit and well and was backed as if defeat was out of the question. At the other end of the scale, last year's winner, the mud-loving Cool Ground, started at 50–1, a fair reflection of his chance on the fast ground.

Sixteen lined up in glorious sunshine as the tapes went up, with Richard Dunwoody deciding to give the Pipe-trained ex-hunter chaser Rushing Wild a positive ride right from the start. Up with the leaders, he jumped to the front at the third fence, with a host of challengers biding their time in behind. Tragedy struck at the seventh fence, when the promising young Cherrykino, trained by Tim Forster and running in the famous Anne, Duchess of Westminster colours, met it all wrong and fell fatally.

Meanwhile, Dunwoody continued to pile on the pressure on Rushing Wild, with Sibton Abbey and Docklands Express trying to keep tabs on the leader as they went out into the country on the second circuit. The Fellow had been held up for a late challenge, but made a couple of errors. With four to go, Rushing Wild looked to be going as well as anything, but Dwyer had Jodami jumping beautifully in behind and was poised to challenge, coming through on the bridle. As they jumped the third last, it looked even at that stage, to be between Jodami and Rushing Wild, just ahead of him. Closing the leader down off the final turn, they were almost level at the second last. Here, Rushing Wild made a slight mistake, handing a slight advantage to Jodami on the stands side.

As the two leaders approached the last clear of their field, Dwyer had Jodami in full flight, knowing a good jump would seal it. They met the last on a stride and landed just ahead of Rushing Wild, before quickening away up the hill. There was only ever going to be one winner from the last, as Jodami kept on strongly to win by a comfortable two lengths. Back in third, the classy Royal Athlete had run the race of his life, running on stoutly up the hill and completing a storming Grand National trial in the process for his trainer Jenny Pitman. The Fellow disappointed in fourth place and the usual criticism was ringing in the jockey's ears as he brought the hot favourite back to unsaddle. Horses are not machines and François Doumen never doubted his stable jockey. In 12 months' time, it would be a very different story.

For now, though, it had been Dwyer's second Gold Cup and he had given Jodami a wonderful ride, timing his run to perfection and using his partner's raking stride to full use throughout the race. At only eight, the son of Crash Course, with a fine turn of speed to match his stamina-laden breeding, had proved himself truly versatile on all types of ground. After the disappointment of 1988 this must have been a wonderful day for Dwyer in particular and it was well-deserved recognition of Beaumont's superb handling of a precocious talent through to the finished article – from a Kelso bumper to the Cheltenham Gold Cup in three years.

Jodami was put away for the season but sadly, a month later, Rushing Wild, the ex-point-to-pointer who had also won the Foxhunters at Cheltenham the previous year, fractured his pelvis on the approach to the top bend in the Irish Grand National at Fairyhouse.

JODAMI (1993)

b.g. 1985 (Crash Course – Masterstown Lucy)
Owned by J.N. Yeadon, trained by P. Beaumont and ridden by M. Dwyer

✣ 1994 ✣

For he's a jolly good Fellow

When The Dikler won the 1973 Gold Cup, it had been a remarkable result, not only for the powerful finish that Ron Barry conjured out of him to collar Pendil in the dying strides, but also as a triumph for longevity. It had been The Dikler's fourth appearance in the race, following a close third the year before, so nobody could say that he was winning out of turn. Just for good measure, he went on to contest the next three Gold Cups as well.

It had been very much the same story for The Fellow and his faithful jockey Adam Kondrat in the early '90s. They lined up for their fourth attempt at a Gallic version of the The Dikler's effort. By 1994, the tall, elegant figure of François Doumen had become a familiar sight at British racecourses. Yet if you had asked the majority of Britain's racing community before Boxing Day of 1987 who François Doumen was, you would probably have got a reply like 'François who?'.

All that changed with Nupsala's shock 25–1 win over Desert Orchid in the King George VI Chase, helped by the last-fence fall of Forgive 'N Forget. Apart from increasing expectation every time he ventured over to Britain, beating the grey wonder did more to raise the trainer's comparatively low profile back home in France than any victory gained on home turf.

The Fellow had kept up the incredible Doumen record in the King George VI Chase, winning both the 1991 and 1992 renewals, and yet the bay son of Italic had agonisingly missed out in two of the last three Gold Cups. The Fellow had the unenviable record of being the only horse to have been beaten a short-head twice in the history of the race. Kondrat, his Polish-born jockey, was back again to try to win that elusive Gold Cup. If he could, the short-head statistic would be rendered meaningless and The Fellow would become the first French-trained horse to win the Gold Cup.

Kondrat proved he has very broad shoulders after the panning he received from certain quarters of the media for 'losing' the Gold Cup in 1992. He was accused of not having done quite enough on the then seven-year-old, his quiet style in total contrast to Adrian Maguire's all-action finish on Cool Ground, which did appear, to the uninitiated, to make the difference between winning and losing in the latter stages of the race. Post-race, Kondrat defended his corner. 'The Fellow doesn't like soft ground and was doing his level best to win. Hitting him would have made no difference.' He added, 'The owner, the Marquesa de Moratalla, detests the use of the whip.'

There was no doubt that coming into the 1993–4 season, the horse at the head of most ten-to-follow lists would have been Jodami, so impressive winning last year's race and still open to considerable improvement. Peter Beaumont, a Yorkshireman not known for talking up his horses out of turn, spoke in glowing terms of how Jodami had come back from his summer break fitter and stronger than ever before and that he hadn't been over-extended in the Gold Cup.

However, it hadn't all been plain sailing for Jodami. By the time March arrived he had enjoyed a particularly topsy-turvy season. He looked superb for his opening race of the season at Wetherby, but fell. A fine victory at Haydock giving the useful Cab On Target no less than fifteen pounds was followed by a poor effort in heavy ground in the Rehearsal Chase at Chepstow, finishing distressed. Jodami came back to form in style in February, winning his second Hennessy Cognac Gold Cup in succession at Leopardstown, putting him spot-on for Cheltenham.

The Fellow had also endured an indifferent season leading up to the Festival, having failed to land his third consecutive King George. He seemed to be going the same way as numerous precocious French-breds over the years, lacking his usual sparkle at Kempton. He finished a well-beaten third behind Barton Bank and Bradbury Star, who fought out a tremendous finish, with Barton Bank, a more than useful seven-year-old, trained by the Duke, just coming out on top.

The Fellow was blinkered on his second start at Auteuil, but was disqualified and placed third for veering across in front of the eventual second. Doumen persisted with the blinkers and The Fellow ran another sound race in the Racing Post Chase back at Kempton, giving lumps of weight away to the winner Antonin, also by the non-thoroughbred French Saddlebred stallion, Italic. In fact, this was a remarkable period for French-breds, which has continued right through to the new millennium.

At this Festival, there was a predominance of French-bred winners, with no less than five winners from nineteen runners. In the Gold Cup itself, with a good-sized field of 15 runners going to post, Jodami was sent off a very warm favourite at only 6–4, ahead of the Josh Gifford-trained Bradbury Star, ridden by his stylish stable jockey Declan Murphy. A rare Josh Gifford entry for the Gold Cup, Bradbury Star was a bit of a Cheltenham specialist and had won the Mackeson Gold Cup in November. However, he was arguably at his best over two and a half or an easy three miles. The Fellow was not unfancied at 7–1 third favourite and Flashing Steel represented the main hope of an Irish upset.

The race went like clockwork for Kondrat, who had been instructed by Doumen to be near the leaders and not to hit the front too soon. After the initial running had been cut out by Run For Free, the seven-year-old Young Hustler and Flashing Steel staked their claims on the far side second time round, with The Fellow and Jodami tracking the leaders. At long last, The Fellow got his favoured fast ground and made every use of it. Kondrat seized his chance two out and struck the front, chased by Jodami, with Mark Dwyer looking a major threat as they came down to the last.

It was at the final fence that Jodami made his only mistake of the race and although he rallied under pressure, he could never quite peg back The Fellow, who held on bravely to win by a length and a half. Young Hustler stayed on well to take third, running the race of his young life, finishing just ahead of Flashing Steel. Whether or not nerves got the better of Doumen is open to debate, but at the ceremony afterwards he managed to drop the Gold Cup as he passed it to his wife! His belief in Kondrat's ability had been rewarded and The Fellow's win was well received by the knowledgeable Cheltenham crowd.

Doumen's successful year in Britain continued through to December with Algan's win in the 1994 King George, giving him his fourth winner of the race in eight years. Doumen's horses, conditioned to running on France's flatter tracks, clearly found Kempton a home from home, more so than Cheltenham's considerable undulations. But the highlight of his year had undoubtedly been the long-awaited Gold Cup victory for The Fellow.

Afterwards, Doumen reflected on a memorable year and the difficulty that Cheltenham poses to both horse and jockey. 'It took Adam Kondrat quite a while to understand Cheltenham and I think the undulations don't help our French horses at all.'

Despite his four appearances dating back to 1991, there was very little chance that The Fellow, or any horse, would ever match The Dikler's record of competing in seven consecutive Gold Cups – a truly remarkable achievement by both horse and trainer, Fulke Walwyn. The Fellow went on to Aintree, attempting to secure the exalted Gold Cup/Grand National double, but the prevailing heavy ground in April was never going to suit him. You have to question the sanity of those prepared to take the incredibly skinny 9–1 on offer at Aintree, in conditions he would have positively hated. Needless to say, he failed to finish, suffering a heavy fall through sheer exhaustion at the twenty-fourth fence.

The following season was a disappointing one for The Fellow as he put in a number of lacklustre efforts, including one in the King George VI Chase at his beloved Kempton, pulling up on soft ground behind his less-fancied stable-companion Algan. It would be the last time The Fellow would race in Britain. After pulling up once more, this time in the Grand Steeplechase de Paris in June 1995, The Fellow, now a ten-year-old, was retired on the spot by the Marquesa, following the death of Ubu III who had won the race but sadly collapsed and died afterwards, suffering a massive haemorrhage.

Doumen's three champion chasers, Ubu III, Ucello II and The Fellow, had been known collectively as the 'Three Musketeers' and all were owned by the Marquesa de Moratalla. Her decision to retire The Fellow was applauded by Sir Peter O'Sullevan, who explained recently, 'After what had happened to Ubu III and Ucello II, the Marquesa didn't want to risk him anymore. He now lives in happy retirement at her Childwick Bury Stud, formerly, owned by the Joel family, near St Albans.' Sir Peter also confirmed that the Marquis de Portago, who had ridden Garde Toi in the 1950 Gold Cup, was in fact the Marquesa's brother, who died in the 1957 Mille Miglia.

The Doumen family have a tremendous pedigree in horseracing and the dynasty will one day continue through the two sons, Xavier, Doumen's assistant, and Thierry, his jockey. Doumen's grandfather was a vet, who set up a veterinary school in Brazil and developed an electrocardiograph machine for horses, while his father was private trainer to brandy baron James Hennessy, for whom he trained many top steeplechasers. François has been a dual-purpose trainer for nearly twenty-five years and has a mixed string of flat horses and jumpers.

THE FELLOW (1994)

b.g. 1985 (Italic – L'Oranaise)
Owned by the Marquesa de Moratalla, trained by F. Doumen and ridden by A. Kondrat

✣ 1995 ✣

Master of all he sowed,

and watched by the Maestro

As we squelched through the winter, there seemed to be a certain inevitability about the outcome of this season's Gold Cup. I'm sure the Lambourn trainer in question, not wishing to pre-empt anything, wouldn't have appreciated me saying so at the time, but I distinctly remember having that feeling of *déjà vu* on Gold Cup day. Perhaps it was because Master Oats reminded me of another Lambourn horse, Burrough Hill Lad – not in looks, but in terms of his improvement as the season progressed.

Following Alderbrook's superb Champion Hurdle victory in only his third hurdle race, Kim Bailey had the Gold Cup favourite fit and ready to run for his life. Bailey had come close in 1992 when Docklands Express ran his heart out to finish a close third in the Gold Cup, but Master Oats was a very different proposition.

Vincent O'Brien watched Gold Cup proceedings from the royal box, on the day that the closing County Hurdle had the honour of bearing the Maestro's name. There was something wholly appropriate about the Champion Hurdle/Gold Cup double being achieved for the first time since the O'Brien-Brabazon combo in 1950, especially with O'Brien himself in attendance and suitably impressed by the winner.

Master Oats was bred by Robin and Scarlett Knipe at their Cobhall Court Stud and sold for five thousand guineas at the Doncaster Sales in 1986. He never ran over hurdles and after pulling up in his first two races (one a point-to-point), he notched his first win in a lowly maiden chase at Southwell in April 1992. At that stage, it is fair to say that it would have been optimistic to suggest that such a top-class performer could possibly emerge from such humble beginnings. However, Bailey eked steady improvement from Master Oats over the coming seasons, especially following a year on the sidelines through injury.

Master Oats enjoyed a superb 1993–94 campaign, winning five of his seven starts, including first time out at Uttoxeter, despite reportedly breaking blood vessels, and winning the Greenalls Gold Cup at Kempton on heavy ground. Again, he ran a race full of promise in Miinnehoma's Grand National, before falling in contention at the thirteenth fence. By the start of the season, Kim Bailey must have known he had a serious Gold Cup challenger on his hands, especially given his favoured soft ground. In December he saw off a determined challenge from a small but select Rehearsal Chase field, which included former Grand National-winning Party Politics and ex-Gold Cup winner Cool Ground.

Bailey now pitched his charge at the re-routed Welsh Grand National, which had been switched to Newbury. Master Oats couldn't have been more impressive, winning on the bridle by 20 lengths from Earth Summit, no mean performer in his own right, who would go on to win both the Welsh and Aintree Grand Nationals. Binoculars were needed to find Party Politics in this race, beaten some 45 lengths by the easy winner, a measure of Master Oats's rate of improvement.

Bailey decided it was all systems go for Cheltenham, with one final prep race and a chance to gain some valuable course experience in the Pillar Property Chase, a recognised Gold Cup trial, run over a furlong shorter than the Gold Cup in March. This would turn out to be a very relevant and informative trial, with the nine-year-old Master Oats turning in yet another impressive performance, beating the mare Dubacilla by a comfortable 15 lengths.

Come Gold Cup day, with two fences omitted due to the state of the ground, Master Oats faced fourteen opponents on officially yielding ground, including Jodami, who had been impressive winning the Hennessy Cognac Gold Cup at Leopardstown in early February, beating Merry Gale by a comfortable three lengths. Merry Gale, a seven-year-old, was trained by Jim Dreaper, who firmly believed that the young horse could be good enough to win a Gold Cup one day, if not here. Bradley had ridden him for the first time in Ireland and stayed loyal to the main hope of Ireland. François Doumen was double-handed with Algan and Val D'Alene. Algan had benefited from Barton Bank's last-fence fall in the King George VI Chase at Kempton on Boxing Day, but there were question marks about his effectiveness around Cheltenham and he was a confirmed mudlark. Dubacilla re-opposed, but connections couldn't realistically expect to turn the tables on Master Oats, so long as he put in a clear round.

During the early part of the race, this didn't look very likely, as Master Oats clattered one or two fences on the first circuit. It was only when Norman Williamson switched him to the outside of the field to get a clear view at the fences that Master Oats began to settle into a rhythm and fence properly. Merry Gale was still in front with two to go but had probably gone too fast for his own good. Barton Bank had fallen at the fifteenth and Jodami ran a puzzling race, uncharacteristically riddled with mistakes, and was well tailed off with two to run. At this point, with none going better, Williamson pressed the button and shot clear of his field, with only Dubacilla doing her best to keep tabs on him. The Grand National winner, Miinnehoma, chased the two leaders at a respectable distance without ever threatening to get involved. Master Oats showed no signs of stopping and cleared the last in splendid isolation, powering up the hill to an impressive 15-length victory. Dubacilla held the Pipe horse by a similar distance, eclipsing many more-fancied horses. Dubacilla's owner, permit-holding Taunton-based farmer Henry Cole, formerly trained the talented mare but decided it would be prudent to send her to a professional in her Gold Cup year – and chose the Duke. After running her usual brave race here, she went to Aintree and finished a creditable fourth to Royal Athlete.

In two seasons, Master Oats had risen nearly sixty pounds up the weights. His attempt to emulate Golden Miller at Aintree ended in glorious failure, running his heart out on totally unfavourable ground but finishing out of the frame. Bailey has no doubts that this performance was his best ever, reflecting afterwards, 'He probably ran about seven pounds better than we did in the Gold Cup, the only difference being the ground was too fast for him. If you look at him three from home, if he'd had the ground he would have won by half the track. Norman Williamson and I agree that he ran the best race of his life.'

Master Oats faced a number of training problems thereafter and like any number of Gold Cup winners never really recaptured the brilliance that took him to the top of the chasing division in 1995. Bailey suffered a drop in fortunes along with Master Oats and has recently moved out of Lambourn to a fresh start in Preston Capes, near Daventry. The move seems to have rekindled the fires within him, and his knowledge and dogged enthusiasm will secure a return to the top very shortly. He's certainly made the right start at his new base and, importantly, Bailey talks sense and has that meticulous approach that all great trainers seem to possess. Given the right ammunition, he will be contesting Gold Cups again in the very near future.

MASTER OATS (1995)

ch.g. 1986 (Oats – Miss Poker Face)
Owned by Mr P.A. Matthews, trained by K.C. Bailey and ridden by N. Williamson

✠ 1996 ✠

Call of the wild

After the domination by Irish-trained horses during the '70s, Dawn Run had been a welcome oasis in the Gold Cup desert. She had broken a losing run for Irish raiders going back to Davy Lad in 1977 and the larder had been bare since that heady day back in 1986. The economy in Ireland was such that exporting their very best talent to cheque book-waving Britain had become a way of life, which had undoubtedly weakened their own challenge at Cheltenham. The paucity of Irish-trained winners reached an all-time low in 1989, with the total eclipse of every Irish raider at the entire Festival – the first whitewash since 1947. Things would be very different towards the end of the '90s, with the Irish economy going through the roof and trainers able to find wealthy businessman at home, willing and in a position to stave off the attentions of their mainland counterparts.

The traditional Anglo-Irish battle for the Gold Cup was in danger of becoming a thing of the past – even Carvill's Hill had managed to find his way to Martin Pipe and a new owner. A virtually unknown chaser, certainly outside Ireland, changed all that. Imperial Call, trained in County Cork by Fergie Sutherland, burst on to the scene with the Gold Cup less than five weeks away. The seven-year-old second season chaser had surprised the jumping world, winning the valuable Hennessy Cognac Gold Cup at Leopardstown.

With Conor O'Dwyer taking over as a last-minute substitute for both Richard Dunwoody and Charlie Swan, Imperial Call had trounced a top-class field with almost contemptuous ease, quickening clear of Master Oats and Monsieur Le Curé, establishing himself as a serious Gold Cup contender. Bookmakers sat up and took notice and Imperial Call was immediately slashed in price to become the new second favourite in many lists, behind the flying grey One Man. I know Paddy Mullins would have approved of Imperial Call's breeding and his dam in particular. Princess Menelek was sired by Menelek out of a mare by Arctic Slave. She had been sent by her breeder, Tom O'Donnell, to visit Callernish, who stood at the Garryrichard Stud alongside another classy national hunt sire, Over The River. Amazingly, the two stallions would sire no fewer than three Gold Cup winners of the '90s between them: Cool Ground, Imperial Call and Cool Dawn. So the blend of speed and stamina was there, the latter in abundance, and it had been the first time Imperial Call had run over further than two and a half miles, which was clearly to the gelding's liking. He had been running with credit against the top two-mile chasers in Ireland and the seven-year-old became the subject of some hefty bids that Lisselan Farms, the owners of the gelding, did well to turn down – with a little help from Fergie Sutherland.

Back in England, One Man, Gordon Richards's 'rubber ball', had been carrying all before him this season. The former Hennessy Gold Cup winner had looked the part in the Tommy Whittle at Haydock, slamming fellow Gold Cup hopeful Monsieur Le Curé. He was then arguably even more impressive for Richard Dunwoody in the re-routed King George VI Chase, which had been switched to Sandown's Mildmay Cazalet meeting in early January. He had beaten a top-class field, including Master Oats, by a comfortable 14 lengths.

But the gnawing doubts remained. Would he see out those extra yards of the Gold Cup up the stamina-sapping hill? One Man went straight for the Gold Cup from the King George and started a short-priced 11-8 favourite against nine opponents, which included the hope of Ireland, the fast-improving Imperial Call.

There had been considerable controversy at this Festival with the number of fatalities that had occurred over the three days. The number would rise to an unacceptable 10 by the end of the three days and, unfortunately, the Gold Cup would be one of the races adding to the eventual total.

Dublin Flyer, the Mackeson winner and third favourite, trained by that eternal pessimist Tim Forster, took them along at a good pace in the early stages of the race. He was brave and consistent and had his supporters, who believed that he could perhaps run the finish out of One Man and the others, as long as Brendan Powell could stretch Dublin Flyer's own suspect stamina by dictating his own pace.

All went smoothly until the sixth fence, where Monsieur Le Curé, the former Sun Alliance Chase winner, paid the ultimate price for a terrible blunder, continuing trainer John Edwards's depressing run of bad luck in the Gold Cup. Back in 1974, his High Ken might have done a 'Norton's Coin' and won at 100-1, had he not come to grief three out bringing down Pendil in the process. In 1989, Yahoo had run his heart out, but found the nation's favourite grey in a stubborn mood. It had only been the classy Monsieur Le Curé that had kept Edwards going in the latter years and by November, with 12 Festival winners to his name, he saw no point in continuing and announced his retirement. Pearlyman, his Grand Annual and dual Queen Mother Champion Chase winner, had been a wonderful servant to the Ross-on-Wye handler over the years, probably never gaining the recognition he deserved, having beaten Desert Orchid on the three occasions they had met. Edwards's claim that Pearlyman was the best chaser of the '80s certainly has some substance to it, if are you prepared to ignore the small matter of versatility, which set Desert Orchid apart from most, Pearlyman included. Now if old Pearlyman had been a grey . . .

Dublin Flyer looked to be going comfortably in front, until he made a mess of the thirteenth. The chasing pack closed in on him and three fences later he had been headed, losing his pitch very quickly. O'Dwyer had been biding his time on Imperial Call and took up the running with Couldn't Be Better, closely attended by One Man, going easily at the time for Dunwoody, and a couple of outsiders: Rough Quest, a former Ritz Club winner and the National-bound Young Hustler.

Couldn't Be Better made a mistake three out, which put paid to his chance, and Imperial Call was joined by One Man, still swinging on the bridle ready to pounce on the leader as they approached the second last. Rough Quest was in behind, tracking the two leaders going well. Over the second last safely enough, Richard Dunwoody asked One Man to quicken up and the response was very limited. While Imperial Call and Rough Quest ran on strongly ahead of him, in total contrast, the favourite curled up very tamely. Ahead of him, Imperial Call had measured the last perfectly and O'Dwyer, responding to an Irish roar that hadn't been heard during a Gold Cup for a decade, pulled clear of Rough Quest up the hill to win quite comfortably. The runner-up kept on well, without ever looking like getting to Imperial Call, who ran out an impressive winner by four lengths. Rough Quest had pulled nearly twenty lengths clear of an exhausted One Man.

Scottish-born Fergie Sutherland had achieved his greatest feat in the twilight of his long career that spanned nearly forty years. However, even the trainer was in danger of missing the boat as he struggled to get into the winners' enclosure. These post-race celebrations made that madcap twenty minutes following Dawn Run's magnificent triumph in 1986 appear positively tame by comparison. Although in danger of being accused of being killjoys, it was important that, under Gillespie's direction, Cheltenham would review security, particularly for the winners' enclosure for next Festival. How nobody got injured in the mêlée is a mystery known only to those watching, as those actually involved were, as ever, totally oblivious to the dangers. Nevertheless, it was a colourful sight, to be sure – a sea of waving tricolour flags. Even O'Dwyer joined in by waving one wildly as he sat astride the new Gold Cup winner, the pride of Ireland.

Needless to say, the Cheltenham management did set about implementing a new system for the following year, yet they must have breathed a collective sigh of relief when Imperial Call, or any other Irish horse, failed to win the Gold Cup the following year.

Imperial Call was the first Cork-trained Gold Cup winner since Cottage Rake in 1950, as well as being the first Festival winner for both his trainer and jockey. Sutherland was an interesting character, not frightened to express his belief in his horse beforehand, knowing that his patience in bringing the horse deftly through the ranks, and not over-facing him, had done the trick.

Sutherland had followed his father into the army via Eton and Sandhurst, having spent his formative years riding out with his great friend and royal trainer (now retired), Dick Hern. Sutherland lost part of his leg in the Korean War, blown off by an exploding mine while fighting with the 5th Royal Inniskillen Dragoon Guards. Moving to Newmarket in 1954 to become pupil assistant to Geoffrey Brooke, before taking out his own licence and training from Carlburg Stables, Sutherland soon enjoyed great success. In his first year of training in 1958, he enjoyed a Queen Mary success at Royal Ascot with A.20, before switching to train at his mother's estate in Cork.

On the back of this and other ultra-cool performances in the saddle, O'Dwyer's services became much sought after. He was approached by Kim Bailey to ride for his stable, which would mean a return to England, having spent some time with Geoff Hubbard some years earlier. Somehow it never quite worked out for O'Dwyer and he returned to Ireland for a second time.

Like so many Gold Cup winners who burst on the scene with an air of invincibility about them, injuries have prevented Imperial Call from so far recapturing the form of his Gold Cup year. His only appearance back at Cheltenham since then has been his abortive attempt at retaining the Gold Cup in 1997, which proved to be a bit of a disaster; his preparations were continually interrupted by injury problems and the prevailing fast ground did not suit.

When Fergie Sutherland retired in June 1998, he had trained at Killinardrish for over thirty years. His assistant, Raymond Hurley, took over the responsibility for training the exuberant Imperial Call, although apart from a brief return to form against Florida Pearl at Punchestown in April 1999, his appearances have been few and far between. It is highly unlikely that Imperial Call will ever return to enjoy further success at Cheltenham. He reigned supreme for a day and brought a thousand of his Cork courtiers with him – no One Man could have stopped him or his entourage in full flow. As Fergie Sutherland told me at the Dublin celebration: 'Imperial Call felt ready to lick creation – and he did.'

IMPERIAL CALL (1996)

br.g. 1989 (Callernish – Princess Menelek)
Owned by Lisselan Farms Ltd, trained by F. Sutherland and ridden by C. O'Dwyer

✣ 1997 ✣

McCoy takes a Chance ride

When he accepted an offer from owner Michael Worcester to train at Folly House Stables in Lambourn in the mid-'90s, not many people outside Ireland had heard of Noel Chance. He had been training on the Curragh, where it had been a daily struggle to make ends meet with only a handful of horses. Chance's opportunity came to move to England and along with it the chance to train Mr Mulligan and a dozen other horses owned by Bristol-based ice cream cone manufacturer Michael Worcester and his wife, Gerry.

A big, rangy chestnut bought privately as a six-year-old by Worcester, following a point-to-point win at Nenagh, Mr Mulligan had only the one run for Kim Bailey, falling at Newbury and injuring vertebrae in his neck. Worcester moved all his horses to Folly House and Mr Mulligan proceeded to win his first four races, before stepping up in grade in his third outing over fences at Ascot in February 1996. He routed a field of useful novices in the Reynoldstown Chase at Ascot, leading from start to finish and winning by 15 lengths, in the manner of a potential star of the future. Cheltenham and the Sun Alliance Chase beckoned for the eight-year-old, but after blundering at the first and not being able to dominate, Richard Johnson did well to get Mr Mulligan back into the race. Another mistake at the third last ended any chance of remaining unbeaten for the season, but they still finished second, some eight lengths behind Nahthen Lad, reserving their placings at Ascot.

Even before the disappointment of the Sun Alliance, Chance knew he had a serious horse to go to war with. 'I have a plan formulated for next season which includes the King George VI Chase, the Hennessy in Ireland, and the Gold Cup – I don't think that's being over-ambitious.'

The plan worked, to a point. Mr Mulligan ran in three races, but was forced to miss his date in Ireland. Chance decided to get a run into him in the Rehearsal Chase at Chepstow in early December, with David Bridgwater in the saddle. Mistakes again cost Mr Mulligan dear, as he finished a disappointing fourth. He had struggled in the soft prevailing ground, rather ironically in a way as he had been held up through a spate of unusually firm ground!

With the King George only a matter of weeks away, Chance had a fight against time to get his charge fit as he had injured his back at Chepstow and then suffered a poisoned near-hind foot to add to his troubles. He arrived at Kempton, according to the trainer, only 75 per cent fit. There was a new face in the saddle, champion jockey Tony McCoy.

One Man, a heavily-backed odds-on favourite, came to mow down Mr Mulligan three from home. Staying on well, and six lengths adrift of Gordon Richards's pride and joy, Mr Mulligan looked assured of second place when he tipped up at the last. It had been an encouraging run, despite a heavy fall which left him extremely stiff and sore with damaged ligaments and severe bruising to his quarters. At least Chance knew that he now had something to build on. McCoy had said he would let him blaze and he had done exactly that. He had been fifteen lengths clear at one stage and had put the other four runners under severe pressure, with only One Man responding to the challenge. One Man was a class act around Kempton and won his second King George in record time, thanks to the scorching gallop set by Mr Mulligan.

But as far as the winner was concerned, the crucial question remained. Would One Man cope any better 12 months on at Cheltenham, having emptied from the last in last season's Gold Cup? Bookmakers still had Imperial Call ahead of One Man, with Mr Mulligan one of the outsiders, but as low as 14-1 with Hills.

It seemed to be a season of falls for Gold Cup hopefuls, with the four principals heading the Gold Cup market in late February, namely Danoli, Coome Hill, Imperial Call and Dorans Pride, all having taken a tumble at some stage of their season. Imperial Call, soundly beaten by Danoli in the Irish Hennessy, had pleased Fergie Sutherland with his racecourse gallop at Clonmel and the champion was ready to do battle again in three weeks' time. Ireland's favourite son, Danoli, still in his novice season, had fractured his off-fore fetlock when winning at Liverpool over hurdles and had been sidelined for nine months, before returning over fences. He still lacked the experience over the larger obstacles, but was held in such high regard that there had been significant money for him ever since the Hennessy win.

Dorans Pride, the former Stayers' Hurdle champion and now a novice with serious credentials for the Gold Cup, had been unbeaten over fences until inexplicably falling in a minor race at Thurles on his latest outing. It was generally thought that, much like Imperial Call, he would need much softer ground than most to be seen at his best. Coome Hill had won the Hennessy Gold Cup at Newbury in November in good style and, following a Sandown fall, had won the Jim Ford at Wincanton impressively without being over-extended. It promised to be one of the most open Gold Cups for years, with so many ifs and buts about a number of the main contenders.

Scorn was poured on Mr Mulligan's chances after a dreadfully poor workout after racing at Newbury, only a couple of weeks before the Gold Cup. This lacklustre display left McCoy scratching his head, wondering if he should be partnering Martin Pipe's novice Cyborgo, despite the fact that the latter would clearly prefer bottomless ground. But McCoy had signed a deal with Guinness and with Mr Mulligan's owner and was therefore committed to riding him. A schooling session a few days later was a massive improvement on the Newbury débâcle.

Cheltenham had turned on their state-of-the-art sprinklers to water the course over the weekend prior to the Festival but a prevailing wind had dried out conditions considerably come Tuesday. With McCoy winning the Champion Hurdle on Make A Stand for Martin Pipe in scintillating style, breaking the course record, it was always going to be a fast run Gold Cup. It was one to remember for McCoy, who said afterwards that Mr Mulligan had given him a totally different feel than at Newbury, even cantering down to the start.

Fourteen hopefuls milled around at the start and when the tapes went up, Dublin Flyer, a confirmed front-runner, took them along at a cracking pace for more than a circuit. Mr Mulligan's inexperience – this was only the tenth run of his life – didn't come into the equation as he bounced off the fast ground, happily taken along by the bold pace-setter. McCoy was at his very best, giving the long-striding chestnut a good view of all his fences.

Dublin Flyer's exertions began to tell as they approached the water second time round. Mr Mulligan, spring-heeled as he had been throughout the first circuit, took over in the lead and proceeded to run the rest of the field into the ground, quickening on at the fifteenth and putting daylight between himself and his rivals. At this point, Barton Bank, now an eleven-year-old, tried valiantly to stay with the new leader, but was always fighting an uphill battle. Nevertheless, he stayed on gamely in the hands of young David Walsh, deputising for the injured Adrian Maguire, but neither he nor Dorans Pride, who would have gone closer in softer ground, could ever get close enough to peg back the runaway leader.

Mr Mulligan, kept up to his work by McCoy, proceeded to run them all into the ground, winning impressively by nine lengths. One Man's challenge petered out tamely between the last two fences, once more flattering to deceive. It was clear he didn't stay the Gold Cup trip and his future would now lie over shorter distances. The favourite on the day, Imperial Call ran no sort of race and was pulled up, reportedly hating the ground. It had been a remarkable performance from a horse that Noel Chance would later describe as 'having the class to win a Gold Cup, even though he wasn't at his best'. This statement confirmed that general opinion in the media that although this hadn't been a vintage renewal, if the winner could return to the form he had shown as a novice winning the Reynoldstown at Ascot, he would have been a match for most Gold Cup winners of the '90s.

After his second outing the following season, winning the Sean Graham Chase at Ayr, Mr Mulligan suffered a near-fore tendon injury, which would require a lengthy spell on the sidelines. The Worcesters decided that the time was right to call it a day at the top. Sadly, Mr Mulligan was put down in June 1999 after his near-fore was fractured just above the knee after being kicked by another horse in a paddock at the Worcesters' farm near Bristol. Michael Worcester, who had been considering bringing him back in training and trying him hunting, paid this compliment to the chestnut with the flaxen mane: 'Gerry and I have been privileged to own such a champion, and his memory will live with us forever.' Mr Mulligan, winner of seven of his twelve races in his short career, never really had the chance to rank alongside the greats of the Gold Cup, but he gave everything in response to the call of his rider, the inspirational Tony McCoy.

McCoy is arguably the greatest jump jockey of all time and you could fill a page with superlatives and still not do justice to some aspect of his brilliance. For me, if there is one aspect of his riding that sets him apart from his contemporaries, it is the use of his legs, particularly in a finish. He will persist in squeezing vice-like every last ounce of effort from a horse, even those horses previously known to have shirked many an issue. Not every horse has the competitive spirit of a Mr Mulligan. At times, this action might not look pretty, but its effect on the unwilling is devastating. It's the legs that have it. They might not look strong, appearing almost Graham Gooch-like, slightly out of kilter with the rest of his body, but that disproportion comes from upper body strengthening, through riding half a ton and more of horseflesh every waking hour.

However, appearances can be quite deceptive. If you were to measure lower leg strength in all current jockeys, it would be an odds-on certainty that McCoy would come out on top, with Andrew Thornton, an immensely strong horseman, running him a close second. Like a karate expert, McCoy focuses power to the desired contact point through his hands and his feet for maximum effect, only to horses, the effect is champion.

MR MULLIGAN (1997)

ch.g. 1988 (Torus – Miss Manhattan)
Owned by Mr and Mrs M. Worcester, trained by N.T. Chance and ridden by A.P. McCoy

✠ 1998 ✠

Dawn rises in Dorset,
while others exit stage right

Cheltenham, under the direction of Edward Gillespie, paid tribute to Ireland's Cheltenham Gold Cup heroes by staging a dinner at Dublin's Fitzpatrick Castle Hotel. The first of three celebration dinners taking place in the final weeks leading up to the Festival, it proved to be a night to remember.

One of the funnier moments of the trip was Edward handing me a blue carrier bag from the boot of his car on our arrival at Birmingham Airport, warning me not to bang it about too much as it had something quite valuable in it. He wasn't joking. Customs took great interest in the innocuous-looking bag that I was idly swinging about as we trudged through the screening facility. To my surprise (and that of the customs officers as well), it turned out to be the current Gold Cup, which Edward was planning to put on display at the dinner that evening. Fortunately, he had the necessary documentation to prove that we weren't stealing it and we were allowed through. But it caused great amusement all round, firstly to see the shape of a trophy come up on the screen in front of us and then to watch the customs officers checking very carefully all over. Ironically, it was the only time that this particular Gold Cup (there is a new one presented each year) ever looked like going to Ireland.

Numerous Gold Cup heroes were present, including winning jockeys Martin Molony, Tommy Carberry, Willie Robinson, Frank Berry and Dessie Hughes, along with winning trainers Mick O'Toole, Jim Dreaper, Francis Flood, Paddy Mullins and Fergie Sutherland. The Maestro himself, Vincent O'Brien, very sensibly spends his winters in the Bahamas these days and his trainer son Charles represented him. It turned out to be quite an evening and a number of us felt a bit fragile by the time we got to Leopardstown the next day.

Something happened there that those present will never forget, including Edward Gillespie. A group of us were admiring the nostalgic pictures on the wall in Leopardstown's superb Hall of Fame when we came across an old photograph of a young Vincent O'Brien on an Alpine skiing trip, pictured on the slopes with none other than Martin Molony, whose company we had all enjoyed so much the previous evening. There was a group of three or four people standing right in front of us, chatting among themselves, also presumably admiring this rare photograph.

I muttered to the others, 'My God, that photograph must have been taken fifty years ago and Martin Molony hasn't changed a bit, has he?' At this point one of the group in front of us, presumably on hearing my remark, spun around, sporting a huge grin. For a split second we were all stunned into silence. It was really weird – it seemed as though Martin Molony had leapt straight out of the photograph and presented himself there, right in front of us. He really hadn't changed at all. In fact, for those of us who never had the good fortune to see him riding in the flesh, he emphatically demonstrated here that his renowned sense of timing hadn't deserted him either!

We were all delighted to see Martin again, wished him well for the day and moved along to the next display. After a while, we realised there was no sign of Edward and eventually we found him across the other side of the room. He was in an uncontrollable state, in fits of laughter, with tears streaming down his face. He explained, 'When Martin appeared seemingly from nowhere, I just didn't know what to do or say. I didn't want to appear rude but I couldn't stop laughing, so I had to make myself scarce and try to get a grip.'

It was comforting to know that even the usually ultra-calm, cool and collected managing director of Cheltenham Racecourse finds at least some situations difficult to handle.

Following the northern Gold Cup winners' celebration in Wetherby, it was my pleasure to eke out all the trainers and jockeys, as well the owners of the first three going back to that first Gold Cup. I also researched and wrote the Gold Cup booklets that went with the Gold Cup luncheon at the course on the Sunday prior to the Festival. There were over four hundred people attending and it was a wonderfully nostalgic event that got the Festival off to a memorable start, on a day when the Irish horses arrive in their droves and many trainers come and assess the state of the ground. There is nothing better than seeing the Irish challengers out exercising or having a roll in the sand (the horses, not the lads), as well as the wealth of preparations ahead of Tuesday, with hundreds of people building all manner of trade stands and marquees. You can feel the unique Festival atmosphere, even at that stage.

The Cheltenham Steeplechase Company would be the first to admit that the ever-increasing popularity of the Festival does have its drawbacks, especially the crush factor. This has been considered and from 1998 on, the crowd limit has been capped at fifty thousand on Gold Cup day. This, for most people, has not come before time. The late Jeffrey Bernard once summed up one particular aspect of the Cheltenham crush and how it affected him. 'I find it fairly sickening that one has to be a rugby player of almost international standard to get to the bars' – never a truer word spoken in jest.

This was one of the warmest Festival weeks anyone could remember. The sun shone for the entire three days and the ground was riding faster day by day, which wasn't going to suit the front four in the Gold Cup betting market. The favourite, Dorans Pride, had been heavily backed on the day, despite the fact that he had won the Irish Hennessy Gold Cup in February on yielding ground and was always thought to be better with a bit of cut. See More Business, the King George VI Chase winner trained in Somerset by former jump jockey Paul Nicholls, drifted badly in the betting, reflecting his apparent dislike of the fast conditions, while Suny Bay and Cyborgo were both better when the mud was flying. Two outsiders that would love the drying conditions were Strong Promise and Cool Dawn. Strong Promise had blotted his copybook with a poor display in the Jim Ford Chase at Wincanton on his last run, but his jockey Norman Williamson had kept faith in him, believing that Geoff Hubbard's seven-year-old would get the Gold Cup trip, despite having looked better over shorter distances.

Cool Dawn had been purchased in 1993 on a trip to Ireland by Robert Alner, a Dorset trainer with a burgeoning reputation for big race winners. He had bought him for seven thousand pounds on behalf of the Hon. Dido Harding, who was looking for a horse to ride in ladies' point-to-points. Cool Dawn, a stamina-laden ten-year-old brown gelding, had been successfully ridden by his owner in point-to-points and had switched to compete in hunter chases two seasons ago, finishing that season with a fine third in the Irish Grand National, ridden by Conor O'Dwyer. More recently, Andrew Thornton, formerly a much underrated jockey, who had won this season's King George VI Chase on See More Business, had struck up quite a partnership with Cool Dawn. They had won three races at Ascot before flopping badly at Sandown on softish ground, at a time when the stable was going through a lean spell with quite a few horses off-colour.

Thornton had started his riding career with Arthur Stephenson and had moved south to Lambourn to join Kim Bailey a few seasons ago – a move that nearly finished his career when he tried to ride as fashionably short as some of his contemporaries. Thornton, nearly six foot tall, made his mind up to revert to his original riding style, which had the desired effect and the renowned horseman once again looked comfortable in the saddle.

The 17 runners constituted the biggest field for 16 years and Thornton was determined to make it a test of stamina from the off. Cool Dawn jumped the first in front and led at a steady pace from the veteran Barton Bank, jumping from fence to fence and looking to be enjoying his front-running role. There was drama on the approach to the seventh fence when Tony McCoy, feeling Cyborgo losing his action behind, pulled his mount out to the right of the fence. Unfortunately, by doing so without warning he had carried out both Indian Tracker and See More Business, who had been close up behind him, towards the outside of the field. It had all happened in a matter of seconds and there was nothing sinister about it, which didn't make it any easier for an unhappy Timmy Murphy, riding See More Business. Nicholls found it very hard to bite his lip, being both angry and disappointed with the early enforced exit of his stable star. But at least he had a future. It wasn't looking good for Cyborgo with a suspected serious pelvic injury.

Meanwhile, up ahead, Cool Dawn had got close in at one or two obstacles, but had been clever at them and was still leading Barton Bank, with Dorans Pride moving up to challenge as the leaders approached the fourth last. It was here that Barton Bank fell back, and Strong Promise, jumping well and still going easily on the bridle, moved up to sit in the leader's slipstream as they jumped the third last. It was here that Dorans Pride made a crucial mistake which cost him a couple of lengths, just as Richard Dunwoody was asking him to close up.

Cool Dawn and Strong Promise skipped around the final turn, a couple of lengths clear of Dorans Pride. They jumped the second last together, with Williamson still holding on to his mount, preparing to strike over the last. Again, they jumped the last in unison, with Dorans Pride still a few lengths adrift in third. Up the hill, Cool Dawn began to drift stands side before Thornton gave him a few smacks with his whip in his right hand to straighten him up. On the far side, Strong Promise had gone a neck up with one hundred yards to go, but no sooner had he got his head in front then he began to send out distress signals. Cool Dawn, finishing by far the stronger, got his head in front again and battled all the way to the line, to score by a length and three quarters. Dorans Pride closed in on the two in front all the way up the hill, without ever looking like catching the first and second.

After the race, Alner explained Cool Dawn's return to form. 'The sun drying out the ground helped him here and we had given him intensive physiotherapy ever since Ascot.' Thornton was equally delighted and explained that he believed that there was nothing between the winner and See More Business and that three months ago, when he won at Ascot, he knew that Cool Dawn had a chance in the Gold Cup, given the right conditions. If you wish to read a full account of Cool Dawn's career, I can recommend *Cool Dawn, My National Velvet* by his owner, Dido Harding.

It had been desperate luck for both Indian Tracker and the second favourite, See More Business. Paul Barber, an enthusiastic lifelong supporter of national hunt racing, and his business partner, John Keighley, were hoping that See More Business could go one better than the ill-fated Rushing Wild's brave second against Jodami five years earlier. All good things come to those who wait and Barber and Keighley would prove to be patient men.

Cool Dawn's fortunes would nose-dive next season, not helped by an unfortunate paddock accident at Wincanton when he reared over and almost crushed his owner. Damaged vertebrae in his withers accelerated retirement for the brave front-running eleven-year-old. Come Cheltenham in March, Cool Dawn would be missing from the line-up, but it promised to be a Gold Cup to savour, especially with a potential champion coming swiftly through the ranks to challenge the mantle of Doran's Pride as Ireland's favourite horse.

The horse in question was the Royal Sun Alliance winner, the outstanding unbeaten novice Florida Pearl, winner of all three of his novice chases, who had bypassed hurdles altogether. He looked a tremendous Gold Cup prospect for next year and trainer Willie Mullins had already spoken of the athletic chestnut in glowing terms. 'God only knows how good Arkle was, but I would hope Florida Pearl is going to be as good as Dawn Run.' Certainly Ireland's new young star seemed to have the scope and, having assisted his father in Dawn Run's glory days, nobody could argue that Mullins wasn't well qualified to make such a bold statement.

After this win, the chestnut was indeed being mooted as the next Arkle. Certainly, there had never been a broader smile on Richard Dunwoody's face as he returned to the winners' enclosure to enjoy the sort of Irish celebrations that befitted their banker bet of the meeting. The sky seemed the limit for the six-year-old and Mullins had already mapped out a plan for next season that would see Florida Pearl returning to Cheltenham next March and the chance of a third successive Festival win for the handsome chestnut, in the Blue Riband of jump racing.

COOL DAWN (1998)

b.g. 1988 (Over The River – Aran Tour)
Owned by Hon. D. Harding, trained by R.H. Alner and ridden by A. Thornton

✤ 1999 ✤

See Less Blunders, See More Gold Cups

When Prince, or symbol, crooned about 1999, the chances were that he didn't have Ditcheat in Somerset or See More Business in mind. Far from the party being over, it has barely started for West Country trainer Paul Nicholls. He could be handling the hottest piece of jumping property for decades in the shape of See More Business.

It had all gone wrong for See More Business in last season's Gold Cup, unluckily carried out before the seventh fence. This season, a change of rider, with newly appointed stable jockey Joe Tizzard stepping into the breech, didn't seem to have that much effect on Paul Nicholls's stable star. He started the season running in the Edward Hanmer at Haydock, running a respectable race, although his fencing left a lot to be desired. It had been a tall order to take try and give weight to the likes of Escartefigue, who David Nicholson pronounced at the time as potentially his best ever chaser. Suny Bay, winning the race for the second year running, had been quite impressive, but always ran well fresh. Although See More Business finished a close fourth, it was still deemed to be a slightly disappointing effort at the time. Subsequently backed to favouritism in the King George VI Chase, See More Business ran no sort of race at all on softish ground, making numerous blunders throughout the race. He was pulled up three out and a routine dope test was ordered. The race had been won in fine style by the grey Teeton Mill, a vastly improved ex-hunter, formerly trained by Caroline Saunders and now with the talented Venetia Williams at Kings Caple in Herefordshire, who looked every inch a potential Gold Cup winner.

This win for Teeton Mill, on the back of an equally impressive victory in the Hennessy Gold Cup at Newbury, propelled the then nine-year-old to vie for Gold Cup favouritism, together with the impressive Florida Pearl.

Martin Pipe as usual had a serious Gold Cup contender, this time in the shape of Cyfor Malta, his young French-bred that won the 1998 Cathcart Chase as a five-year-old, before going on to tame the Aintree fences a few weeks later in the John Hughes. He followed up in impressive style in the Murphys Gold Cup before beating none other than See More Business and Go Ballistic in the Pillar Chase at the end of January 1999, before injury struck and kept him off for the season. It must have been worse than first believed, as he hasn't been seen on a racecourse since.

One negative factor to consider regarding these battle-hardened French imports is that it is very rare for them to continue to produce the goods for more than two, possibly three, seasons in total. Maybe Cyfor Malta's enforced absence could buck that trend. If he does bounce back from his injury, he will still only be eight years old come 2001 and Pipe is a past master at bringing horses back, particularly after a long lay-off. Following some considerable Gold Cup disappointments in recent years, Pipe firmly believed this horse was the genuine article – the one that would win the Gold Cup and complete the Pond House set. In the meantime, there will probably be another six Cyfor Maltas in the Pipe kindergarten, squealing for their Gold Cup chance.

The number of horses *chez* Pipe is expanding at such a rate that he will probably need to buy a large part of neighbouring Devon to house them all. Perhaps that explains why he runs so many horses at various meetings across the country: he simply doesn't have room to accommodate them all at Pond House at the same time!

Florida Pearl had taken the Hennessy Cognac Gold Cup at Leopardstown in workmanlike fashion by a couple of lengths from Escartefigue. Having fallen and lost his unbeaten record at Leopardstown on his first run of the season, this had been a satisfactory Gold Cup trial for the Mullins horse. The trainer took the view that he didn't want to over-face the horse, but at the same time he didn't want to 'cotton wool' him either. Richard Dunwoody was confident of his chances, declaring, 'It is his travelling and cruising speed that is the key to him. He can really quicken for a three-mile chaser and I can't think of another that I have sat on that can pick up like he does.' Unfortunately, other Mullins fancied horses, such as the unbeaten Alexander Banquet, would all run disappointingly earlier in the week and there were question marks hanging over the wellbeing of the stable's runners at just the wrong time.

Ireland's other hope, Dorans Pride, was bidding to make it third time lucky in the race, having picked up bronze for the past two years. He had profited from Florida Pearl's fall in the Ericsson Chase at Leopardstown in December and had been deliberately kept fresh for the Gold Cup, in contrast to previous years.

Nicholls would be double-handed in the race with Double Thriller and See More Business. The former, an ex-hunter chaser owned by permit-holder and local farmer Reg Wilkins of Double Silk fame, had been ridden by Joe Tizzard to beat Teeton Mill in a hunter chase at Cheltenham in April 1998. The least exposed of all the Gold Cup hopefuls, he had won his two starts this season with consummate ease, beating Wayward King a distance at Wincanton in the Jim Ford Chase, and was attempting to win the Gold Cup *en route* to taking his chances at Aintree on a very favourable mark. Double Thriller was the more fancied of the two Nicholls runners in the betting, but Nicholls had been making encouraging noises about See More Business, warning the media not to write off See More Business.

There had been much talk about Escartefigue running in blinkers, as he had done when racing in his native France, hoping they would see a return to his best form. A similar plan of applying blinkers to See More Business was announced by the Nicholls team, as the gelding had apparently worked brilliantly in them in the hands of Nicholls's brother-in-law, Mick Fitzgerald, who was coming in for the plum ride, with Tizzard keeping faith with Double Thriller. There never was going to be the problem of Fitzgerald being claimed to ride in the Gold Cup by his boss Nicky Henderson. For some unknown reason, and despite his fantastic Festival record, Henderson has only ever had one Gold Cup runner, Raffi Nelson, unplaced way back in 1981.

Norman Williamson had been saved a difficult choice between the Edward O'Grady-trained novice Nick Dundee and Teeton Mill. The former's connections, at a very late stage, decided to go for the Sun Alliance instead of the Gold Cup, which left Williamson free to ride Teeton Mill. Nick Dundee had been travelling like the winner for Williamson in the novices' Gold Cup, when he came to grief three out and chipped a bone above his left-hind hoof. Sadly, a probable Gold Cup winner of the future, he continued the O'Grady run of bad luck with his best horses and would never race again.

Martin Pipe, in the absence of Cyfor Malta, ran the useful novice chaser Unsinkable Boxer. Paul Green's powerful bay had landed a monster gamble over hurdles at last year's Festival, but had struggled to get his act together, despite winning unimpressively in novice events. He would struggle here, too.

With the ground officially good to soft, good in places, weight of money on the day came for Florida Pearl and Dorans Pride, split in the betting by Teeton Mill, many people's idea of the winner, albeit with slight reservations about getting the trip up the hill. It would prove to be a dramatic race, as Senor El Betrutti took the 12 runners along at a brisk pace over the first few fences, until headed by Double Thriller, who had failed to settle and seemed to be very keen to get to the head of affairs. Dorans Pride, in the hands of Paul Carberry, was ridden up with the pace and raced on the outside of the new leader. Teeton Mill, who had made an uncharacteristic error at the seventh, was suddenly pulled out of the race lame, without jumping the tenth. It transpired that he had slipped a tendon off a hock and would require surgery to save his career.

Up ahead and with a circuit to go, See More Business moved quietly up to track the leaders in third place, with northern hope, Simply Dashing, living up to his name and pressing forward on See More Business's outside. See More Business's jumping had been a bit sticky at one or two fences down the far side, but he was going well enough, with Florida Pearl beginning to take closer order on the leading five or six. With Escartefigue never really getting into the race, it was left to the Duke's second string, Go Ballistic, to make good headway in the hands of Tony Dobbin to lead four out from Double Thriller. The 66–1 shot was going as well as anything as he cleared the third last, with Florida Pearl and See More Business taking much closer order on Go Ballistic as he rounded the turn for home. Only a length separated the three leaders as they jumped the second last. It was here that Florida Pearl began to fall back.

Dobbin and Fitzgerald had the race between them as they both drove their horses into the last fence, jumping it in unison. Fitzgerald managed to get slightly the better jump and, having ridden Go Ballistic to six of his wins, knew exactly what his opponent would find under pressure. Slowly but surely, See More Business began to edge ahead and, try as he might, Dobbin couldn't raise a further effort from the brave ten-year-old. See More Business stayed on in fine style to win by a length at the line. It had been the second West Country winner in a row and the masterstroke of applying blinkers had done the trick.

After the race, Fitzgerald, coming in to receive the plaudits after riding yet another superb race, his fifth winner of the week and his first Gold Cup, enthused, 'I feel on top of the world – this is the one that everyone in racing wants to win.'

Joint-owner dairy farmer Paul Barber had completed his wish of milking a thousand cows and winning a Gold Cup and Nicholls clearly enjoyed every minute of it, receiving the best tonic of all for his upset stomach. There would be a barrel or two of cider drunk down in Shepton Mallet that night.

According to Willie Mullins, it was 'back to the drawing board' with Florida Pearl. Yet how could he be too disappointed with his seven-year-old, who had finished third in a high-quality Gold Cup? I had visited the Mullins County

Carlow yard in the autumn of 1998 and you couldn't fail to be impressed by the set up. Watching Florida Pearl working round and round Mullins's all-weather oval was an experience – the bay was emitting the sound known in the game as 'high blow', the trademark of a supremely relaxed athlete. Willie Mullins knows there is better to come and was hoping to get a few more runs into Florida Pearl in the millennium Gold Cup season. However, following a setback or two, this hasn't quite happened.

See More Business was described by connections as 'lazy' and hence the need for blinkers to sharpen his concentration. It is safe to say that See More Business would never have been the horse he now clearly is without them. Looking back, even his 1997 King George win had been riddled with errors, and, although not entirely foot-perfect here, he made no semblance of a serious error at any stage.

See More Business's win meant that Nicholls became the first trainer since Michael Dickinson, with Bregawn and Badsworth Boy in 1983, to record the Festival chasing Championship double – the Gold Cup and the Queen Mother Champion Chase – in the same season.

A jump jockey in the '80s, Nicholls rode plenty of good horses for West Country trainer David Barons, winning two Hennessy Gold Cups on Broadheath and Playschool, the latter winning the 1987 Welsh National and the unplaced favourite for the 1988 Cheltenham Gold Cup. Nicholls took out a training licence in late 1991 and See More Business, co-owned by his principal owner and landlord, Paul Barber, has been the highlight of many Nicholls successes this season, capped by his three Festival winners. Nicholls, Bristol-born and son of a policeman, could never be described as a shrinking violet. He is clearly ambitious and realises the importance of projecting the right image to attract owners and in that respect has done a fantastic job, more than trebling the number of horses in his stable since 1992. Success breeds success and training his first Festival winners in 1999 can only swell the numbers still further. But he retains a slightly traditional view towards training, declaring, 'I don't believe in all the science and I've never given a horse a tracheal wash and rarely take a blood test.' This is not to say he lives in the past. He has bowed to using Pipe's well-documented method of interval training to keep his horses supremely fit.

Paul Barber's Manor Farm stables had been the base of Jim Old before he left, and Nicholls has taken over at the helm, having previously assisted his former employer, David Barons. Paul Nicholls's principal owner had been hoping that See More Business could wipe away the memory of being carried out 12 months ago. He had also narrowly missed out in 1993, when the ill-fated Rushing Wild found Jodami too good, the gelding running in the Hunt and Co. (Bournemouth) colours.

Will Nicholls ever visit the Dome's Rest Zone? There's probably more chance of him taking March off and going on safari for a month with Martin Pipe! Someone more likely to want to be elsewhere when the Festival comes round each March is Richard Dunwoody. 'The Prince', as he became known in the weighing room from the days of Peter Scudamore, was forced to retire in mid-December 1999, following a long-term injury to his right arm that wouldn't respond to treatment – another fall could have meant risking paralysis of the arm, or worse. With the additional pain caused by a cyst on his spinal cord, courtesy of a fall many years ago, you begin to understand why Dunwoody had no choice but to retire, five years before he actually wanted to. Dunwoody is nobody's fool and, as you would expect of him, he did the correct and sensible thing. He's already admitted that he'll desperately miss riding, but not as much as we'll all miss seeing him make it look so easy. Dunwoody was always a fine ambassador for his sport and honed his every skill to perfection – style, strength, timing and a killer instinct which set him apart from the majority of his peers – a true professional in every sense of the word.

Terry Biddlecombe knows talent when he sees it and a few years ago told the *Express* how he felt Dunwoody compared to the greats of his riding days, while discussing how jump racing had changed. 'It's a money game now – it wasn't like it in my day. You rode for death and glory and lived hard. That might sound romantic claptrap but it's true. Men like Fred Winter, Jeff King, Johnny Haine, David Mould, Michael Scudamore and, of course, Josh Gifford were great riders. They may look prettier in the saddle these days but I doubt whether they're any better horsemen than we were, if as good. I'd make an exception for Richard Dunwoody. In my view, he'd stand comparison with anyone. In fact, he is one of the all-time greats.'

Dunwoody has a thriving sports promotion company, as well as media interests to keep him occupied. If he needs someone within racing to entertain clients for his on-course corporate entertainment, he could do worse than employ the young amateur and comedian Paul Flynn. Based at Philip Hobbs's base in the West Country, Flynn is taking the same R. Dunwoody route through the amateur ranks to the top. Like his hero, he will turn professional sooner rather than later and for me is the most talented rider I've clapped eyes on since A.P. McCoy burst on to the scene a few years ago. Flynn is fearless, in your face without being cocky, and appears to be a bit of a case. But anyone who is headhunted by top jockeys' agent Dave Roberts has to be special.

Flynn is hungry for success, and horses run for him – just two of many qualities he shares with McCoy. He will be kept on his toes by Robert Widger, another talented youngster vying for rides down at the Hobbs yard. For me, though, it will be Flynn, who can talk the backside off a donkey, who will hopefully make the quantum leap to challenge his compatriot McCoy in future years. But only if he can keep his feet firmly on the ground – and he's in the best place to do so, as Philip and Sarah Hobbs will keep a good eye on him. It's also in their interest to keep the predators at bay. And no, we're not talking women here, Mr Flynn! His timing is actually even better than I thought. As I write this, he's larking about again in front of the cameras on the Racing Channel. There's a touch of young Carberry about this one.

Since his Gold Cup win, See More Business has earned rave reviews for his re-appearance and subsequent King George wins at the end of 1999. If the blinkers continue to have the desired effect, Nicholls can look forward to further success with his stable star, for at least another couple of seasons. After all, See More Business hasn't got much mileage on the clock, even less if you consider that he has hardly been out of third gear since the blinds have been applied.

SEE MORE BUSINESS (1999)

b.g. 1990 (Seymour Hicks – Miss Redlands)
Owned by Mr P.K. Barber and Mr J.A. Keighley, trained by P.F. Nicholls and ridden by M.A. Fitzgerald

See More Gold Cup victories, and a Pipe dream

One wonders what the reaction would be if a certain M.C. Pipe ever finds himself in the fortunate position of repeating the Dickinson 1-2-3-4-5 feat. Certainly, few people (apart from a few bookmakers and one or two of Pipe's green-eyed peers) would begrudge him a Gold Cup winner, never mind the first five home, in his only missing 'classic'. But would the Cheltenham faithful display the same warmth of feeling for Pipe as they so readily did for the Dickinsons, on their victorious Gold Cup days?

The answer would have to be an emphatic no. But why? Perhaps the Dickinsons stood for true Yorkshire grit and were very much the 'traditional national hunt racing family'. It would be difficult to try and describe the Pipes in similar fashion, unless of course you substitute 'Somerset' for 'Yorkshire' and emphasize the term 'bookmaker'. Even Pipe's principal owner, David Johnson, has described his trainer as 'still a bookmaker at heart'. Not that such conjecture would ruffle the Pipe feathers anyway. Even without that elusive Cheltenham Gold Cup winner he is still the ultimate in winning machines, displaying terrier-like qualities to retain his trainers' championship year after year.

Pipping his arch-rival Nicholls in 1999, Pipe proved emphatically that you can never write him off. The ammunition is always there, waiting to be reloaded. Nicholls must have thought he was home and hosed after scooping his three Festival winners and extending his lead in prize money terms out of the reach of all – bar one. Staving off such a potent threat as Nicholls would have given Pipe a real buzz. He's ultra-competitive, beavering away under that brown trilby, making sure he is ahead of the game. Pipe is a man of contradictions. He will think nothing of spending over one hundred thousand pounds on a piece of technical equipment for his laboratory, yet unless Raleigh Cycles come along and offer him a sponsorship deal with a racing bike thrown in, he will keep using his tatty old bike to get around the yard. He must be quite attached to it by now – it has been there longer than most of his horses and he even rode it on that memorable Countryside March in Hyde Park! The televised *Cook Report* in May 1991 tried to expose some supposed 'darker aspects' of the Pipe success story, yet failed miserably. Even eight years ago, Pipe was too much of a professional to lie down and let a clearly slanted attempt at devaluing everything he stood for be seen to hold any water. Countless trainers' championships later, he doesn't seem to have done too much wrong, but a genuine rival in the burly shape of Nicholls has arrived to try and push Pipe off that bicycle.

Nicholls is making his presence felt in no uncertain fashion. The Gold Cup and Queen Mother Champion Chase double in 1999 spoke volumes for his ability to mix it with the best. Realistically, as things stand, only Pipe and Nicholls have the fire-power necessary to secure future championships, although former jockey Philip Hobbs, another West Country trainer, is steadily improving the quality of his horses and could be the next trainer from Zummerset to make the big breakthrough. Knowing Pipe, he won't relax – he hardly ever does. He will be burning the midnight oil, eyes darting from screen to screen, gleaning vital information from his video mountain of race recordings. Trying to keep one stride ahead of the opposition and proving as much on the track, that's the buzz for Pipe. You couldn't blame him for thinking Carvill's Hill would bring the Gold Cup back to Pond House, but it wasn't to be. However, he will keep on chipping away, until he can mould that Gold Cup horse.

It is possible that the horse in question is already safely ensconced at Pond House. It might well be the sidelined Cyfor Malta or even Make A Stand, if he can ever come back and jump a fence like he could a hurdle. It could even be one of his multitude of French-breds that seem to arrive in their lorryloads each week. However, Pipe suffers disappointments just like any other trainer, but can't afford to let it get to him. With the fire-power he has, it is inevitable there are problems to be sorted out on a daily basis.

A perfect example of how to conduct yourself when faced with the inevitable ups and downs of racing were never better illustrated than by Gordon Richards and his special grey, One Man. He defended his 'rubber ball' to the press pack in the unsaddling enclosure at Ascot, following a disappointing loss in the 1997 Comet Chase. His post-race demeanour in the face of some aggressive questioning by the press was typical of the great man's patience and understanding of matters equine and human. His unswerving faith in One Man was total and connections were rewarded with a memorable victory to Cheltenham in the 1998 Queen Mother Champion Chase. The 'Man or Mouse?' taunt in the *Sporting Life* after the Ascot defeat was, to say the least, wide of the mark – and Richards knew it and kept his mouth shut. It was a tragedy that both Richards and his rubber ball would die within months of each other, but not before One Man had gained a special Festival win in the Queen Mother Champion Chase, which must have meant so much to his trainer. The Gold Cup itself always proved beyond them both, but not for lack of trying. One Man always gave 100 per cent – only what you would expect from a champion. To enrich the Gold Cup scene, you don't need to be a winner. The likes of the spring-heeled One Man proved that.

Strangely, that particular renewal of the Comet Chase threw up its share of stories. The winner, Strong Promise, went on to finish a brave second to Cool Dawn in the 1998 Gold Cup, but has struggled, following injury problems, to return to anything like his old form. The only other runner, Sound Man, was owned by Davis Cup captain David Lloyd, with whom I happened to watch the race that day. Like thousands of owners, he would dearly love a Festival winner and has been agonisingly close on a couple of occasions. Lloyd had enjoyed many memorable days with the exciting Sound Man, but this certainly wasn't one of them. As we watched the race unfold, Sound Man virtually ploughed through every fence on his way to finishing a distant third. I can still see the look of shock and disbelief etched on Lloyd's face that afternoon. Sadly, it was the last time that his pride and joy, trained by Edward O'Grady in Tipperary, would ever be seen on a racecourse. Weeks later, the day after Mr Mulligan's Gold Cup win to be precise, word reached the *Sporting Life* newsdesk that all was not well with Sound Man. He had been taken out of the Queen Mother Champion Chase, with the explanation that he had been injured and therefore wouldn't be making the journey to Cheltenham. What nobody would clarify was the severity of the injury. Lloyd couldn't (or didn't want to) shed any more light on things, so I tried to contact J.P. McManus, one of Sound Man's co-owners, at his home in Ireland, leaving a message with his wife to ask him to call me on his return. The other lads thought I was being a tad optimistic, thinking that J.P. wouldn't bother to ring back. Within minutes he had phoned, and although he wasn't prepared to actually admit that Sound Man had been put down, he did seem to be quite emotional about it, stressing how much the horse had meant to all of the co-owners.

Contacting the nearest veterinary practice to the O'Grady stable, I was fortunate enough to speak to the vet who had been called out to Sound Man the previous week. He confirmed immediately that because of the seriousness of the leg injury sustained on the gallops he had no other option but to put down Sound Man. It seemed that, quite understandably, O'Grady had just wanted to get Cheltenham over and done with, without having to face the inevitable questions concerning Sound Man's death. It can't have been an easy time for him.

Despite his enviable Festival record in other races, O'Grady has yet to train a Gold Cup winner, but he has been desperately unlucky in recent years, losing more than his fair share of potential champions, most notably Golden Cygnet and Ventana Canyon. Nick Dundee is the latest to suffer an injury that will end a promising career. At least he has survived, but he will never race again.

Looking ahead to the Gold Cup picture of the next century, it would be exciting to start the new millennium with a champion capable of achieving greatness. See More Business could be that horse. Ever since the masterstroke of applying blinkers, a brave move in a Gold Cup, it has worked and now seems to be virtually bomb-proof. Avoiding injuries and extremes of ground apart, he could well become the first horse since Arkle to win three Gold Cups. If he is as good as he currently looks, then the Cyborgo incident in the 1998 Gold Cup might have been far more significant than it appeared at the time. Like Gordon Richards, Paul Nicholls has always had great faith in his horse and now that he has found the key to keeping the gelding's mind on the job in the hurly-burly of championship races, this could be the real thing. He might not display the extravagance of a Mill House or an Arkle, but his jumping is now famously swift and economical. Not at all flashy and certainly not over big, he is a champion in disguise – hence the shades!

Time will tell whether See More Business scales further heights to reach 'Arkledom'. He has already beaten Ireland's hope, the flashy chestnut with the flashy name, Florida Pearl. A pearl can be at best a prized gem, a paragon or finest example, at worst a cataract of the eye, or a tubercle of an antler burr, even a lustrous globule! But the jury is still out on The Pearl, despite two impressive Festival wins. His trainer knows a class act when he sees it, but doesn't go shouting it from the rooftops. Willie Mullins learnt that much from his father and will do his level best to hone the talents of his Carlow warrior.

If the next 25 years of the Cheltenham Gold Cup are anything like as good as the first 75, then we should be in for a bit of a treat. Could we really expect, even in our wildest dreams, to see another miller, rake, Arkle (deference complied with, m'lady), saint, prince, mandarin, snail, owl, thinker and a lone, grey orchid for good measure? All that's missing is the pea green boat. But the frightening thing about it all is that it actually happened at Cheltenham and thankfully without the strains of 'Colonel Bogey' reverberating through you every half-hour. Soon there will be Lord Kitchener posters to accompany the jolly jaunt at certain tracks. Inspirational? No, just annoying – extremely. Each and every one of this Gold Cup menagerie represented a few months, a year, or even a lifetime of mortal hope. Like moths attracted to a powerful light, some lingered rather longer than others, some got too close for comfort and paid the price. Some seemed to know just when to flit in and out. One or two, every once in a while, would just get too damn lucky!

Willie Mullins, who always looks as though he doesn't have a care in the world, told me, 'If you are not careful, it can do your head in, this game.' Although impossibly ambiguous, you catch the drift of what he was saying. He is meticulous, which seems to be one essential quality needed to become a great trainer. But that isn't enough on its own. There will never be a set formula for winning a race like the Cheltenham Gold Cup. The results, over the years, have proved that winners come in all shapes, sizes and colours. But they all have one thing in common: the ability to climb the hill. According to Jonjo O'Neill, 'It's like trying to get to Heaven, trying to get to that winning post.' It is the ultimate dream.

Gold Cup Results

1924
12 March

1 Red Splash (ch g Copper Ore – La Manche)	5.11.5	5–1	F. Rees
2 Conjurer II (b g Garb Or – dam by Juggler)	12.12.0	7–1	Mr H.A. Brown
3 Gerald L (b g Captivation – Larenne)	10.12.0	5–1	J. Morgan

Runners: 9
Owner: Major H. Wyndham
Trainer: F.E. Withington
Distances: hd, nk
Time: not taken
Also ran: Forewarned, Hawker, Old Tay Bridge, Ardeen, Royal Chancellor
Prize money: £685

1925
11 March

1 Ballinode (ch m Machakos – Celia)	9.12.0	3–1	E. Leader
2 Alcazar (b h Yerres – Good and Gracious)	9.12.0	8–13	F. Rees
3 Patsey V (ch g Lord Garvagh – dam by Walmesgate)	11.12.0	10–1	Mr B. Lemon

Runners: 4
Owner: Mr J.C. Bentley
Trainer: F. Morgan
Distances: 5, dist.
Time: 7 min 29.6
Also ran: Conjurer II
Prize money: £880

1926
9 March

1 Koko (b g Santoi – Persister)	8.12.0	10–1	J. Hamey
2 Old Tay Bridge (ch g Bridge of Earn – Broken Reed)	12.12.0	3–1	J. Hogan
3 Ruddyglow (br g Ruddygore – Nell)	8.12.0	6–5	Mr W. Filmer-Sankey

Runners: 8
Owner: Mr F. Barbour
Trainer: A. Bickley
Distances: 4, 5
Time: 7 min 11.0
Also ran: Postinio, Mansin, Trentino, Vive, Gerald L
Prize money: £880

1927

8 March

1 Thrown In (ch g Beau Bill – Va Largo)	11.12.0	10–1	Hon. H. Grosvenor
2 Grakle (br g Jackdaw – Lady Crank)	5.11.5	5–1	J. Moloney
3 Silvo (b g Minter – Ever True)	11.12.0	13–8	F. Rees

Runners: 8
Owner: Lord Stalbridge
Trainer: O. Anthony
Distances: 2, 0.5
Time: 7 min 28.0
Also ran: Gerald L, Postinio, Grecian Wave, Amberwave, Hackdene
Prize money: £780

1928

13 March

1 Patron Saint (b.g St Girons – V.M.C.)	5.11.5	7–2	F. Rees
2 Vive (br g Minter – Ever True)	13.12.0	8–1	L.B. Rees
3 Koko (b g Santoi – Persister)	10.12.0	4–5	P. Powell

Runners: 7
Owner: Mr F. W. Keen
Trainer: H. Harrison
Distances: 4, 2
Time: 7 min 29.6
Also ran: Aruntius, Rathowen, Meleaston, Sprig
Prize money: £780

1929

12 March

1 Easter Hero (ch g My Prince – Easter Week)	9.12.0	7–4	F. Rees
2 Lloydie (ch g Vedanta – Lizzie Lane)	7.12.0	100–9	R. McCarthy
3 Grakle (br g Jackdaw – Lady Crank)	7.12.0	11–4	K. Piggott

Runners: 10
Owner: Mr J.H. Whitney
Trainer: J. Anthony
Distances: 20, 2
Time: 6 min 57.0
Also ran: Knight Of The Wilderness, May King, Koko, Breconian,
        Kilbrain, Wild Edgar, Bright's Boy
Prize money: £776

1930

11 March

1 Easter Hero (ch g My Prince – Easter Week)	10.12.0	8–11	T. Cullinan
2 Grakle (br g Jackdaw – Lady Crank)	8.12.0	10–1	K. Piggott
3 Gib (b g The Jabberwock – Bettyville)	7.12.0	13–8	F. Rees

Runners: 4
Owner: Mr J.H. Whitney
Trainer: J. Anthony
Distances: 20, remounted
Time: 7 min 6.0
Also ran: Donzelon
Prize money: £670

1931
No race

1932
2 March

1 Golden Miller (b g Goldcourt – Miller's Pride)	5.11.5	13–2	T. Leader
2 Inverse (br g St Girons – Inversion)	6.12.0	8–1	R. Lyall
3 Aruntius (b g Call of the Wind – Wine Gall)	11.12.0	20–1	D. McCann

Runners: 6
Owner: Hon. D. Paget
Trainer: B. Briscoe
Distances: 4, bad
Time: 7 min 33.4
Also ran: Gib, Kingsford, Grakle
Prize money: £670

1933
8 March

1 Golden Miller (b g Goldcourt – Miller's Pride)	6.12.0	4–7	W. Stott
2 Thomond II (ch g Drinmore – dam by St Luke)	7.12.0	11–4	W. Speck
3 Delaneige (b g Santair – Kylestrame)	8.12.0	20–1	J. Moloney

Runners: 7
Owner: Hon. D. Paget
Trainer: B. Briscoe
Distances: 10, 5
Time: 7 min 33.0
Also ran: The Brown Talisman, Kellsboro' Jack, Holmes, Inverse
Prize money: £670

1934
7 March

1 Golden Miller (b g Goldcourt – Miller's Pride)	7.12.0	6–5	G. Wilson
2 Avenger (br g St. Girons – Inversion)	5.11.5	6–1	R. Lyall
3 Kellsboro' Jack (b g Black Gauntlet – Vendramina)	8.12.0	10–1	D. Morgan

Runners: 7
Owner: Hon. D. Paget
Trainer: B. Briscoe
Distances: 6, 6
Time: 7 min 4.6
Also ran: Royal Ransom, Delaneige, Inverse, El Hadjar
Prize money: £670

1935
14 March

1 Golden Miller (b g Goldcourt – Miller's Pride)	8.12.0	2–1	G. Wilson
2 Thomond II (ch g Drinmore – dam by St Luke)	9.12.0	5–2	W. Speck
3 Kellsboro' Jack (b g Jackdaw – Kellsboro' Lass)	9.12.0	100–7	D. Morgan

Runners: 5
Owner: Hon. D. Paget
Trainer: B. Briscoe
Distances: 0.75, 5
Time: 6 min 30.0

Also ran: Avenger, Southern Hero
Prize money: £670

1936
14 March

1 Golden Miller (b g Goldcourt – Miller's Pride)	9.12.0	21–20	E. Williams
2 Royal Mail (bl g My Prince – Flying May)	7.12.0	5–1	Mr F. Walwyn
3 Kellsboro' Jack (b g Jackdaw – Kellsboro' Lass)	10.12.0	10–1	D. Morgan

Runners: 6
Owner: Miss D. Paget
Trainer: O. Anthony
Distances: 12, 2
Time: 7 min 5.2
Also ran: Brienz, Fouquet, Southern Hero
Prize money: £670

1937
No race

1938
10 March

1 Morse Code (b or ch g Pilot – Heliograph)	9.12.0	13–2	D. Morgan
2 Golden Miller (b g Goldcourt – Miller's Pride)	11.12.0	7–4	H. Nicholson
3 Macauley (br g Bolingbroke – Conette)	7.12.0	3–1	D. Butchers

Runners: 6
Owner: Lt.-Col. D.C. Part
Trainer: I. Anthony
Distances: 2, 3
Time: 6 min 35.2
Also ran: Southern Hero, Airgead Sios, Red Hillman
Prize money: £720

1939
9 March

1 Brendan's Cottage (b g Cottage – Brendan's Glory)	9.12.0	8–1	G. Owen
2 Morse Code (b or ch g Pilot – Heliograph)	10.12.0	4–7	D. Morgan
3 Embarrassed (b g Embargo – Lady Georgie)	6.12.0	25–1	Capt. P. Herbert

Runners: 5
Owner: Mrs A. Smith-Bingham
Trainer: G. Beeby
Distances: 5, bad
Time: 7 min 34.2
Also ran: L'Estaque, Bel et Bon
Prize money: £1,120

1940
20 March

1 Roman Hackle (b g Yutoi – Waraya)	7.12.0	1–1	E. Williams
2 Black Hawk (b g Eagle Hawk – Black Lamb)	9.12.0	20–1	T.F. Rimell
3 Royal Mail (bl g My Prince – Flying Day)	11.12.0	100–1	D. Morgan

Runners: 7

Owner: Hon. D. Paget
Trainer: O. Anthony
Distances: 10, 2
Time: 6 min 46.4
Also ran: Rightun, Bel et Bon, Up Sabre, Hobgoblin
Prize money: £495

1941

20 March

1 Poet Prince (ch g Milton – Welsh Princess)	9.12.0	7–2	R. Burford
2 Savon (b g Schiavoni – Saffron)	9.12.0	10–3	G. Archibald
3 Red Rower (b g Rameses II – Red Maru)	7.12.0	8–1	D. Morgan

Runners: 10
Owner: Mr D. Sherbrooke
Trainer: I. Anthony
Distances: 3, sh
Time: 6 min 15.6
Also ran: Teme Willow, Red Prince, Dominick's Cross, Callaly, Roman Hackle, Knight of Troy, The Professor II
Prize money: £495

1942

21 March

1 Médoc II (b g Van – Menthe Poivre)	8.12.0	9–2	H. Nicholson
2 Red Rower (b g Rameses II – Red Maru)	8.12.0	3–1	D. Morgan
3 Asterabad (b g Asterus – Carissima)	11.12.0	20–1	T. Carey

Runners: 12
Owner: Lord Sefton
Trainer: R. Hobbs
Distances: 8, 4
Time: 6 min 38.0
Also ran: Schubert, Golden Knight, Sawfish, Dixie Kid, Solarium, Roman Hackle, Broken Promise, Golden Luck, Poet Prince
Prize money: £495

1943

No race

1944

No race

1945

17 March

1 Red Rower (b g Rameses II – Red Maru)	11.12.0	11–4	D.L. Jones
2 Schubert (b g Lightning Artist – Wild Music)	11.12.0	11–2	C. Beechener
3 Paladin (b g Birthright – Saint Joan)	11.12.0	10–3	G. Conlon

Runners: 16
Owner: Lord Stalbridge
Trainer: Owner
Distances: 3, 1.5
Time: 6 min 16.2

Also ran: Poet Prince, Nobletoi, Red Prince, India II, Rightun, The Hack, Way Out, Farther West, Ghaka, National Hope, Flying Saint, Peaceful Walter, Elsich
Prize money: £340

1946
14 March

1 Prince Regent (b g My Prince – Nemaea)	11.12.0	4–7	T. Hyde
2 Poor Flame (b g Flamenco – Poor Dale)	8.12.0	5–1	T.F. Rimell
3 Red April (b g April The Fifth – Red Maru)	9.12.0	9–2	G. Kelly

Runners: 6
Owner: Mr J.V. Rank
Trainer: T. Dreaper
Distances: 5, 4
Time: 6 min 47.6
Also ran: African Collection, Jalgreya, Elsich
Prize money: £1,130

1947
12 April

1 Fortina (ch h Formor – Bertina)	6.12.0	8–1	Mr R. Black
2 Happy Home (b g Cottage – Golden Emblem)	8.12.0	3–1	D.L. Moore
3 Prince Blackthorn (br g Embargo – Alice Maythorn)	9.12.0	8–1	R. Turnell

Runners: 12
Owner: Lord Grimthorpe
Trainer: H. Christie
Distances: 10, 6
Time: 6 min 41.2
Also ran: Fabiano, Chaka, Comique, Leap Man, Bricett, Nack, Rearmament, Coloured Schoolboy, Elsich
Prize money: £1,140

1948
4 March

1 Cottage Rake (b or br g Cottage – Hartingo)	9.12.0	10–1	A. Brabazon
2 Happy Home (b g Cottage – Golden Emblem)	9.12.0	6–1	M. Molony
3 Coloured Schoolboy (br g Grand Colours – Alpha Virginis)	8.12.0	10–1	E. Vinall

Runners: 12
Owner: Mr F.L. Vickerman
Trainer: M.V. O'Brien
Distances: 1.5, 10
Time: 6 min 56.4
Also ran: Salmiana II, The Diver, Freddy Fox, Revelry, Gallery, Klaxton, Red April, Cool Customer, Barney's Link
Prize money: £1,911

1949
11 April

1 Cottage Rake (b or br g Cottage – Hartingo)	10.12.0	4–6	A. Brabazon
2 Cool Customer (b g Mr Toots – Never Worry)	10.12.0	13–2	P. Murphy
3 Coloured Schoolboy (br g Grand Colours – Alpha Virginis)	9.12.0	8–1	E. Vinall

Runners: 6
Owner: Mr F.L. Vickerman

Trainer: M.V. O'Brien
Distances: 2, 6
Time: 6 min 36.0
Also ran: Finnure, Royal Mount, Red April
Prize money: £2,817

1950

9 March

1 Cottage Rake (b or br g Cottage – Hartingo)	11.12.0	5–6	A. Brabazon
2 Finnure (ch g Cacador – Hazelly)	9.12.0	5–4	M. Molony
3 Garde Toi (ch g Le Grand Cyprus – Grey Cloth)	9.12.0	100–1	Marquis de Portago

Runners: 6
Owner: Mr F.L. Vickerman
Trainer: M.V. O'Brien
Distances: 10, 8
Time: 7 min 00.6
Also ran: Nagara, Clarendon, Rideo
Prize money: £2,936

1951

25 April

1 Silver Fame (ch g Werwolf – Silver Fairy)	12.12.0	6–4	M. Molony
2 Greenogue (b g Knight of the Garter – Miss Muffsie)	9.12.0	100–8	G. Kelly
3 Mighty Fine (b g Pretorious – Miss Maureen)	9.12.0	10–1	J.A. Bullock

Runners: 6
Owner: Lord Bicester
Trainer: G. Beeby
Distances: sh, 2
Time: 6 min 23.4
Also ran: Freebooter, Lockerbie, Manicou
Prize money: £2,783

1952

6 March

1 Mont Tremblant (ch g Gris Perle – Paltoquette)	6.12.0	8–1	D.V. Dick
2 Shaef (gr g Mansur – Rispana)	8.12.0	7–1	F. Winter
3 Galloway Braes (br g Norwest – Isola)	7.12.0	66–1	R. Morrow

Runners: 13
Owner: Hon. D. Paget
Trainer: F. Walwyn
Distances: 10, 4
Time: 7 min 2.30
Also ran: Nagara, Cushenden, Café Crème, Silver Fame, Greenogue, Lord Turbot, Freebooter, Knock Hard, E.S.B., Injunction
Prize money: £3,233

1953

5 March

1 Knock Hard (ch g Domaha – Knocksouna)	9.12.0	11–2	T. Molony
2 Hallowe'en (br g Court Nez – My Blue Heaven)	8.12.0	5–2	F. Winter
3 Galloway Braes (br g Norwest – Isola)	8.12.0	33–1	R. Morrow

Runners: 12

Owner: Mrs M.H. Keogh
Trainer: M.V. O'Brien
Distances: 10, 4
Time: 6 min 28.40
Also ran: Mont Tremblant, Mariner's Log, Stormhead, Cushenden, Teal, Lanveoc Poulmic, E.S.B., Rose Park, Statecraft
Prize money: £3,258

1954
4 March

1 Four Ten (b g Blunderbuss – Undue Praise)	8.12.0	100–6	T. Cusack
2 Mariner's Log (ch g Archive – She Gone)	7.12.0	20–1	P. Taaffe
3 Hallowe'en (br g Court Nez – My Blue Heaven)	9.12.0	100–6	G. Slack

Runners: 9
Owner: Mr A. Strange
Trainer: J. Roberts
Distances: 4, 4
Time: 7 min 12.20
Also ran: Mont Tremblant, Knock Hard, Rose Park, Galloway Braes, Stormhead, Shaef
Prize money: £3,576

1955
10 March

1 Gay Donald (b g Gay Light – Pas de Quatre)	9.12.0	33–1	A. Grantham
2 Hallowe'en (br g Court Nez – My Blue Heaven)	10.12.0	7–2	F. Winter
3 Four Ten (b g Blunderbuss – Undue Praise)	9.12.0	3–1	T. Cusack

Runners: 9
Owner: Mr P J. Burt
Trainer: J.J. Ford
Distances: 10, 8
Time: 6 min 59.20
Also ran: Early Mist, Galloway Braes, Bramble Tudor, Crudwell, Pointsman, Rose Park
Prize money: £3,775

1956
8 March

1 Limber Hill (ch g Bassam – Mindoon)	9.12.0	11–8	J. Power
2 Vigor (b g Victrix – Château Neil Gow)	8.12.0	50–1	R. Emery
3 Hallowe'en (br g Court Nez – My Blue Heaven)	11.12.0	100–8	F. Winter

Runners: 11
Owner: Mr J. Davey
Trainer: W. Dutton
Distances: 4, 1.5
Time: 6 min 42.0
Also ran: Cruachan, Pointsman, Lochroe, Wise Child, Sam Brownthorn, Four Ten, Bramble Tudor, Glorious Twelfth
Prize money: £3,750

1957
14 March

1 Linwell (br g Rosewell – Rubia Linda)	9.12.0	100–9	M. Scudamore
2 Kerstin (br m Honor's Choice – Miss Kilcash)	7.12.0	6–1	G. Milburn

3 Rose Park (ch g Pactolus – Primulas)   11.12.0   100–8   G. Nicholls
Runners: 13
Owner: Mr D. Brown
Trainer: C. Mallon
Distances: 1, 5
Time: 6 min 55.6
Also ran: Pointsman, Lochroe, Sam Brownthorn, Dovetail, E.S.B., Wise Child, Sir Ken, Gay Donald,
        Sea Captain, Stroller
Prize money: £3,996

1958

13 March
1 Kerstin (br m Honor's Choice – Miss Kilcash)   8.12.0   7–1   S. Hayhurst
2 Polar Flight (br g Iceberg II – More Pure)   8.12.0   11–2   G. Slack
3 Gay Donald (b g Gay Light – Pas de Quatre)   12.12.0   13–2   F. Winter
Runners: 9
Owner: Mr G.H. Moore
Trainer: Major C. Bewicke
Distances: 0.5, bad
Time: 6 min 55.6
Also ran: Jack V, Limber Hill, Hall Weir, Game Field, Linwell, Mandarin
Prize money: £5,778

1959

6 March
1 Roddy Owen (b g Owenstown – Desla's Star)   10.12.0   5–1   H. Beasley
2 Linwell (br g Rosewall – Rubia Linda)   11.12.0   11–2   F. Winter
3 Lochroe (b g King Hal – Loch Cash)   11.12.0   100–9   A.R. Freeman
Runners: 11
Owner: Lord Fingall
Trainer: D. Morgan
Distances: 3, 10
Time: 7 min 28.4
Also ran: Hart Royal, Game Field, Jack V, Taxidermist, Kerstin, Pas Seul, Flame Royal, Caesar's Helm
Prize money: £5,363

1960

10 March
1 Pas Seul (b g Erin's Pride – Pas de Quatre)   7.12.0   6–1   W. Rees
2 Lochroe (b g King Hal – Loch Cash)   12.12.0   12–1   D. Mould
3 Zonda (b g Dornot – Zanthene)   9.12.0   9–1   G.W. Robinson
Runners: 12
Owner: Mr J. Rogerson
Trainer: R. Turnell
Distances: 1,5
Time: 7 min
Also ran: Roddy Owen, The Bell, O'Malley Point, Polar Flight, Knightsbrook, Mac Joy, Lotoray,
        Kerstin, The Major
Prize money: £5,414

1961
9 March

1 Saffron Tartan (br g Tartan – Kellsboro Witch)	10.12.0	2–1	F. Winter
2 Pas Seul (b g Erin's Pride – Pas de Quatre)	8.12.0	10–3	D.V. Dick
3 Mandarin (b g Deux pour Cent – Manada)	10.12.0	100–7	P.G. Madden

Runners: 9
Owner: Col. G.R. Westmacott
Trainer: D. Butchers
Distances: 1.5, 3
Time: 6 min 49.8
Also ran: Frenchman's Cove, Olympia, King, Reprieved, Devon Customer, Knucklecracker
Prize money: £6,043

1962
15 March

1 Mandarin (b g Deux pour Cent – Manada)	11.12.0	7–2	F. Winter
2 Fortria (b g Fortina – Senria)	10.12.0	3–1	P. Taaffe
3 Cocky Consort (b g Happy Monarch – Sporty Ann)	9.12.0	50–1	C. Stobbs

Runners: 10 ran
Owner: Mme K. Hennessy
Trainer: F. Walwyn
Distances: 1, 10
Time: 6 min 39.4
Also ran: Duke of York, Pas Seul, King's Nephew, The Rip, John O'Groats, Knucklecracker
Prize money: £5,720

1963
14 March

1 Mill House (b g King Hal – Nas na Riogh)	6.12.0	7–2	G.W. Robinson
2 Fortria (b g Fortina – Senria)	11.12.0	4–1	P. Taaffe
3 Duke of York (b g Flush Royal – Queen of the Dandies)	8.12.0	7–1	F. Winter

Runners: 12
Owner: Mr W.H. Gollings
Trainer: F. Walwyn
Distances: 12, 4
Time: 7 min 8.4
Also ran: Longtail, Pride of Ivanhoe, Caduval, Frenchman's Cove, Olympia, King's Nephew, Nicolaus Silver, Cannobie Lee, Rough Tweed
Prize money: £5,958

1964
7 March

1 Arkle (b g Archive – Bright Cherry)	7.12.0	7–4	P. Taaffe
2 Mill House (b g King Hal – Nas na Riogh)	7.12.0	8–13	G.W. Robinson
3 Pas Seul (b g Erin's Pride – Pas de Quatre)	11.12.0	50–1	D.V. Dick

Runners: 4
Owner: Anne, Duchess of Westminster
Trainer: T.W. Dreaper
Distances: 5,25
Time: 6 min 45.6
Also ran: King's Nephew
Prize money: £8,004

1965

11 March

1 Arkle (b g Archive – Bright Cherry)	8.12.0	3–10	P. Taaffe
2 Mill House (b g King Hal – Nas na Riogh)	8.12.0	10–3	G.W. Robinson
3 Stoney Crossing (br g North Riding – Sunlit Stream)	7.12.0	100–1	W. Roycroft

Runners: 4
Owner: Anne, Duchess of Westminster
Trainer: T.W. Dreaper
Distances: 20, 30
Time: 6 min 41.2
Also ran: Caduval
Prize money: £7,986

1966

17 March

1 Arkle (b g Archive – Bright Cherry)	9.12.0	1–10	P. Taaffe
2 Dormant (ch g Domaha – Miss Victoria)	9.12.0	20–1	M. Scudamore
3 Snaigow (b g Vulgan – Nicotania)	7.12.0	100–7	D. Nicholson

Runners: 5
Owner: Anne, Duchess of Westminster
Trainer: T.W. Dreaper
Distances: 30, 10
Time: 6 min 54.2
Also ran: Sartorius, Hunch
Prize money: £7,674

1967

16 March

1 Woodland Venture (b g Eastern Venture – Woodlander)	7.12.0	100–8	T.W. Biddlecombe
2 Stalbridge Colonist (gr g Colonist II – Eesofud)	8.12.0	11–2	S. Mellor
3 What A Myth (ch g Coup de Myth – What A Din)	10.12.0	3–1	P. Kelleway

Runners: 8
Owner: Mr H.H. Collins
Trainer: T.F. Rimell
Distances: 0.75, 2
Time: 6 min 59.2
Also ran: Dormant, Dicky May, Fort Leney, Foinavon, Mill House
Prize money: £7,999

1968

21 March

1 Fort Leney (b g Fortina – Leney Princess)	10.12.0	11–2	P. Taaffe
2 The Laird (br g Border Chief – Pré Fleuri)	7.12.0	3–1	J. King
3 Stalbridge Colonist (gr g Colonist II – Eesofud)	9.12.0	7–2	T.W. Biddlecombe

Runners: 5
Owner: Col. J. Thomson
Trainer: T.W. Dreaper
Distances: neck, 1
Time: 6 min 51.0
Also ran: Bassnet, Mill House
Prize money: £7,713

1969

20 March

1 What A Myth (ch g Coup de Myth – What A Din)	12.12.0	8–1	P. Kelleway
2 Domacorn (br g Domaha – Spring Corn)	7.12.0	7–2	T.W. Biddlecombe
3 Playlord (b g Lord of Verona – Playwell)	8.12.0	4–1	R. Barry

Runners: 11
Owner: Lady Weir
Trainer: H.R. Price
Distances: 1.5, 20
Time: 7 min 30.8
Also ran: Arab Gold, King Cutler, Stalbridge Colonist, Dicky May, Furtive, Castle Arbour, Kellsboro Wood, The Laird
Prize money: £8,129

1970

19 March

1 L'Escargot (ch g Escart III – What A Daisy)	7.12.0	33–1	T. Carberry
2 French Tan (br g Trouville – Kilted Angel)	8.12.0	8–1	P. Taaffe
3 Spanish Steps (b g Flush Royal – Tiberetta)	7.12.0	9–4	J. Cook

Runners: 12
Owner: Mr R.R. Guest
Trainer: D.L. Moore
Distances: 1.5, 10
Time: 6 min 47.4
Also ran: Freddie Boy, The Laird, Gay Trip, Larbawn, The Dikler, Titus Oates, Kinloch Brae, Herring Gull, Arcturus
Prize money: £8,103

1971

18 March

1 L'Escargot (ch g Escart III – What A Daisy)	8.12.0	7–2	T. Carberry
2 Leap Frog (b g Trouville – Maggie's Leap)	7.12.0	7–2	V. O'Brien
3 The Dikler (b g Vulgan – Coronation Day)	8.12.0	15–2	B. Brogan

Runners: 8
Owner: Mr R.R. Guest
Trainer: D.L. Moore
Distances: 10, 15
Time: 8 min 0.6
Also ran: Into View, Fortina's Palace, Herring Gull, Glencaraig Lady, Royal Toss
Prize money: £7,995

1972

16 March

1 Glencaraig Lady (ch m Fortina – Luckibash)	8.12.0	6–1	F. Berry
2 Royal Toss (br g Royal Challenger – Spinning Coin)	10.12.0	22–1	N. Wakley
3 The Dikler (b g Vulgan – Coronation Day)	9.12.0	11–1	B. Brogan

Runner: 12
Owner: Mr P. Doyle
Trainer: F. Flood
Distances: 0.75, hd
Time: 7 min 17.8
Also ran: L'Escargot, Crisp, Spanish Steps, Bighorn, Gay Trip, Leap Frog, Titus Oates, Dim Wit, Young Ash Leaf
Prize money: £15,255

1973

15 March

1 The Dikler (b g Vulgan – Coronation Day)	10.12.0	9–1	R. Barry
2 Pendil (b g Pendragon – Diliska)	8.12.0	4–6	R. Pitman
3 Charlie Potheen (br g Spiritus – Irish Biddy)	8.12.0	9–2	T.W. Biddlecombe

Runners: 12
Owner: Mrs D.W. August
Trainer: F. Walwyn
Distances: sh, 6
Time: 6 min 37.2
Also ran: L'Escargot, Crisp, Spanish Steps, Bighorn, Gay Trip, Leap Frog, Titus Oates, Dim Wit, Young Ash Leaf
Prize money: £15,125

1974

14 March

1 Captain Christy (b g Mon Capitaine – Christy's Bow)	7.12.0	7–1	H. Beasley
2 The Dikler (b g Vulgan – Coronation Day)	11.12.0	5–1	R. Barry
3 Game Spirit (ch g Game Rights – Castile)	8.12.0	20–1	T.W. Biddlecombe

Runners: 7
Owner: Mrs J.M.A. Samuel
Trainer: P. Taaffe
Distances: 5, 20
Time: 7 min 5.5
Also ran: Charlie Potheen, Inkslinger, High Ken, Pendil
Prize money: £14,572

1975

13 March

1 Ten Up (b g Raise You Ten – Irish Harp)	8.12.0	2–1	T. Carberry
2 Soothsayer (b or br g Mystic II – Sagoma)	8.12.0	28–1	R. Pitman
3 Bula (b g Raincheck – Pongo's Fancy)	10.12.0	5–1	J. Francome

Runners: 8
Owner: Anne, Duchess of Westminster
Trainer: J. Dreaper
Distances: 6, 0.5
Time: 7 min 51.4
Also ran: Glanford Brigg, High Ken, Bruslee, The Dikler, Captain Christy
Prize money: £17,757

1976
18 March

1 Royal Frolic (b g Royal Buck – Forward Miss)	7.12.0	14–1	J. Burke
2 Brown Lad (b g Sayajirao – Calcos)	10.12.0	13–8	T. Carberry
3 Colebridge (b g Vulgan – Cherry Bud)	12.12.0	12–1	F. Berry

Runners: 11
Owner: Sir E. Hanmer
Trainer: T.F. Rimell
Distances: 5, 5
Time: 6 min 40.1
Also ran: Money Market, Glanford Brigg, Bula, Otter Way, The Dikler, Roman Bar, Flashy Boy, What A Buck
Prize money: £18,134

1977
17 March

1 Davy Lad (b g David Jack – Château)	7.12.0	14–1	D.T. Hughes
2 Tied Cottage (b g Honour Bound – Cottage Ray)	9.12.0	20–1	T. Carberry
3 Summerville (b g Bowspit – Stella d'Oro)	11.12.0	15–1	J. King

Runners: 13
Owner: Mrs J. McGowan
Trainer: M.A. O'Toole
Distances: 6, 20
Time: 7 min 13.8
Also ran: April Seventh, Fort Fox, Tamalin, Master H, Banlieu, Bannow Rambler, Even Up, Fort Devon, Zarib, Lanzarote
Prize money: £21,990

1978
12 April

1 Midnight Court (b g Twilight Alley – Strumpet)	7.12.0	5–2	J. Francome
2 Brown Lad (b g Sayajirao – Calcos)	12.12.0	8–1	T. Carberry
3 Master H (ch g Master Owen – Last Resort)	9.12.0	18–1	R. Crank

Runners: 10
Owner: Mrs O. Jackson
Trainer: F. Winter
Distances: 7, 1
Time: 6 min 57.3
Also ran: Bachelor's Hall, Fort Devon, Cancello, Forest King, Otter Way, Fort Fox, Royal Frolic
Prize money: £23,828

1979
15 March

1 Alverton (ch g Midsummer Night – Alvertona)	9.12.0	5–1	J.J. O'Neill
2 Royal Mail (ch g Bally Royal – Lency)	9.12.0	7–1	P. Blacker
3 Aldaniti (ch g Derek H – Renardeau)	9.12.0	40–1	R. Champion

Runners: 14
Owner: The Snailwell Stud Co. Ltd
Trainer: M.H. Easterby
Distances: 25, 20
Time: 7 min 1.0
Also ran: Casamayor, Brown Lad, Gaffer, Night Nurse, Bit of Manny, Mighty Honour, Royal Frolic, Strombolus, Otter Way, Tied Cottage, Bawnogues
Prize money: £30,293

1980
13 March

1 Master Smudge (ch g Master Stephen – Lily Pond II)	8.12.0	14–1	R. Hoare
2 Mac Vidi (b g Vidi Vici – Jockette)	15.12.0	66–1	P. Leach
3 Approaching (ch g Golden Vision – Farm Hill)	9.12.0	11–1	B.R. Davies

Runners: 14
Owner: Trainer
Trainer: A. Barrow
Distances: 5, 2.5
Time: 7 min 14.2
Also ran: The Snipe, Border Incident, Jack of Trumps, Royal Mail, The Vintner, Diamond Edge, Kas, Kilcoleman Narribinni, Secret Progress, Chinrullah (disq.), Tied Cottage (disq.)
Prize money: £35,997

1981
19 March

1 Little Owl (Cantab – Black Spangle)	7.12.0	6–1	Mr A.J. Wilson
2 Night Nurse (b g Falcon – Florence Nightingale)	10.12.0	6–1	A. Brown
3 Silver Buck (br g Silver Cloud – Choice Archlesse)	9.12.0	7–2	T. Carmody

Runners: 15
Owner: Mr R.J. Wilson
Trainer: M.H. Easterby
Distances: 1.5, 10
Time: 7 min 9.9
Also ran: Spartan Missile, Diamond Edge, Jack of Trumps, Royal Judgement, Approaching, Midnight Court, Tied Cottage, Chinrullah, Fair View, Raffi Nelson, Royal Bond, So And So
Prize money: £44,258

1982
18 March

1 Silver Buck (br g Silver Cloud – Choice Archlesse)	10.12.0	8–1	R. Earnshaw
2 Bregawn (ch g Saint Denys – Miss Society)	8.12.0	18–1	G. Bradley
3 Sunset Cristo (b g Derek H – Sunset Rambler)	8.12.0	50–1	C. Grant

Runners: 22
Owner: Mrs C. Feather
Trainer: M.W. Dickinson
Distances: 2, 12
Time: 7 min 11.3
Also ran: Diamond Edge, Captain John, Grittar, Venture To Cognac, Royal Bond, Tied Cottage, Two

Swallows, Lesley Ann, Sugarally, Peaty Sandy, Earthstopper, Border Incident, Drumroan, Henry Bishop, Master Smudge, Night Nurse, Snow Flyer, Straight Jocelyn, Wansford Boy

Prize money: £48,386

1983

17 March

1 Bregawn (ch g Saint Denys – Miss Society)	9.12.0	10–3	G. Bradley
2 Captain John (ch g Mon Capitaine – Aprolon Light)	9.12.0	11–1	D. Goulding
3 Wayward Lad (br g Royal Highway – Loughanmore)	8.12.0	6–1	J.J. O'Neill

Runners: 11

Owner: Mr M. Kennelly

Trainer: M.W. Dickinson

Distances: 5, 1.5

Time: 6 min 57.6

Also ran: Silver Buck, Ashley House, Richdee, Midnight Love, Combs Ditch, Fifty Dollars More, Brown Chamberlain, Whiggie Geo

Prize money: £45,260

1984

15 March

1 Burrough Hill Lad (br g Richboy – Green Monkey)	8.12.0	7–2	P. Tuck
2 Brown Chamberlain (br g Space King – Jocelin)	9.12.0	5–1	J. Francome
3 Drumlargan (b g Twilight Alley – Avro Jet)	10.12.0	16–1	F. Codd

Runners: 12

Owner: Mr R. S. Riley

Trainer: J. Pitman

Distances: 3, 8

Time: 6 min 41.4

Also ran: Scot Lane, Fifty Dollars More, Bregawn, Canny Danny, Royal Bond, Observe, Wayward Lad, Foxbury, Everett

Prize money: £47,375

1985

14 March

1 Forgive 'N Forget (ch g Precipice Wood – Tackienne)	8.12.0	7–1	M. Dwyer
2 Righthand Man (b g Proverb – Gleann Buidhe)	8.12.0	15–2	G. Bradley
3 Earls Brig (br g New Brig – Naughty Tara)	10.12.0	13–2	P. Tuck

Runners: 15

Owner: T. Kilroe and Sons Ltd.

Trainer: J. Fitzgerald

Distances: 1.5, 2.5

Time: 6 min 48.3

Also Ran: Drumadowney, Half Free, Boreen Prince, Combs Ditch, Wayward Lad, Homeson, Door Latch, Ballinacurra Lad, Sointulla Boy, Bregawn, Rainbow Warrior, Greenwood Lad

Prize Money: £52,560

1986

13 March

1 Dawn Run (b m Deep Run – Twilight Slave)	8.11.9	15–8	M. Dwyer
2 Wayward Lad (br g Royal Highway – Loughanmore)	11.12.0	8–1	G. Bradley
3 Forgive 'N Forget (ch g Precipice Wood – Tackienne)	9.12.0	7–2	M. Dwyer

Runners: 11

Owner: Mrs C.D. Hill
Trainer: P. Mullins
Distances: 1, 2.5
Time: 6 min 35.0
Also ran: Run and Skip, Righthand Man, Observe, Combs Ditch, Earls Brig, Von Trappe, Castle
    Andrea, Cybrandian
Prize money: £54,900

1987
19 March

1 The Thinker (ch g Cantab – Maine Pet)	9.12.0	13–2	R. Lamb
2 Cybrandian (b g Prince Regent (Fr) – Lavenham Rose)	9.12.0	25–1	C. Grant
3 Door Latch (ch g Cantab – Kelly's Door)	9.12.0	9–1	R. Rowe

Runners: 12
Owner: T.P. McDonagh Ltd.
Trainer: W.A. Stephenson
Distances: 1.5, 2.5
Time: 6 min 56.1
Also ran: West Tip, Wayward Lad, Golden Friend, Forgive 'N Forget, Mr Moonraker, Bolands Cross,
    Combs Ditch, Earls Brig, Charter Party
Prize money: £55,500

1988
17 March

1 Charter Party (b g Document – Ahoy There)	10.12.0	10–1	R. Dunwoody
2 Cavvies Clown (b g Idiot's Delight – Cavallina)	8.12.0	6–1	S. Sherwood
3 Beau Ranger (ch g Beau Chapeau – Sand Martin)	10.12.0	33–1	P. Scudamore

Runners: 15
Owner: Mrs C. Smith and Mrs J. Mould
Trainer: D. Nicholson
Distances: 6, 10
Time: 6 min 58.9
Also ran: Nupsala, Yahoo, West Tip, Kildimo, Golden Friend, Run and Skip, Playschool, Forgive 'N
Forget, Rhyme 'N Reason, Cybrandian, Foyle Fisherman, Stearsby
Prize money: £61,960

1989
16 March

1 Desert Orchid (gr g Grey Mirage – Flower Child)	10.12.0	5–2	S. Sherwood
2 Yahoo (Trombone – Coolroe Aga)	8.12.0	25–1	T. Morgan
3 Charter Party (b g Document – Ahoy There)	11.12.0	14–1	P. Scudamore

Runners: 13
Owner: Mr R. Burridge
Trainer: D.R.C. Elsworth
Distances: 1.5, 8
Time: 7 min 17.6
Also ran: Bonanza Boy, West Tip, Ballyhane, Cavvies Clown, Pegwell Bay, Slalom, Ten Plus, The
    Thinker, Carvill's Hill, Golden Freeze
Prize money: £68,371

1990

17 March

1 Norton's Coin (ch g Mount Cassino – Grove Chance)	9.12.0	100–1	G. McCourt
2 Toby Tobias (Furry Glen – Aurora Lady)	8.12.0	8–1	M. Pitman
3 Desert Orchid (gr g Grey Mirage – Flower Child)	11.12.0	10–11	R. Dunwoody

Runners: 12
Owner: Trainer
Trainer: S.G. Griffiths
Distances: 0.75, 4
Time: 6 min 30.9
Also ran: Cavvies Clown, Pegwell Bay, Maid of Money, Yahoo, Bonanza Boy, Nick The Brief, Ten of Spades, Kildimo, The Bakewell Boy
Prize money: £67,003

1991

14 March

1 Garrison Savannah (b g Random Shot – Merry Coin)	8.12.0	16–1	M. Pitman
2 The Fellow (b g Italic – L'Oranaise)	6.12.0	28–1	A. Kondrat
3 Desert Orchid (gr g Grey Mirage – Flower Child)	12.12.0	4–1	R. Dunwoody

Runners: 14
Owner: Autofour Engineering
Trainer: J. Pitman
Distances: sh, 15
Time: 6 min 49.8
Also ran: Cool Ground, Kildimo, Nick The Brief, Celtic Shot, Yahoo, Arctic Call, Carrick Hill Lad, Twin Oaks, Norton's Coin, Party Politics, Martin d'Or
Prize money: £98,578

1992

12 March

1 Cool Ground (ch g Over The River – Merry Spring)	10.12.0	25–1	A. Maguire
2 The Fellow (b g Italic – L'Oranaise)	7.12.0	7–2	A. Kondrat
3 Docklands Express (b g Roscoe Blake – Southern Moss)	10.12.0	16–1	M. Perrett

Runners: 8
Owner: Whitcombe Manor Racing Stables Ltd
Trainer: G.B. Balding
Distances: sh, 1
Time: 6 min 47.5
Also ran: Toby Tobias, Carvill's Hill, Golden Freeze, Norton's Coin, Kings Fountain
Prize money: £98,028

1993

18 March

1 Jodami (b g Crash Course – Masterstown Lucy)	8.12.0	8–1	M. Dwyer
2 Rushing Wild (b g Rushmere – Lady Em II)	8.12.0	11–1	R. Dunwoody
3 Royal Athlete (ch g Roselier – Darjoy)	10.12.0	66–1	B. De Haan

Runners: 16
Owner: Mr J.N. Yeadon
Trainer: P. Beaumont
Distances: 2, 7
Time: 6 min 34.4
Also ran: The Fellow, Sibton Abbey, Docklands Express, Garrison Savannah, Run For Free, Cool Ground, Tipping Tim, Chatam, Topsham Bay, Cahervillahow, Black Humour, Very Very Ordinary, Cherry Kino
Prize money: £99,448

1994

17 March

1 The Fellow (b g Italic – L'Oranaise)	9.12.0	7–1	A. Kondrat
2 Jodami (b g Crash Course – Masterstown Lucy)	9.12.0	6–4	M. Dwyer
3 Young Hustler (ch g Import – Davett)	7.12.0	20–1	C. Llewellyn

Runners: 15
Owner: Marquesa de Moratalla
Trainer: F. Doumen
Distances: 1.5, 4
Time: 6 min 40.7
Also ran: Flashing Steel, Bradbury Star, Docklands Express, Miinnehoma, Deep Bramble, Run For Free, Topsham Bay, Chatam, Blazing Walker, Capability Brown, Garrison Savannah, Ebony Jane
Prize money: £118,770

1995

16 March

1 Master Oats (ch g Oats – Miss Poker Face)	9.12.0	10–3	N. Williamson
2 Dubacilla (b m Dubassoff – Just Camilla)	9.12.0	20–1	D. Gallagher
3 Miinnehoma (b g Kambalda – Mrs Cairns)	12.12.0	9–1	R. Dunwoody

Runners: 15
Owner: Mr P.A. Matthews
Trainer: K.C. Bailey
Distances: 15, 15
Time: 6 min 55.9
Also ran: Merry Gale, Young Hustler, Monsieur Le Curé, Beech Road, Jodami, Commercial Artist, Barton Bank, Flashing Steel, Algan, Nuaffe, Val d'Alene, Deep Bramble
Prize money: £122,540

1996

14 March

1 Imperial Call (br g Callernish – Princess Menelek)	7.12.0	9–2	C. O'Dwyer
2 Rough Quest (b g Crash Course – Our Quest)	10.12.0	12–1	M.A. Fitzgerald
3 Couldn't Be Better (br g Oats – Belle Bavard)	9.12.0	11–1	G. Bradley

Runners: 10
Owner: Lisselan Farms Ltd.
Trainer: F. Sutherland
Distances: 4, 19

Time: 6 min 42.3
Also ran: Barton Bank, Young Hustler, One Man, King of the Gales, Dublin Flyer, Lord Relic,
Monsieur Le Curé
Prize money: £131,156

1997
13 March

1 Mr Mulligan (ch g Torus – Miss Manhattan)	9.12.0	20–1	A.P. McCoy
2 Barton Bank (br g Kambalda – Lucifer's Daughter)	11.12.0	33–1	D. Walsh
3 Dorans Pride (ch g Orchestra – Marians Pride)	8.12.0	10–1	J.P. Broderick

Runners: 14
Owner: Mr and Mrs M. Worcester
Trainer: N.T. Chance
Distances: 9, 0.5
Time: 6 min 35.5
Also ran: Go Ballistic, Challenger Du Luc, One Man, Coome Hill, Cyborgo, Banjo, Danoli, Dublin
Flyer, Imperial Call, Nahthen Lad, Unguided Missile
Prize money: £134,810

1998
19 March

1 Cool Dawn (br g Over The River – Aran Tour)	10.12.0	25–1	A. Thornton
2 Strong Promise (br g Strong Gale – Let's Compromise)	7.12.0	14–1	N. Williamson
3 Dorans Pride (ch g Orchestra – Marians Pride)	9.12.0	9–4	R. Dunwoody

Runners: 17
Owner: Miss D. Harding
Trainer: R.H. Alner
Distances: 1.75, hd
Time: 6 min 39.7
Also ran: Senor El Betrutti, Suny Bay, Simply Dashing, Challenger Du Luc, Barton Bank, Strath
Royal, Yorkshire Gale, Go Ballistic, Addington Boy, Couldn't Be Better, Cyborgo, Rough
Quest, Indian Tracker, See More Business
Prize money: £148,962

1999
16 March

1 See More Business (b g Seymour Hicks – Miss Redlands)	9.12.0	16–1	M.A. Fitzgerald
2 Go Ballistic (br g Celtic Cone – National Clover)	10.12.0	66–1	A. Dobbin
3 Florida Pearl (b g Florida Son – Ice Pearl)	7.12.0	5–2	R. Dunwoody

Runners: 12
Owner: Mr P.K. Barber and Mr J.A. Keighley
Trainer: P.F. Nicholls
Distances: 1, 17
Time: 6 min 41.9
Also ran: Double Thriller, Addington Boy, Simply Dashing, Escartefigue, Dorans Pride, Senor El
Betrutti, Unsinkable Boxer, Suny Bay, Teeton Mill
Prize money: £149,600

Photographer Bernard Parkin was born in Cheltenham and has lived close to Prestbury Park all his life. As a child he was taken to see the last three of the great Golden Miller's five Cheltenham Gold Cups, but it was not until Poet Prince's year (1941) that he became infatuated with horseracing. Since then he has missed very few meetings at 'the home of steeplechasing'. A professional artist since leaving school, Bernard took up racecourse photography at the age of 18. The two vocations have run successfully in parallel ever since. He has been supplying The Royal Household with his work since 1957, holds a royal warrant and is Racing Photographer to Her Majesty Queen Elizabeth, The Queen Mother. In 1977, Bernard Parkin was appointed the official photographer to The Steeplechase Company (Cheltenham) Ltd and still holds that position.